CONDUCTING CLINICAL SOCIOMETRIC EXPLORATIONS:

A MANUAL FOR PSYCHODRAMATISTS AND SOCIOMETRISTS

BY ANN E. HALE

1985, First Workbook Edition, Royal Publishing Company
1981, First Printing, Ann E. Hale

Library of Congress Cataloging in Publication Data

Hale, Ann E. (Ann Elisabeth), 1942–
    Conducting clinical sociometric explorations.

    Bibliography: p.
    Includes index.
    1. Sociometry. 2. Moreno, J. L. (Jacob Levy),
1892-1974. 3. Psychodrama. 4. Small groups.
I. Title.
HM253.H25 1985   302'.072   85-60745
ISBN 0-931571-01-4

Printed in the United States of America

Royal Publishing Company
Roanoke, Virginia

DEDICATION

To My Students

TABLE OF CONTENTS

CHAPTER I
SOCIOMETRIC THEORY OF JACOB LEVY MORENO

Canon of Creativity 1
Biographical Overview 3
Philosophical Basis of Moreno's Sociometric Theory 4
Cornerstones of Sociometry 4
    Spontaneity 6
    Cultural Conserve 6
    Creativity 6
Major Theories 7
    Science of Action 7
    Role Theory 7
    Sociometry and the Science of Society 8
        Social Reality 9
        Social Networks 10
    Theory of Interpersonal Relations 11
Bibliography 13

CHAPTER II
THE SOCIAL ATOM

Introduction 17
Historical Background of the Social Atom 17
Streetlight Sociometry 18
Social Atom Explorations 18
    Moreno's Social Atom 20
    Social Atom Collectives Exploration 21
    Perceptual Social Atom Sociogram 22
    Psychological Social Atom 23
    Fantasy Family Social Atom 24
    Social Atom Explored in Action 25
    Social Atom Exploration with Streetlight Sociometry Notational System 26
    Target for Use in Social Atom Explorations 27
Bibliography 28

CHAPTER III
THE SOCIOMETRIC TEST

Introduction 31
The Warming-up Phase 31
    Warm-up of the Sociometrist 31
    Warm-up of the Group 32
The Action Phase 33
    Selecting Criteria of Choice 33
    Classifications of Criteria 33
    Wording of Criteria 34
    Revealing Sociometric Data 35
    Declaring Choices and Reasons for Choice 35
        Positive Choice 36
        Negative Choice 36
        Neutral Choice 36
    Making Perceptual Choices 37
    Revealing Choices in Face to Face Interaction 38
The Sharing Phase 38
The Analysis Phase 39
    Constructing the Sociomatrix 39
    Determining Mutuality and Incongruity 42
    The Perceptual Sociomatrix 44
    Sociogram Construction 45
        How to Draw a Sociogram 45
        Notational System for Sociogram Construction 47
        The Target Sociogram 48

Analysis of Choices 50
   The Sociometric Star 50
   Isolate and Isolated Dyad 50
   Cliques and Sub-groups 50
   Pivotal Persons and Linkages 50
Interpretation of Data 51
   Emotional Expansiveness 52
   Mutuality and Incongruity 53
   Perceptual Data 55
   Cleavage 55
   Identifying Leaders 55
   Reliability of Data 56
Sociometric Intervention Phase 56
   Enacting a Group Sociogram 56
   Making Assignments 57
     Pairs 57
     Small Groups 57
   Criteria Selection for Identifying Act Hunger 58
   Role Training 58
   Identifying Criteria for Future Tests 58
Quasi or Near Sociometry 59
Bibliography 63
Appendices 65
   I. Flow Chart of Phases of Sociometric Test 65
   II. Stages in a Group's Development When the Sociometric Test Would Be a Choice ... 70
   III. Description of the Sociometric Test 71
   IV. Ranking Criteria of Choice by Relevance, Threat and Type 73
   V. Data Sheets (Objective and Perceptual) 75
   VI. Sociomatrix Format 77
   VII. Exploring Your Sociometric Set 79
   VIII. Sample Devices 85
     a. Leisure Role Cluster Exploration 85
     b. Sociometric Test of Leisure Role Cluster 86
     c. Staff Role Exploration 87
     d. Staff Encounter Exploration 88
     e. Sociometric Choice for Central Roles 89

CHAPTER IV
ENCOUNTERING MORENO-STYLE

Introduction 93
Role Reversal 93
   Role Reversal Training Tips 94
   Reflective Listening 95
Warm-up to an Encounter 95
   Constructive Communicative Relationships 96
   Structured Warm-ups in Action 98
   Conflict Warm-up (pen and paper) 100
Conflict Resolution 101
   Role Diagram of Conflict Resolution Facilitation 102
   Analyzer Function 103
   Communicator Function 103
   Conflict Manager Function 104
   Conflict Resolution Facilitator Training Model 105
   The Model 105
   The Role of Facilitator/Director 106
   The Role of Training Director 107
   Conclusion 108
Bibliography 109

CHAPTER V
THE ROLE DIAGRAM EXPANDED

Introduction 113
Basic Role Diagram Construction 113
   Compiling the List of Roles 113
   Choosing the Point of Time 114

Selecting the Role Diagram Format 114
   Intrapersonal Role Diagram 115
   Interpersonal Role Diagram 116
   Combined Intrapersonal and Interpersonal 117
   Expanded Role Diagram (Extramural Roles) 118
   Bilateral Role Diagram 119
   Multilateral Role Diagram 120
   Sample Role Diagram Expanded 121
  Indicating Responses to Roles 122
Interpreting the Role Diagram and Moving into Action 123
  Encounter 124
  Unlearning and De-conserving Roles 124
  Role Training 124
  Future Projection and Role Testing 125
Bibliography 126
Appendices 127
  I. Instructions to Participants 127
  II. Role Diagram Data Sheet 128
  III. Role Diagram Notation 129
  IV. Examples of Role Diagrams 130
   Example 1. Role Diagram of the Psychodrama Director 130
   Example 2. Group Member Role Diagram 137
  V. Sample Forms 139
   Sample 1. Interpersonal Role Diagram 139
   Sample 2. Interpersonal Role Diagram (Perceptual Aspect) 140
   Sample 3. Multilateral Role Diagram 141
   Sample 4. Bilateral Role Diagram 142

CHAPTER VI
ACTION SOCIOMETRY: A GUIDE FOR GROUP LEADERS

Introduction 145
Recognizing the Criterion of Choice in Action 145
Auxiliary Ego Role Choice Chart 146
Using Action Sociometry for Dealing with Issues of Inclusion 147
Counteracting the Sociodynamic Effect 147
Forming Pairs and Small Groups in Action 149
Act Hunger 149
Bibliography 152
Appendices 153
  I. Group Exploration of Act Hunger for Role of High Value 153
  II. Exploring Your Act Hunger 154

WORKBOOK PAGES OF FORMS, SAMPLE DEVICES

Moreno's Social Atom 167
Psychological Social Atom 168
Social Atom Collective 169
Perceptual Social Atom Sociogram 170
Target for Social Atom 171
Target for Social Atom 172
Ranking Criteria of Choice 173
Ranking Criteria of Choice (continued) 174
Objective Data Sheet for Sociometric Test 175
Perceptual Data Sheet for Sociometric Test 176
Objective Data Sheet for Sociometric Test 177
Perceptual Data Sheet for Sociometric Test 178
Objective Data Sheet for Sociometric Test 179
Perceptual Data Sheet for Sociometric Test 180
Sociomatrix 181
Sociomatrix 182
Sociomatrix 183
Sociometric Choice for Central Roles 184
Conflict Warm-up 185
Role Diagram Data Sheet 186
Interpersonal Role Diagram 187
Interpersonal Role Diagram (Perceptual Aspect) 188

Multilateral Role Diagram 189
Bilateral Role Diagram 190
Group Member Role Diagram 191
Exploring Your Act Hunger 192
Group Exploration of Act Hunger 193
Group Exploration of Act Hunger (continued) 194
Auxiliary Ego Role Choice 195
Auxiliary Ego Role Choice 196

PREFACE

This workbook edition makes more readily available sociometry as developed by J.L. Moreno and as extended and expanded by his colleagues and students. The focus is upon classical sociometry and particularly upon clinical application of the method. Clincial Sociometry is that aspect of sociometric methodology devoted to psychological and socio-emotional change, relationship theory and active intervention in the social network of individuals. The first edition in 1981 (a limited edition of 500 copies in notebook form) was well received, and fulfilled an ambition I shared with Moreno, providing a student edition to his work. In January, 1974, while I was Director-in-residence at the Moreno Institute, Moreno and I spent several hours, two or three times a week, on the project of a student's edition to *Who Shall Survive?* until he became too ill to continue.

A major revision to this edition can be found in Chapter 1. My intention has been to present sociometric theory as an aspect of Moreno's unified philosophical system, and to identify for the reader how sociometry is interconnected with action method, creativity, dynamic social change and the therapeutic process. The revision was prompted by experiences I have had as a trainer and guest workshop leader. A tendency exists to reserve sociometry to specialized workshops and divorce these methods from action method and therapeutic approaches. The result is to diminish the potency of the Morenean system.

My involvement in sociodrama and action method in a variety of settings outside of, and including, the clinical, has demonstrated to me the fear of spontaneity, action and change which exists and affects so many. The methods which result from Moreno's theoretical system have been proven effective, yet there is still reluctance to use them. Many colleagues of mine question this and offer reasons why this is so—methods not known, books about them difficult to access, the time it takes to become competent, etc. I believe the methods have been used and discarded as too difficult to manage. The methods were employed by persons who proceeded into action without first having the understanding and skills to deal with act hunger, inhibiting sociodynamic conditions, and the sheer complexity of the process. The revision in Chapter 1 seemed necessary to me as it provides for the novice an overview of the methods as a social-therapeutic philosophy, thereby generating a perspective, or map, to the system. My hope is that the "map" can be absorbed and available to consult when the methods produce the unexpected.

My revisions also include an expansion of Chapter 6, giving more attention to action sociometry, action method in general, and providing more guidance to action methods leaders. My special appreciation is extended to the New Zealand teachers' college lecturers who attended the first "Seminars on Action Method" held at Wellington Teachers College, March 11-13, 1985. Colin Martin, the course director, involved me as resource person in this seminar which proved to me that the success and continued use of action method is dependent upon anticipated results and well-handled, meaningful surprises. Colin Martin, my sincere thanks for your encouragement and appreciation.

These revisions were also influenced by the attention given to Moreno's philosophical system by Peter Dean Mendelsson and by Linnea Carlson-Sabelli and Hector Sabelli. Mendelsson's dissertation focuses on the reunification of Moreno's theory, philosophy and methods. The Sabelli's have been developing a process theory, based on the unity of opposites to which they are applying to the Morenean system. I am also indebted to colleagues John Nolte and Jonathan Fox for sharing their well-developed understanding of spontaneity and creativity, and Alton Barbour for his assistance with small group behavior.

The workbook edition offers several features for student use. Inserted into the book is a clear, see-through sociomatrix reader, an improvement on the printed one. Also, at the back of the book are twenty pages of sociometric forms which are perforated for ease of detachment. This makes it possible for the forms contained in the text portion (as examples) to remain there. Permission is given for exercises and forms contained in the book to be duplicated.

ANN E. HALE, 1985
Roanoke, Virginia

CHAPTER I
SOCIOMETRIC THEORY OF JACOB LEVY MORENO

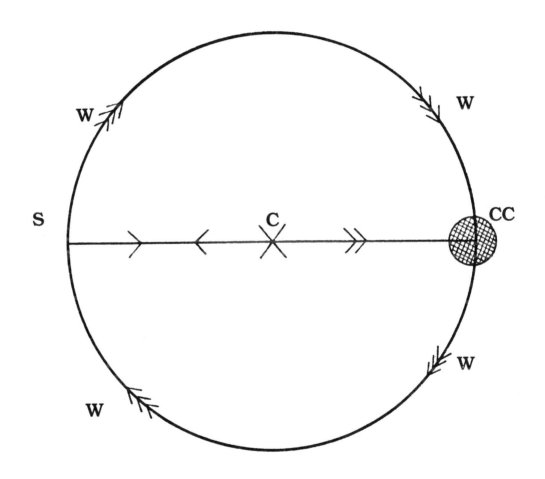

CANON OF CREATIVITY

J.L. Moreno, "Field of Rotating Operations between Spontaneity-Creativity and the Cultural Conserve" in *Who Shall Survive?*, p. 46. (The W indicates the warming-up process, the "operational expression of spontaneity".)

SOCIOMETRIC THEORY OF JACOB LEVY MORENO

Biographical Overview of Moreno's Life

Jacob Levy Moreno was born on May 20, 1889 in Bucharest, Romania, the oldest of six children of the well-to-do exporter Nissom Moreno and his wife Pauline Wolf Moreno. At age five the family moved to Vienna. The Moreno family was of a sephardic Jewish community; however, J.L. Moreno did not partake of any formalized religious training. It is known that Moreno formed a society of friends called "the religion of the encounter" at the age of eighteen. Religion was a major focus in Moreno's life and certainly it occupied his thoughts and imagination during his student days.[1]

From 1910-1912 Moreno studied philosophy and mathematics at the University of Vienna, and from 1912-1917 he attended the University of Vienna Medical School from which he received his M.D. in 1917. It was at this time that Moreno used to visit the Augarten near the Archduke's palace and tell stories to the children who would gather there. During these fairy tale sessions with children Moreno began to investigate spontaneity. "It was not as much what I told them, the tale itself, it was the act, the atmosphere of mystery, the paradox, the unreal become real."[2]

During this time Vienna was in the midst of World War I. The cultural city with its famed coffeehouses was greatly politicized. The expresssions of this politicization were in daily papers and public debates. It was during this time that Moreno became the editor of *Daimon,* a monthly magazine devoted to existential philosophy, the arts, and theoretical discussions. Martin Buber was a contributor to *Daimon.* These years (1918-1920) were the years that Moreno began to formulate his conception of God, spontaneity, creativity, the philosophy of the here and now, sociometry, axiodrama (1918), socio-drama (1921) and in 1923 Das Stegreiftheater.

In the years between 1919 and 1925, Moreno published his books anonymously, including *Words of the Father,* which he had written in red ink on the walls of an Austrian castle. In 1925 Moreno came to an ideological crossroads. It became important to choose a home for his ideas, a place where his beliefs about humanity could be investigated and could flourish. He chose the United States: "I preferred to be the midwife to an incoherent, confused, democratic way of life, than the commisar of a highly organized world."[3]

Moreno began a medical practice in New York, working psychodramatically with children at the Plymouth Institute in Brooklyn. In 1928 he demonstrated his role playing techniques with children at the Department of Pediatrics at Mt. Sinai Hospital and worked at the Mental Hygiene Clinic. Moreno opened the Impromptu Group Theatre and for three years conducted thrice-weekly programs at Carnegie Hall.

In 1932, with the help of his friend, Dr. William Alanson White, Moreno was successful in organizing a conference on group methods at the American Psychiatric Association meeting in Philadelphia. Moreno writes that he was discouraged by the "lukewarm reception" and reported that White said to him: "First you will attract the social psychologists, then the sociologists, then the anthropologists and next the psychologists. Many years will go by before the physicians will listen, but the last of all will be the psychiatrists." And thus it has come about.[4]

From 1932-1938 Moreno conducted a long-range sociometric study with Helen Hall Jennings of the New York State Training School for Girls at Hudson, New York. Many of his formulations and hypotheses were contained in the 1934 edition of *Who Shall Survive? A New Approach to the Problem of Human Relations.* A later edition which appeared in 1954 contained detailed accounts and socio-grams of these investigations.

"Moreno coined most of the terms which are now universally used by all schools of group psychotherapists, 'group therapy,' 'group psychotherapy,' 'warming up,' 'group catharsis,' 'social catharsis,' 'action catharsis,' 'acting out techniques,' etc. He has been the actual leader and prime mover of the group psychotherapy movement since 1931. He initiated or guided most of the Group Psychotherapy conferences within the American Psychiatric Association during the last twenty years, which has aided probably more than anything else to raise the medico-psychological status of the new discipline. His journal *Sociometry* (1937) was the first to open its pages to contributions on group psychotherapy, which led ten years later to the establishment of a special journal. In 1942 he opened the Sociometric Institute, organized for the purpose of training besides sociometrists, group psychotherapists and psychodramatists, and spreading these ideas throughout the world. In 1942 he formed the first scientific society which had the term 'group psychotherapy' in its name, the American Society of Group Psychotherapy and Psychodrama, which published a quarterly Bulletin of Psychodrama and Group Psychotherapy since May, 1943. In 1947 he started **Sociatry,** Journal of Group and Intergroup Therapy, the title of which was changed to **Group Psychotherapy** two years later (1949). In 1951 his nationwide petition for a Section on Group Psychotherapy within the American Psychiatric Association brought about the support of more than fifteen hundred psychiatrists and, in consequence, the establishment of a Symposium on Group Psychotherapy and Psychodrama within the American Psychiatric Association now in their third year. In 1951 he formed an International Committee on Group Psychotherapy in Paris, and State Committees on Group Psychotherapy within the U.S.A. in all its forty-eight states."[5]

Moreno taught at the New School for Social Research, Teachers College, Columbia University and was on the faculty of the Graduate School of Arts and Sciences at New York University. Moreno married Florence Bridge and had a daughter, Regina. Later they divorced and Moreno married Zerka Toeman, who collaborated with him in many publications from 1941. Zerka and J.L. had a son, Jonathan David Moreno, who grew up in Beacon, New York, on the estate which housed the Moreno Institute. Publications, travels, organizational pursuits and training occupied Moreno until his death at his home in Beacon, May 14, 1974. His last public appearance in February, 1974, was at the Medical Society of New York annual meeting held in New York City. He was cited as the "Psychiatrist of the Century." His reply to this honor was to thank his colleagues: "The older I get, the more I realize, how much I have learned from people like you."[6]

The acknowledgement which is due Moreno appears in the occasional publication or foreword. Moreno's view of the failure to recognize his work was that the controversy about his methods had more to do with his own personality, than with his unorthodox action methods. He also saw the development of a scientific system as a participative event: "Whereas the 'genius' method made the participation in the sciences and arts an exception, the scientific method strives toward making the participation universal. This may mean that the brave world of men needs not only to be shared but also **co-produced;** that it is to be created not only by one or a few geniuses but through the efforts of all people."[7]

The Philosophical Basis for Moreno's Sociometric Theory

"I suffered from an *idee fixe,* from what might be called then an affectation, but of which might be said today, as the harvest is coming in, that is was by "the grace of God." The *idee fixe* became my constant source of productivity; it proclaimed that there is a sort of primordial nature which is immortal and returns afresh in every generation, a first universe which contains all beings and in which all events are sacred. I liked that enchanted realm and did not plan to leave it, ever."[8]

Moreno was "trying to plant the seeds of a diminutive creative revolution" as he engaged others—sick or healthy; not a social revolution, or even a psychiatric revolution (which it was later called) but a religious revolution. Moreno envisaged a religion based upon acknowledging God-likeness in each person and the capacity to bring out the creator in every person. The expression of these religious beliefs would be in action, interaction with others according to principles based on the sacredness of spontaneity and creativity in every individual.

It was in the first edition of **Who Shall Survive? A New Approach to the Problem of Human Relations** (1934) that Moreno's theories were presented as a unified body, with his "Canon of Creativity" as the cornerstone. Supporting branches of this theory to be discussed here are Moreno's (1) Role Theory, (2) Theory of Interpersonal Relations, (3) the Science of Action, and (4) Sociometry and the Science of Society. See Figure 1 on the following page which depicts the interrelationship of these theories and the resulting action methodologies.

Cornerstones of Sociometry

Moreno saw God as the supreme Creator, and the robot, which is the delight of many technocrats, as the complete antithesis, the cultural conserve, as this drawing indicates:

ROBOT ◄─────────────── Additions of Spontaneity ───────────────► GOD
(Cultural Conserve)   (Creativity)

The Canon of Creativity (depicted on the frontispiece for this chapter, p. 1) is concerned with the

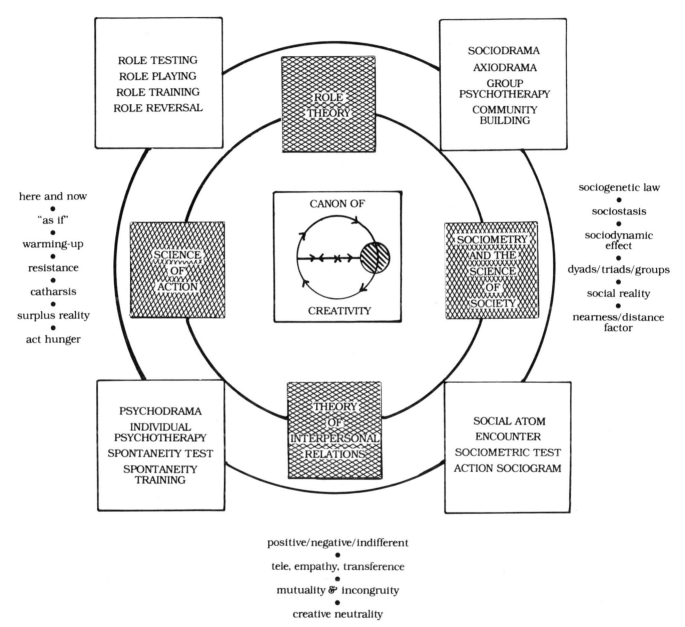

Figure 1. Interrelationship of Moreno's Theories/Methods

Shaded boxes indicate major theories. Larger outer boxes indicate
action methodologies. Key concepts of the theories are in outer margins.

process of creation and the creation as an end product. Simply stated, Moreno saw existing creations (he called these the cultural conserve) as the springboard to creativity through a process which involves more and more additions of spontaneity. A person encounters an already existing product and begins to imagine the alteration or expansion of it, or a departure from it. Following one's imagination into action enables spontaneity to come into being. In the imagining one "plays" with the idea of something new before "creating" with it. Spontaneity emerges as the play begins and increases, thereby generating an emotional energy in response which sustains the creative process.

Spontaneity is the ingredient in the creative process which provokes creativity. An unconservable factor, spontaneity has the capacity for freshness, originality, and usefulness. Moreno (1965) identified three kinds of spontaneity:

1. Pathological spontaneity—this form of spontaneity is in evidence when a person makes a novel response to a situation but one which is not useful or adequate. For example, it might be novel to exit a building by walking backward, but by doing so, a person is unable to see where the steps begin. Hardly useful or adequate.

2. Stereotyped spontaneity—"It consists of a spontaneous response which is adequate to the situation, but which lacks sufficient novelty or significant creativity to be fruitful to the situation. The comedian's repetitive reaction to a situation soon loses its novelty, and although it may continue to provoke some laughter, it soon ceases to be a spontaneous response."

3. True spontaneity—"Is a high grade creativity variety of genius. In this type there is an adequate response accompanied by characteristics that are both novel and creative . . . to be truly spontaneous, the results must be in some way new and useful for some purpose."[9]

Spontaneity exists in the here and now and is related to the readiness factor of any act. Spontaneity can become distorted. When the imagination is contained and the person's desire to move into action restrained by others (or conditions) the energy committed to the new creation and which has been mobilized will need to be dispelled. Following the imagination, preparing for a novel or useful application now ceases to be the controlling factor; rather, the concern becomes simply the release of energy. This phenomenon has been termed "act hunger", the main ingredient of pathological spontaneity. Should the creative process continue unencumbered toward the direction of usefulness, novelty and adequacy, the release of energy is spontaneous, producing completion of the creation.

The Cultural Conserve

The cultural conserve is comprised of the mass of all existing creations: ideas and information, form and design, all structures, one's life experience, and the finished products of any creative process. The capacity for usefulness of the cultural conserve lies dormant until a person comes into contact with it. Then, ". . . the cultural conserve plays an even more significant role as the springboard for enticing spontaneity toward creativity."[10] In the drawing of the Canon of Creativity (p. 1) Moreno has depicted a circle leading from the cultural conserve (CC) which then returns to it and interacts with it. The creator may return to the cultural conserve again and again until he/she has generated sufficient momentum to "spin off" into the direction of creativity (shown in the drawing as the mid-line). This return to the cultural conserve is an important aspect of the creative process. The interaction with all existing knowledge and experience provides a "feedback loop" for the usefulness, originality and adequacy of the new creation. The cultural conserve is not the enemy of spontaneity. The enemy are those critics who fear spontaneity, preferring to be safe and secure within convention and past achievement.

Creativity

"The realization of fulfillment of creativity in man takes many forms. Among them are two outstanding categories of the creator: (1) the devotee of the truly perfect; and (2) the devotee of the truly imperfect, the lover of spontaneity.

The devotee of the truly perfect upholds the conserve as the ultimate value and is skeptical of spontaneity. He is the devotee of theory and the master of words. That is why he is compulsive, authoritarian, and critical of those who act. He loves to develop magnificent theoretical systems, physical, social and cultural projects. He sponsors theories of religion, altruism, of love, and preferably on the theoretical reflective level. He shrinks from experimenting existentially with religious or theoretical creativity. He does not strive for the embodiment of sainthood in his own life.

The improvising creator, in contrast, is devoted to experimentation in all forms—religious, therapeutic, scientific. He is the improvisor in art, science and religion. Rather than writing books and formulating systems he loves to act and create. Whereas the "truly perfect" is loved by an elite, the improvisor is loved by the multitude. It is a profound contrast between the aristocrat and the people's leader."[11]

It is this improvising creativity that connects Morenean philosophy to eastern religion/philosophy. The existence of the flaw, the imperfection, in works of art is central to Zen art. For instance, in studying oriental painting one is told to contemplate the unpainted portion of the canvas, the white spaces. In directing a psychodrama the student is told to give attention to what is missing, what hasn't happened yet. In the creative process the creator engages with the cultural conserve, notices what is missing, notices the incompletions, and imagines something new. It was apparent to Moreno that society had tended to organize itself in ways to mask imperfections, no need to create, no need to act. Moreno's philosophical system was formulated to assure a place for his approach to the evolution of mankind.

The Science of Action

The greatest challenge in life is to be present, in the here and now, and to act. The science of action is concerned with preparation for action, barriers to action (resistance), inability to be in the moment, and therapeutic methods designed to assist the creative process in life. The task of action methods is to explore those events and situations in which a person has learned attitudes and behaviors preventing spontaneity and creativity. The usual instruction is, "Show me. Don't tell me." Verbal communication is the activity of speaking; however, it is less direct, describing rather than demonstrating. Showing, rather than telling, provides access to observing and measuring, the scientist's tools for study, hypothesizing and invention. Thus, the name, science of action.

The science of action begins with the crucial concern of the warming up process. This phase begins in the here and now and involves externalizing the encounter one has with him/herself, and the unspoken dialogue one has with another. Continued externalization makes concrete the situations, stories, dynamics as if it is happening now, providing a stage for action, which is dramatic, both for the individual and for the social network in which he/she relates. The warming up begins with the cultural conserve, the repository of the person's (group's) life experience. The externalization in action provides an opportunity to expand on the experience and to "play out" an actual situation, clearly and fully. Barriers to spontaneity become evident, can be confronted, studied, evaluated, and changes proposed by introducing "what if" situations (surplus reality).

Moreno is not content with insight, nor is this the scientist's goal. The science of action theory is firmly based on the belief that what has been learned in action must also be un-learned in action. And, as this learning has taken place among others, either as interactors or as audience, the learning has been co-produced. It is for this reason that Moreno developed the branch of the social sciences, sociometry, to provide a framework for exploring the involvement of interactors in the development of one's personal cultural conserve.

Role Theory

Each person is born into an existing culture (social network). The reality of that culture is both personally and collectively defined. As the infant interacts with his/her world the self emerges. Moreno explains: "The tangible aspects of what is known as "ego" are the roles in which it operates."[12] "Role emergence is prior to the emergence of the self. Roles do not emerge from the self, but the self may emerge from roles."[13] It is helpful to refer again to the philosophy of spontaneity and creativity. The role is an abstraction which exists to put a name to certain actions. The self is the potential creator of the self by engaging in the implied actions of the role and giving the role a personal definition. The identity of a person depends upon the interaction with the role conserve, using it as a "springboard" for creativity within the role repertoire. Figure 2 below depicts this process and its relationship to the Canon of Creativity:

Figure 2.   Role Development Related to Canon of Creativity (Hale)

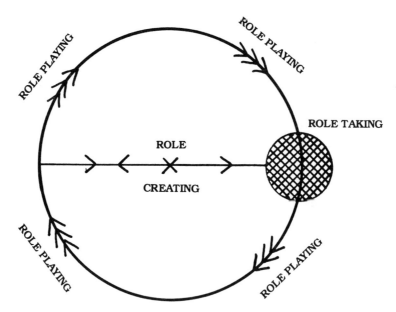

Moreno's role theory also involves a process of role development which is explained in depth in "The Spontaneity Theory of Child Development" to be found in **Psychodrama,** vol. 1. When a person first encounters a role it is usually being enacted, or it is described in words. The **perceptions** about what the role is, and the **expectations** one has for the **enactment** of the role is prescribed. Often, the first response is to observe the role, imitate it as a way to become familiar with the role. Through interactions with others a person receives feedback on their role enactment. Based on this feedback the person makes a decision on whether or not to incorporate the role into his/her repertoire as is, or to experiment further. The role may also be discarded.

Moreno described three categories of roles:

1. somatic roles—roles defined by physical realities
2. socio/cultural roles—roles collectively defined by systems and cultures
3. psychodramatic roles—roles defined by a person's imagination

Also of concern to role development is the awareness of roles in ascendence and roles in descendence. When a role is new to one's repertoire there is more anxiety as the role is underdeveloped and still experimental. The well-developed role is one where there is sufficient spontaneity present to produce novelty and usefulness. Roles in descendence are most often overdeveloped roles and rigidity becomes more evident.

Access to roles becomes vital to the development of the self. The ego must have roles in which to operate. This is where sociometric study becomes extremely useful, for it is through careful and thoughtful exploration of access to roles that members of groups begin to co-produce the growth of one another. The group studies their choices of each other in order to evaluate the **collective** impact of their choices on each individual's opportunity for roles of high value, and their access to the process of role creating.

Sociometry and the Science of Society

Moreno developed a socio-atomic theory of the socius which is a composite of persons viewed from the perspective of one person or viewed collectively by a group. The structure of the socius which Moreno referred to as *social reality* is made up of two factors:

1. external reality—"consists of visible, overt and observable groups"
2. sociometric matrix—the interpenetration of numerous less visible dynamics, both quantitative and qualitative.

Social reality denotes "the historically growing, dynamic social groupings of which the actual universe consists." [14]

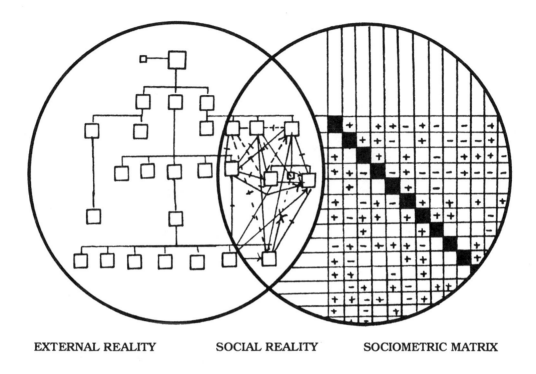

Figure 3. Social Reality

The structure of society is complex as are the dynamics forming it. Sociometric networks may be explored via numerous investigative methods. A person identifies the groups of which he or she is a member and can then proceed to explore **group dynamics** via the individual social atom, sociograms which result from the sociometric test, and target sociograms depicting connections of group members' choices on multiple selection criteria; or, **individual dynamics** via the social network map, psychological social atom, and role diagram. An overview of the methodological system is presented in Figure 4.

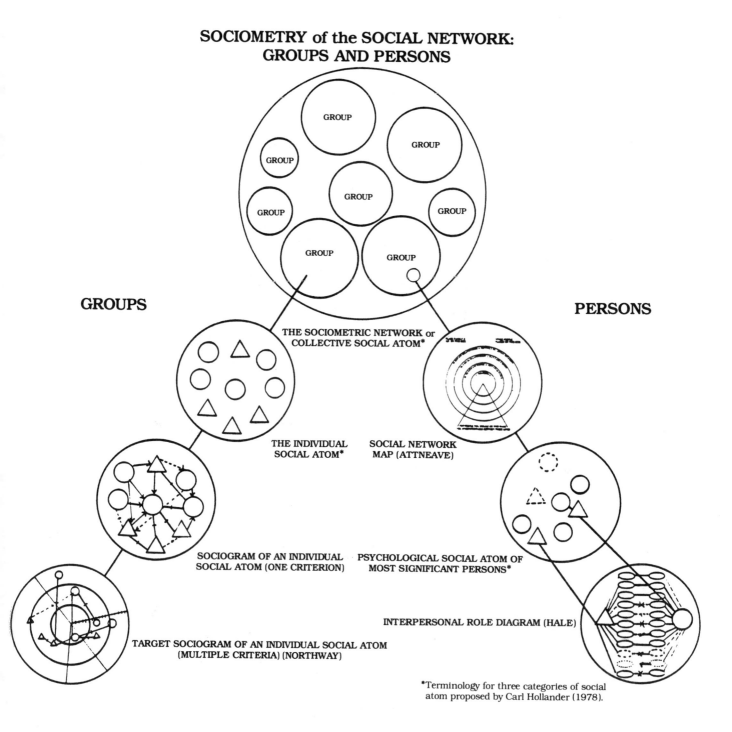

Figure 4.   Sociometry of the Social Network: Groups and Persons

Sociometric Networks may be explored via numerous investigative methods. A person identifies the groups he or she is a member of and can proceed to explore group dynamics (individual social atom, sociograms which result from the sociometric test, and target sociograms depicting connections of group members on multiple criteria) OR individual dynamics (social network map, psychological social atom, and role diagrams). By Ann E. Hale, 1980.

Moreno wanted people to view social structure in the same manner as one may view other cultural conserves—the existing structures have the same potential for creative change. The purpose of sociometric methods designed by Moreno and his co-researchers in the 1930's through 1950's, is to make it possible for every person to take part in creating the structure for a universe which ". . . can (not) have less of an objective than the whole of mankind."[15] Participants in sociometric explorations become, according to Moreno: co-researcher, co-scientist, co-observer, co-therapist, co-creator.

The involvement of **all** persons as research actors is crucial if one believes that all persons have a right to a place in the world, a place where he/she belongs, where he/she has access to roles of high value, where the creative/spontaneous self can survive. Persons need to be aware and present on an everyday basis in order to monitor three prevailing social phenomena: sociogenetic law, sociostasis, and the sociodynamic effect.

> **Sociogenetic law**—This law acknowledges the "inheritance" each generation and each person has in terms of natural groupings. It refers to that tribal element which is inherent in each of us, and which has developed over centuries into rituals, custom, territoriality. It is observable in groups of children who form and re-form their groups based on these unlearned, but "assimilated" codes of behavior.[16]

> **Sociostasis**—Every person (and hence, every group) has an observable and measurable sociometric set: a quantity and quality of relationships which he/she must maintain in order to experience social equilibrium. The set varies by individual. A person may be in crisis or experience stress when sociostasis is not maintained. (See "Exploring Your Sociometric Set," Chapter 3, Appendix VII, p. 78.) The therapeutic objective for disequilibrium is to repair the social atom.

> **Sociodynamic effect**—This phenomenon results when the wealth of choices fall to a small number of people and when only a few choices must be spread over a large number of people. Access to roles, including access to role-taking, role-playing and role creating so important to the emergence of the self, is denied by the sociometric selection process and by external reality. The result to the chosen few is rigidity, controlling behavior, overwork and depersonalization. The result to the underchosen is isolation, apathy, competition, and reduced activity.

Sociometry becomes a methodological necessity for the conscientious group leader who has the responsibility to "share the wealth" of his/her knowledge in order that leadership roles, as well as other group roles, are accessible.

Theory of Interpersonal Relations

In order for sociometric study to succeed participants will need to be able to account for the choices they make for interactors, to understand motivation for choice and underlying feelings of attraction and repulsion. The **science** of the method is in the valence (strength) of positive and negative response, in chosen or not chosen, near or distant. Because this is observable and measurable, a person or group can recognize a particular structure resulting from their combined choice-making, evaluate it and propose any change they may wish to make. The discomfort of revealing (and knowing) such personal details as motivation for choice, is offset by the value of change, the value of continued creativity as individuals and group members. It helps to have a language for understanding and describing those feelings.

Tele, Transference and Empathy

Moreno coined the term **tele** to describe that current of feeling which flows between two persons. Tele, an abstraction, is responsible for reciprocity, mutuality and cohesion in groups. "Moreno defines tele as 'insight into,' 'appreciation of,' and 'feeling for,' the 'actual makeup' of the other person."[16] Tele affects a relationship by preceding the actual meeting with feelings projected across space.[17] Tele exists when the perception one has of another matches the perception that person has of him/herself.

Transference exists when the attraction or repulsion to another person has only to do with an image which is projected onto that person. It does not match that person's image of him/herself. It may have nothing at all to do with that person; or , it is possible that the person being projected onto may have, or exhibit, mannerisms which evoke a particular memory. A person whose response to another is based on transference will be unable to role reverse with accuracy until the transference figure has been dealt with.

Empathy is referred to as one-way tele. A person is able to see another person as they really are, but that person is unable to reciprocate. Empathy is a necessary ingredient for persons and groups who elect to engage in group psychotherapy.

Transference and the projective process may be used creatively to act on the unresolved areas of one's life experience. Using dramatic methods, Moreno encouraged his clients to freely project onto trained therapeutic assistants (auxiliary egos). The projection is played out with the intention of finding its source and resolving the barrier preventing a telic response from emerging. In order to be successful, empathic conditions must exist.

Moreno envisaged a world beyond the therapeutic "auxiliary world" of trained assistants. He wants all men to engage one another, face to face, to meet, and to develop the capacity for "creative neutrality," that empathic response which takes precedence over positive and negative feelings.

Summary

Moreno's tools for world-making rely on fully knowing the extent of his philosophy, which involves the Canon of Creativity, the Science of Action, Role Theory, Sociometry and the Science of Society, and the Theory of Interpersonal Relations. Moreno's philosophy is a philosophy of life, which places value on freedom, change, action, play, truth, role reversal, and being present in the moment. It is a subversive philosophy. It has enormous room for the scientific, but mostly it is intended for the humane.

CHAPTER 1
FOOTNOTES

1. Biographical information for this chapter has been compiled from the following sources: "Preludes to the Sociometric Movement" in *Who Shall Survive?* (1978) edition by J.L. Moreno, N.Y.: Beacon Press, 1978; American Sociological Association *Footnotes* by Robert Boguslaw, November, 1974; "Obituary: J.L. Moreno," *The Beacon News,* May 15, 1974; Peter Dean Mendelsson, *Rethinking Sociometry: Toward the Reunification of Theory, Philosophy, Methodology and Praxis,* Ph.D. Dissertation, St. Louis, Washington University, 1976; and Walt Anderson, "J.L. Moreno and the Origins of Psychodrama: A Biographical Sketch" in Ira A. Greenberg, Ed., *Psychodrama: Theory and Therapy,* N.Y.: Behavioral Publns., 1974, pp. 205-211. Zerka T. Moreno supplied information to me personally.

2. J.L. Moreno, "Preludes to the Sociometric Movement" in *Who Shall Survive?,* Beacon, N.Y.: Beacon House, 1978, p. xviii.

3. *Ibid.,* p. xxxix.

4. *Ibid.,* p. lvi.

5. Walt Anderson, "J.L. Moreno and the Origins of Psychodrama: A Biographical Sketch" in *Psychodrama: Theory and Therapy,* Ira A. Greenberg, Ed. New York: Behavioral Publns., 1974, p. 208.

6. Personal communication, Zerka T. Moreno.

7. J.L. Moreno, *Who Shall Survive?,* p. 23.

8. *Ibid.,* p. xviii.

9. J.L. Moreno, "The Creativity Theory of Personality: Spontaneity, Creativity and Human Potentialities," *Arts and Sciences,* New York University Bulletin, Vol. 66, no. 4 (January 24, 1966), p. 20.

10. *Ibid.*

11. *Ibid.,* p. 21-22.

12. J.L. Moreno, *Who Shall Survive?,* p. 75.

13. *Ibid.,* p. 76.

14. *Ibid.,* p. 81.

15. *Ibid.,* p. 3.

16. *Ibid.,* p. 215.

17. Gordon W. Allport, "Comments on: J.L. Moreno, Transference, Countertransference and Tele," *Group Psychotherapy,* Vol. 7 (1957), p. 307.

BIBLIOGRAPHY

Allport, Gordon W., "Comments on: J.L. Moreno, Transference, Countertransference and Tele", *Group Psychotherapy,* Vol. 7 (1954), p. 307.

Anderson, Walt, "J.L. Moreno and the Origins of Psychodrama: A Biographical Sketch," in Ira A. Greenberg, Editor, *Psychodrama: Theory and Therapy,* New York, Behavioral Publications, 1974, pp. 205-211.

Borgatta, Edgar F., Robert Boguslaw, Martin P. Haskell, "On the Work of Jacob L. Moreno", *Sociometry,* Vol. 38, no. 1 (1975), pp. 148-161.

Bratescu, Gheorghe, "The Date and Birthplace of J.L. Moreno", *Group Psychotherapy and Psychodrama,* Vol. 28, (1975), pp. 2-4.

Hart, Joseph W., "Identifying Ways of Distinguishing 'Choice Activity' from 'Closure Movements' When Administering Pictorial Sociometric Techniques (PST) to the Mentally Retarded", *Group Psychotherapy, Psychodrama and Sociometry,* Vol. 29 (1976), pp. 121-126.

Mendelsson, Peter Dean, *Rethinking Sociometry: Toward the Reunification of Theory, Philosophy, Methodology and Praxis.* Ph.D. Dissertation, St. Louis, Missouri, Washington University, 1976.

Meyer, Henry J., "The Sociometries of Dr. Moreno," *Sociometry,* Vol. 15, no. 3-4 (August-November, 1952), pp. 354-363.

Moreno, J.L., *Psychodrama,* Volume I, Beacon, N.Y., Beacon House, 1946.

————, "The Creativity Theory of Personality: Spontaneity, Creativity and Human Potentialities," *New York University Bulletin, Arts and Sciences,* Vol. 66, no. 4 (January 24, 1966), pp. 19-24.

————, et. al., *The Sociometry Reader,* Glencoe, Illinois, The Free Press, 1960.

————, *Who Shall Survive? Foundations of Sociometry, Group Psychotherapy and Sociodrama,* Beacon, N.Y., Beacon House, 1978.

Wysong, William J., *ACORNography, a Slide Presentation* (Presented at the 39th Annual Meeting of the American Society of Group Psychotherapy and Psychodrama, New York, April 13, 1981), Colorado Springs, Colorado, 1980.

CHAPTER II
THE SOCIAL ATOM

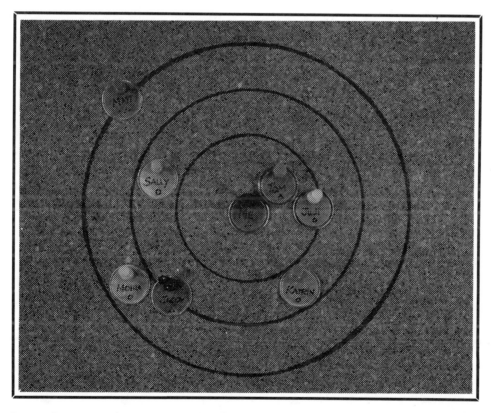

A social atom utilizing Whiteley's "streetlight sociometry" notational system.

(See page 26)

THE SOCIAL ATOM

The social atom is that nucleus of persons to whom one is connected. The connections between persons have a "nearness to distant" factor; some persons being more significant than others; some more peripheral. When people explore their social atom they identify **who** is included and **who** is excluded, **what** is the basis of choice, and **where** do these persons fit in relation to each other. Often this is accomplished by using the sociometric test which is described in Chapter III. Moreno described in **Who Shall Survive?** (1953) that:

> "One can look at the social atom from two directions, from an individual towards the community and from the community towards the individual." [1]

The sociometric test is designed to facilitate the community or collective view of combined social atoms and the impact of choices upon the group. This chapter will focus upon ways to explore the social atom from the point of view of the individual.

> "In the . . . 'individual-centered' social atom, one can see how the feelings radiate from him into many directions towards individuals who respond to him by likes, dislikes or indifferences and of whom he is aware, or who choose, reject or are neutral toward him without (sic) that he is aware of their participation in his social atom. This may be called the psychological aspect of the social atom." [2]

Historical Background of the Social Atom

Since the formal introduction of the concept of the social atom in the 1934 edition of **Who Shall Survive?** there have been changes and refinements in what is meant by the term. In the beginning Moreno defined a social atom and cultural atom. The term social atom was used to signify "a pattern of attractions, repulsions and indifferences which exist between individuals" [3] and "the focal pattern of role-relations around the individual" was the definition of the cultural atom. In the book **Sociometry, Experimental Method and the Science of Society** (1951), Moreno states that "the distinction between social and cultural atom is artificial. It is pertinent for construction purposes but it loses its significance within a living community." [4]

The complexity of sociometric structures had become apparent by this time. Moreno had been constructing maps of whole communities. The linkages between social atoms, the identification of psycho-social networks, and the clear distinction between kinds of groups made it necessary to reexamine the organization of the concept of the social atom.

One major impact on the concept of the social atom was the work of Helen Hall Jennings in the area of leadership. In 1943 Jennings identified two groups, **psychegroups and sociogroups:**

> "(I) sociogroups, i.e., groups where sociometric structure is based on a criterion which is collective in nature . . .
>
> (II) psychegroups, i.e., groups where sociometric structure is based on strictly **private** criterion which is **totally** personal in nature . . ." [5]

Charles Loomis and Harold Pepinsky in their ten-year summary of sociometry recommended that work concerning the individual social atom take into account these two groupings of criteria. [6]

Moreno's last writings about the social atom maintain that there is **one social atom** which is viewed from many perspectives. The individual-centered social atom, the collective-centered social atom are two such perspectives.

In 1972 Sharon Leman and Carl Hollander began to work with the organization of the social atom concept, and identified three distinct forms: [7]

1) Collective Social Atom—refers to the minimum number of meaningful groups to which we belong.

2) Individual Social Atom—refers to the smallest number of people required to maintain membership in a collective.

3) Psychological Social Atom—refers to the smallest number of people required by an individual in order to be in a state of sociostasis or social equilibrium.

When asked about this re-organization, Sharon Hollander replied, "We wanted to make the social atom more meaningful for everyday use." [8] The Hollanders use the three forms of social atom in their publications and the terms have gained wider usage. [9] One of the significant contributions of the Hollanders is the reminder one is given in these definitions of social atoms, that numbers are important. To be among the minimum or smallest number implies significance. At a time in the study of the social atom when the focus is on the complexity of the sociometric structure, it is good to be reminded that there is a "smallest number" which is sought and can be identified.

The concept of the social atom has now become incorporated into social psychology. Many of Moreno's ideas and theories have been found in the work of other sociologists, re-discovered or newly invented. It is important to sociometrists and psychodramatists to be aware of the many new constructions and contributions which exist in this area. One example is the work of psychologist Carolyn Attneave. Her book *Family Networks* (1973) with joint author Ross Speck has focused attention on the treatment of persons within their social network. Attneave has developed the Social Network Map, which offers another perspective on the exploration of the collective social atom.

Streetlight Sociometry

Streetlight Sociometry is a notational system which uses a color coding system for the choices that people make which is found in everyday life: the traffic light. It is also a method for depicting choices which allow for maximum movement, without erasures and being in action. This is accomplished by the use of color-coded push-pins used with key discs (pink for females and blue for males) which may be affixed on a corkboard. Marko Whiteley developed this method in 1979 as a way to "bring the advantages of sociometry back to universality." [10] "I was trying to think of some way to simplify the process and make it more available to the public when the idea hit me that relationships were very similar to the interaction with traffic signals. Some relationships gave you a clear green for go and some a definite rejection or stop signal. Many others remained indifferent or gave the caution signal." [11]

The Streetlight Sociometry system can be applied to every sociometric procedure, the sociometric test, the role diagram, encounter, and the various social atom explorations.

"The expression of positive feelings in a relationship on any of the graphs could be done with a green line drawn between character symbols and the negative ones with a red line. The feelings of indifference could be expressed with the yellow.

"As I applied this color scheme to sociograms, I realized how visually they were easier to read. In addition to simplifying the charting procedures, the words like positive, negative and indifference were replaced by go, stop and caution." [12]

The use of this notational system enhances the possibility that group members will want to participate as co-researchers. A common language has been introduced, a language which is connected with helping the traffic to move smoothly. It simplifies without distorting. The fact that it is simple to comprehend helps to overcome the difficulty some people have with putting "fancy language to their feelings". It approximates the choice category and by doing so the Streetlight notational system can be used as a starter.

Social Atom Explorations

As stated previously, there are a number of perspectives from which to explore the social atom. As well, there are various ways to display the information gathered: on paper, by moveable graphics, and in action. The following approaches to the exploration of the social atom have been included in this chapter, beginning on page 20.

1) Moreno's Social Atom of persons emotionally related to the subject (1936) which is used to depict consummated relationships, wished for relationships and the person's acquaintance volume.

2) Social Atom Collectives Exploration (1957) by James Vander May and edited by Ann E. Hale, which is used to depict the significant collectives to which a person belongs and the interconnectedness of those collectives.

3) Perceptual Social Atom Sociogram (1975) by James Vander May and edited by Ann E. Hale, is

used to depict the feelings of attraction, repulsion and indifference which exist between persons in a group.

4) Psychological Social Atom Exploration (1981) by Ann E. Hale is used to identify those persons central to a person's existence and sociostasis.

5) Fantasy Family Social Atom (1976) by Ann E. Hale is used to explore an imaginary family constellation and whom in an existent group could take the roles of those fantasy family members.

6) Social Atom Explored in Action is a description of an action exploration of a group according to how central each person believes he or she is to the operation of the group and where each person feels him or herself to be in relation to others in the group—by Alton Barbour.

7) Streetlight Sociometry Notational System applied to the social atom has been developed by Marko Whiteley (1979). This system makes it practical to use and easy to change.

MORENO'S SOCIAL ATOM*
Nucleus of Persons Emotionally Related to You

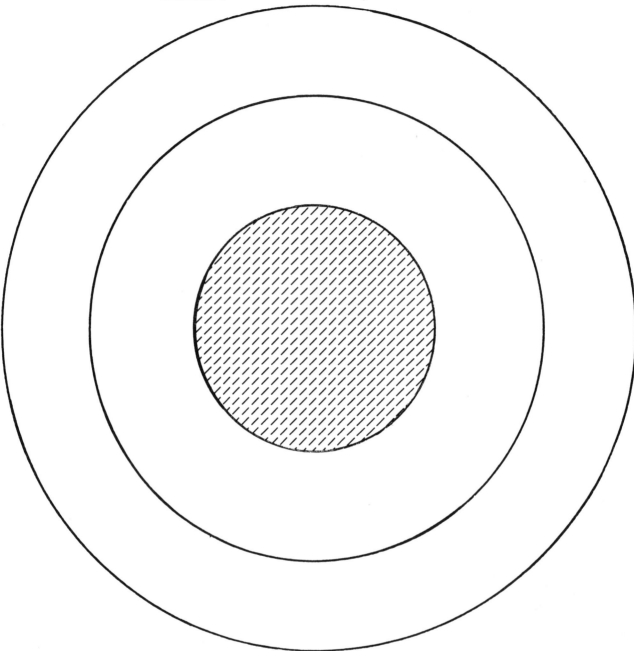

*For additional information see J.L. Moreno, *Sociometry, Experimental Method and the Science of Society.* Beacon, N.Y.: Beacon House, 1951, pp. 57-69.

This exercise is designed to help you identify (1) those people to whom you feel emotionally related, (2) those with whom you wish to have a relationship, and (3) those persons who are acquaintances.

INSTRUCTIONS:

First   Make a list of the persons you know and indicate in the margin the number 1, 2, or 3 depending on whether they fit the category as described above.

Second   Using the symbols of circles for females ◯ and triangles for males △ place yourself in the inner nucleus and position those persons to whom you feel emotionally related within the inner circle, using nearness or distance to indicate their significance to you. Continue with category (2) placing persons in the middle circle, and (3) the outer circle.

Third   Be aware of what you experience as you proceed. Discuss the meaning this exploration has had for you with another person, or share it with the group.

SOCIAL ATOM COLLECTIVES EXPLORATION*

This exploration will bring into focus the collectives which are significant to you and the interconnectedness of those collectives. Because each collective implies a role repertoire, shifts and changes in your choices for these groups affect your interactions with others and how you identify yourself.

1. Make a list of the groups that are significant to you. Be sure to include significant groups even if you are no longer active in them, or groups to which you have wanted to belong.

2. Take a sheet of paper and place yourself in a circle on the page. Giving each group, or collective a name, draw circles on the page for each group, using the size of the circle to indicate its importance to you relative to the other groups. Draw lines from you to each group using the notational system given below.

3. If possible to do so in the space allowed, list the individuals in each group who are significant to you. Number them in the order of their importance to you *here and now.* Remember, importance and significance to you does not always mean that you feel positive or attracted to that person. Your feeling for the person(s) can be explored using the Perceptual Social Atom Sociogram.

4. Identify for yourself those persons who appear in more than one collective or group.

5. Identify the reason for each group's significance to you. Evaluate which groups you could do without. Of these groups, which have to be existent in order for you to feel social equilibrium or sociostasis.

6. Examine missing groups, the wished for group or the group that is inactive. How do you manage without these groups, and what plans have you for the future?

7. Discuss this exploration with another person or share what you have experienced with the group.

NOTATIONAL SYSTEM

a. Attraction _____

b. Rejection __ __ __ __

c. Indifference . . . .

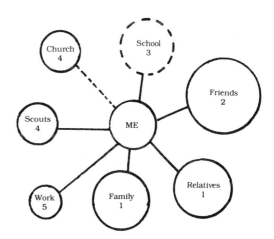

___

*This exercise is an edited version of an exercise by James Vander May: "A Perceptual Social Atom Sociogram", *Group Psychotherapy and Psychodrama,* Vol. 28 (1975), p. 129-132. Edited by Ann E. Hale, M.A.

PERCEPTUAL SOCIAL ATOM SOCIOGRAM*

The following exercise is designed to focus the feelings of attraction, repulsion, or indifference which exist between you and others by first identifying your feelings for others and, secondly, making perceptual guesses about the feelings others may have for you.

1. Identify a collective (or group) you wish to explore.

2. Make a list of names of the members of this group. If it is a large group, list the names of persons with whom you have a significant relationship, including strained relationships or persons who are deceased or who have left the group.

3. Rank each person in the collective according to their significance to you. Place a number next to each person's name. Several persons may have the same degree of significance.

4. Take a sheet of paper and place yourself in a circle at the center of the sheet. Using circles for females ◯ and triangles for males △ place each person on the sheet according to where you perceive them to be in relation to you. (This does not mean where you want them to be, or where they may want to be, but your best guess of where they stand in relation to you.) Place the ranking number to the right of their name.

5. Using the following notational system to indicate the feeling you have for each person **here and now**, draw a line using the code half-way between your circle and the symbol for the other person. Do this for each person in the collective.

6. Now make a perceptual guess about how each person in the collective may feel toward you **here and now**. In order to maximize the perceptual accuracy of the sociogram, it is necessary for you to role reverse with each person. Using the code, draw a line from each person to meet the line drawn half-way from your place on the sociogram.

7. Review the relationship you have with each person and identify what the reasons are for your feelings for each person and for their feelings for you.

8. If you are unsure or disturbed about the information which appears, find a way to check your perceptions with the persons involved. Discuss your feelings and reaction with another person or with the group.

NOTATIONAL SYSTEM:

a. Mutual attraction ——————————
b. Mutual rejection — — — — — — — — —
c. Mutual indifference ··················
e. Attraction - Indifference ———————— ······
f. Rejection - Indifference — — — — — ·····

Female ◯   Male △   Missing Person ⬚ △

SOCIOGRAM EXAMPLE:

———————
*This exercise is an edited version of an exercise by James Vander May: "A Perceptual Social Atom Sociogram," *Group Psychotherapy and Psychodrama*, Vol. 28 (1975), p. 128-134. Edited by Ann E. Hale, M.A.

PSYCHOLOGICAL SOCIAL ATOM

The smallest number of people required by you in order to feel a social equilibrium (sociostasis) is called psychological social atom.* When someone who has become central to your life is missing (temporarily or permanently) the energy that would normally be given to creative, productive endeavors becomes channeled into coping with the loss, managing the feelings evoked and searching for another person who can fit a similar place in your life. Becoming familiar with your psychological social atom and studying the dynamics of maintaining these connections can help you understand the moods and changes that occur in your life and suggest ways to handle them.

The following questions, taken from an article on intimacy by Vick Rubin,** are offered here as a means for focusing you on those persons who are central to you. In the space following each question, note the names of persons who come to mind.

1. I feel that I can confide in ＿＿＿＿＿＿＿＿＿＿＿ about virtually everything.

2. I would do almost anything for ＿＿＿＿＿＿＿＿＿＿＿ .

3. If I could never be with ＿＿＿＿＿＿＿＿＿＿＿ , I would feel miserable.

4. If I were lonely, my first thought would be to seek ＿＿＿＿＿＿＿＿＿＿＿ out.

5. One of my primary concerns is ＿＿＿＿＿＿＿＿＿＿＿ 's welfare.

6. I would forgive ＿＿＿＿＿＿＿＿＿＿＿ for practically anything.

7. I feel responsible for ＿＿＿＿＿＿＿＿＿＿＿ 's well being.

8. I would greatly enjoy being confided in by ＿＿＿＿＿＿＿＿＿＿＿ .

9. It would be hard for me to get along without ＿＿＿＿＿＿＿＿＿＿＿ .

Review the names of persons listed above. Are there other people in your life who feel central to you? *Make a list* of those persons whom you perceive to comprise the smallest number of people who you need in your life to feel a social equilibrium.

Next take a sheet of paper and place your name in a circle on the page. Using circles for females ◯ and triangles for males △ place each person on the page in proximity to you according to how close or distant you feel you are *here and now.* If you feel that you are becoming closer to each other draw an arrow towards you; and, if you are feeling an increasing distance between you and the other person, draw an arrow indicating moving further away.

As you diagram your psychological social atom, note the feelings that arise. Discuss what you are experiencing with another person or share your feelings with the group.

If it seems important to diagram the feelings which exist *here and now* between you and the persons who comprise your psychological social atom, follow the directions for the Perceptual Social Atom Sociogram.

---

*Hollander, Carl E., and Sharon Hollander, *Action Relationships in Learning* Denver, Colorado, Snow Lion Press, 1978.

**Rubin, Vick, "Lovers and Other Strangers: The Development of Intimacy in Encounter and Relationships," *American Scientist,* Vol. 62, pp. 182-190.

FANTASY FAMILY SOCIAL ATOM

A person has no choice over which family he or she is born into. The decisions about how many brothers and sisters you have is often a decision which does not include your vote. This exercise is designed to evoke (1) a fantasy of the family you missed having, and (2) to identify who in this group could take the role of the various family members of your fantasy family social atom.

1. Imagine a family you would have liked to have had. Select an age when it would have been important to you to have had this family. _____ years old.

2. List your fantasy family below, and identify whom in the group you would choose to have in the role of each fantasy family member.

FAMILY MEMBER (SPECIFY OR IMPLY AGE AND SEX)	GROUP MEMBER FOR THE ROLE	WHY I HAVE CHOSEN HIM OR HER FOR THE ROLE

3. Make perceptual guesses about the role other members of this group may have chosen for you in their fantasy family social atom.

GROUP MEMBER	ROLE	WHY I HAVE BEEN CHOSEN FOR THE ROLE

4. Discuss with group members the roles you have chosen for them. Share the reasons you have given and discuss the perceptions you had of who would choose you for certain roles.

5. Group members may wish to enact a scene at the age specified, having the members of their fantasy family social atom around them. Appropriate time should be available for integration and closure.

6. Discuss what you have experienced from this exercise with another person or share your feelings with the group.

7. The group may need to close with a de-roling exercise in which group members take back the role they have projected onto another group member.

SOCIAL ATOM EXPLORED IN ACTION
By Alton Barbour, Ph.D., University of Denver

This exercise is designed for a collective or group to explore group composition and structure. Each individual places him- or herself on an imaginary target according to his or her own perception of where they fit in the group. Taken into consideration is the positioning of other group members, thereby producing a group action sociogram.

1. Imagine yourselves on a large target with each concentric "ring" about a yard wide. The center of the target indicates the center of the group.

2. Be spontaneous and honest in your responses rather than reflective and analytic.

3. Position yourself on the target taking into consideration two things:

   a. Place yourself near the people that you feel genuinely close to and far from the people that you feel less close to. Use the physical space as an analogue for psychological space for closeness and for distance.

   b. Place yourself close to the center of the target to the extent that you believe yourself included in the group and central to the group operation. Place yourself farther from the center as you see yourself as less included and less central to the group operation.

In making both of the estimates, consider only where you are *now* relative to the others in the group—not last week or where you might be later.

Know where you are before you move there. Don't let others make up your mind for you. If you choose a place which feels wrong when you take it, step out again. Make another decision.

4. Let each person, one at a time but in any order, address the group as a whole.

   This is how I see my position in the group ⎯⎯⎯⎯⎯⎯⎯⎯⎯⎯⎯⎯⎯⎯⎯⎯⎯⎯⎯ .

   This is how I feel about my position in the group ⎯⎯⎯⎯⎯⎯⎯⎯⎯⎯⎯⎯⎯⎯⎯⎯ .

   This is what it tells me about myself ⎯⎯⎯⎯⎯⎯⎯⎯⎯⎯⎯⎯⎯⎯⎯⎯⎯⎯⎯⎯⎯ .

   These statements are made while the group *holds its position* physically on the target. Persons may need to be asked to be brief.

5. When the physical-spatial part of this exercise is completed and each person has had a chance to respond, the group may draw together if it wishes for interaction and sharing.

Editor's Note: Often persons may wish to explore what it would be like to have a different position in the group. A role reversal with someone who has the desired position may be indicated. Group discussion could focus on what has to happen within yourself and within the group in order for each person to have or maintain the position they want in the group.

SOCIAL ATOM EXPLORATIONS
WITH STREETLIGHT SOCIOMETRY NOTATIONAL SYSTEM

For this exercise you will need the following supplies:

1 **corkboard** per person (minimum 8½x11 inches; or a carpet with a closely woven nap)

1-1½ inch metal-rimmed **key tags** in sufficient numbers for one for each person in each social atom depicted, approximately 20 per person

1 **light-blue leaded pencil** per person

1 **pink leaded pencil** per person

Push pins in colors: green, red, and yellow (they can be purchased in boxes of 100)

The Streetlight Sociometry Notational System was developed by Marko Whiteley (1979) to make use of a color coding system in everyday usage, familiar to persons in all walks of life, and to make it practical for a person to examine his social atom as frequently as he wishes.

1. Select the social atom or collective you wish to explore.

2. Write the names of each person in the collective on a key tag. Lightly shade key tag with blue pencil for males, and pink pencil for females.

3. Next determine how you are feeling about each person *here and now.* Use the following notational system:

GREEN PUSH-PIN   GO: Positive, growing, movement possible
YELLOW PUSH-PIN   CAUTION: Uncertain, cautious feelings, tentative movement, slow
RED PUSH-PIN   STOP: Negative feelings stopping the relationship, stuck, angry feelings

4. Take a push-pin for how you are feeling about yourself here and now and use it to fix the key tag with your name on it onto the cork board. The cork board represents your life space at the moment, your social atom.

5. Place the other key tags which represent the other members of the collective on the cork board, using the push pins to represent the feelings you have about each person; OR, you can do the perceptual aspect of the social atom by using a push-pin to represent the feeling *you perceive* that they have about you.

6. Identify the feelings you have had as you have proceeded with this exercise. What interpretation have you of your social atom? What seems important for you to do at this point in time about the inter-actions you have with the members of this collective?

7. Discuss what you have experienced in this exercise with another person or share with the members of the group.

Whiteley suggests that people keep their cork board in a handy location and make brief explorations everyday. If recording the results are important, the information can be written down or a photograph taken.

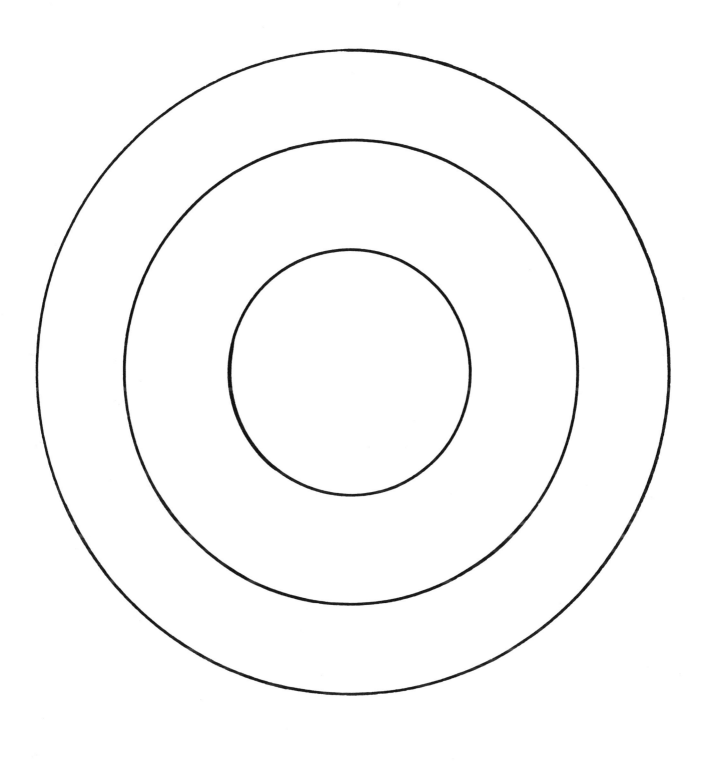

Name _____   Date _____

Criterion: _____

TARGET FOR USE IN SOCIAL ATOM EXPLORATIONS

CHAPTER II

FOOTNOTES

1. Moreno, J.L., *Who Shall Survive?,* Foundations of Sociometry, Group Psychotherapy and Sociodrama, Beacon, N.Y., Beacon House, 1953 ed., p. 294.

2. *Ibid.*

3. *Ibid.,* pp. 69-70.

4. Moreno, J.L., *Sociometry, Experimental Method and the Science of Society,* Beacon, N.Y., Beacon House, 1951, p. 147.

5. Jennings, Helen Hall, "Sociometric Differentiation of the Psychegroup and the Sociogroup," *Sociometry,* Vol. X, No. 1 (February, 1947) p. 71.

6. Loomis, Charles P. and Harold B. Pepinksy, *Sociometry, 1937-1947: Theory and Methods* (Sociometry Monographs, 20), Beacon, N.Y., Beacon House, 1949, p. 5.

7. Hollander, Carl E. and Sharon L. Hollander, "Sociometry" *Sensorsheet,* Boulder, Colorado, Winter, 1973, pp. 4-6.

8. Conversation with Sharon Hollander, May 2, 1981.

9. These concepts are described in greater detail. See Bibliography, Carl Hollander (1978), Sharon Hollander (1974; 1978) and Vander May (1975).

10. Whiteley, Marko, *Streetlight Sociometry* (a one-page description), North Hollywood, California, 1979.

11. _____, *Streetlight Sociometry, A Self-Actualizing Portfolio,* Los Angeles, California, 1980, p. 4.

12. *Ibid.*

BIBLIOGRAPHY

Attneave, Carolyn. *Social Network Map.* Seattle, Washington, 1975.

Barbour, Alton. "Group Composition and Structure," an unpublished exercise. Denver, Colorado, University of Denver, n.d.

Hale, Ann E., "Fantasy Family Social Atom," an unpublished exercise. Roanoke, Virginia, 1976.

Hollander, Carl E. and Sharon L. Hollander, *Action Relationships in Learning.* Denver, Colorado, Snow Lion Press, 1978.

_____. "Sociometry" in *Sensorsheet,* a publication of the Earth Science Educational Program, Boulder, Colorado, Winter, 1973, pp. 4-6.

Hollander, Sharon L. *Social Atom: An Alternative to Imprisonment.* Denver, Colorado, Snow Lion Press, 1978. (also in: *Group Psychotherapy and Psychodrama,* Vol. 27 (1974), pp. 173-183.)

Jennings, Helen Hall, *Leadership and Isolation.* New York: Longmans, Green, 1943.

_____. "Sociometric Differentiation of the Psychegroup and the Sociogroup," *Sociometry,* Vol. X, no. 1 (February, 1947) pp. 71-79.

Loomis, Charles P. and Harold B. Pepinsky, *Sociometry, 1937-1947: Theory and Methods.* (Sociometry Monograph, no. 20), Beacon, N.Y., Beacon House, 1949.

Moreno, J.L. *Sociometry, Experimental Method and the Science of Society.* Beacon, N.Y., Beacon House, 1951.

_____, editor, et. al. *The Sociometry Reader,* Glencoe, Illinois, Free Press, 1960.

_____, *Who Shall Survive?* Beacon, N.Y., Beacon House, 1953. Third edition, 1978.

Mueller, Barbara and Penny MacElveen-Hoehn, "The Use of the Network Concepts in an Educational Model" *Group Psychotherapy, Psychodrama and Sociometry,* Vol. 32 (1979) pp. 165-172.

Rubin, Vick. "Lovers and Other Strangers: the Development of Intimacy in Encounter and Relationships," American Scientist, Vol. 62, pp. 182-190.

Speck, Ross and Carolyn Attneave. *Family Networks,* New York, Vintage, 1973.

Vander May, James. "Social Atom Exercise" an unpublished exercise. Grand Rapids, Michigan, 1973.

_____. "Perceptual Social Atom Sociogram," *Group Psychotherapy and Psychodrama,* Vol. 28 (1975), p. 128-134.

Whiteley, Marko, *Streetlight Sociometry, a Self-Actualizing Portfolio.* Los Angeles, Calif., 1980.

Note: A Glossary of Terms used in this chapter may be found in the Appendices.

CHAPTER III
THE SOCIOMETRIC TEST

THE CLASSICAL SOCIOMETRIC TEST

Introduction

The primary purpose of a sociometric exploration of a group is to reveal information to the group and its leaders about itself, specifically focusing on the connections which exist between group members and the reasons for those connections. Moreno developed a number of devices which accomplish this purpose to varying degrees. This chapter describes the *sociometric test,* an exploration of the choices group members make for each other as partners for specific activities.

The sociometric test has been in use since 1934[1] in many settings[2] and in combination with other research procedures. Consequently, the procedure has undergone expansion and refinement. The writer has chosen to present the classical sociometric test in detail, as a process, with a warming-up phase, an action phase, a sharing phase, an analysis phase and a future projection/intervention phase. Following this detailed process the reader is referred to Chapter VI which is devoted to action sociometry.

The Warming-Up Phase

The decision to use a sociometric test may result from pre-session planning, or it may arise as an answer to an immediate group need. Also, a group may decide to learn about the procedure by "doing one." The *intent,* those reasons for choosing this particular procedure, becomes a central element in the design of the sociometric test and consequently affects the warming-up phase. The decision to use the sociometric test assumes a thorough understanding of the procedure on the part of the person conducting the exploration (sociometrist) and an ability to describe the process to participants.[3] The sociometrist needs to be clear about ways the sociometric test will meet an expressed need of the group here and now and the impact it may have on group member interactions in the future.

The Warm-up of the Sociometrist

The person conducting the sociometric test in a group is involved in directing a number of persons in a collective exploration of a highly sensitive personal process: choice. Preparation of oneself to engage in this procedure means anticipating group concerns and reactions and being ready to confront these concerns directly and confidently. It also involves examining oneself for anxieties, fears, prejudices and covert issues which might inhibit the confidence and honesty with which one handles the exploration.

Some questions which focus the sociometrist on his own warming-up phase[4]

(These questions are posed to evoke reflection and to generate an internal dialogue which can result in "spontaneous collaboration,"[5] that of the sociometrist with the group, utilizing his or her perceptions and pointing the way to those areas where more information is required.)

Can I identify when it was and what was happening in the group which prompted me to consider using the sociometric test?

What advantages do I foresee to its use? For me? For the group?

What disadvantages do I foresee for its use? For me? For the group?

What could happen which would affect my confidence? Who is likely to be involved if this happens? How do I imagine handling this situation if it occurs?

Is there any aspect of the procedure I am unsure of? What do I need to know, and where can I find an answer to my questions?

What alternatives to the sociometric test have I in mind which could assist the group in its present stage of development and readiness?

Will I take part in the exploration as a participant and share the role of co-researcher with the other members of the group? How will this decision be handled in the group?

The Warm-up of the Group

The first concern the sociometrist faces is the group's need to know what a sociometric test is, what is expected of them, what is going to happen.

> "A full and lucid presentation, first perhaps to small and intimate groups, and then in a town meeting if necessary, is extremely helpful."[6]

The writer has prepared two appendices to this chapter which will be useful at this stage of the process. Appendix I, a-e, is a modified flow chart of the steps involved in the classical sociometric test. This chart can be used in outlining the procedure to a group; it can be used by group members as a guide which they can follow. Appendix III, Description of the Sociometric Test for the First-time Participant, is a short guide which can be handed out to participants beforehand and used for discussion in those "small and intimate groups" Moreno suggested.

The manner in which the introductory phase is handled will greatly influence the level of fear and resistance in group members' responses. It is important that the sociometrist remember that anxiety affects attention and retention. He or she may have to repeat instructions and to clarify a point more than once.

These are concerns which are expressed with some frequency by groups as they contemplate involving themselves in the sociometric test. The following is a list of some frequently asked questions:[7]

What is tele?

What is meant by neutrality?

Why not just ask us whom we like and dislike?

Since you say that the group's structure is constantly changing, depending on what we are doing, how important can it be to get a picture of the group's structure for only one activity and one point in time?

Can't this cause a lot of hard feelings in our group? How can it possibly help someone for them to find out that they have been rejected?

I don't see how doing this can really change anything. Don't most people know where they stand by now?

I don't see the usefulness of bring negative feelings out into the open. Look at how we dealt with Judy and Carl's situation. It was never resolved. Why would we want to generate more conflict if we are not able to handle it?

Some frequently asked questions about the process of choosing:

What if I want to choose someone who is not here?

There is someone I could put under both choose to and choose not to. What do I do about the fact that to me they belong under both places?

Is there any way we could do this without showing the choices to anybody?

There are several people I would put as my third choice. I really can't distinguish between them. Is that allowed?

Won't people think I'm conceited if I guess that a lot of people are going to choose me?

Is it okay if I drop out? I really don't want to do this. I thought that I could go along with it, but as I do this I find it fits my worst fear of what could happen in a group like this.

These questions reflect the nature of the group members' readiness to proceed or the source of their anxiety if they are unable to continue. These concerns can be the topic of discussion in smaller subgroups. The less anxiety that exists the greater the potential for spontaneous choice-making.[8] It is important to proceed more slowly if that allows the group to be respectful of other group members' concerns and their status of co-researcher.

Meeting in small groups provides for a release of tension which may have been built up during the discussion in the larger group. The smaller group gives persons more opportunity to speak informally and to reveal the source of fears and anxieties. Persons eager to begin the sociometric test can use this opportunity to share the source of their positive feelings for the process.

What if the group decides not to proceed with the sociometric test?

Each person in the group should be willing to involve themselves. If a person or persons seriously object, the group needs to consider an alternative exploration which can be all-inclusive. Moreno's first sentence in *Who Shall Survive?* (1934) makes this quite clear.

> "A truly therapeutic procedure cannot have less an objective than the whole of mankind." [9]

There are times when a group may wish to proceed, despite the refusal of a member, or members, to participate. There are times when the objections have to do with the choice, "I choose not to choose." This is the stance of the true isolate. It would be important for that group member, or those group members, to experience the impact of their position on the structure of the group. The isolate is not to be confused with a person who is making a statement of refusal to involve himself based on lack of trust in the procedure of the sociometric test and the group's ability to use the information productively and humanely. In this instance the group should not proceed.

The group can refer to the Sharing Phase (see Appendix I.c) and share the feelings they have about what has taken place, what they expected to occur, what surprised them and what unfinished business has resulted from considering the sociometric test for use in the group.

The group may need to engage in less-threatening activities, even quasi-sociometric ones, in order to develop visible positive regard for each other, to create a more trusting group climate and to test out their skills in handling interpersonal conflict. Most group members are healthily reluctant to reveal negative choices in a group if they perceive the leadership and/or the group as incapable of facilitating conflict resolution. [10]

The Action Phase

The action phase of the sociometric test refers to the process of determining the criterion on which to base choices, declaring the choices, making perceptual guesses, and interacting with group members, sharing the objective and perceptual data with each person.

Selecting the Criterion on Which to Base the Sociometric Test

The criterion is designed to fit the situation in which the sociometric exploration is to be applied, specifically, what the group or the investigator wishes to know about the group. For example, a group which had become frustrated and unproductive when two of its "key members" were sick might want to explore the potential for leadership in the group. This might be done by asking the question, "Of the persons in the group who have not yet been in focus as leaders, whom would you choose to take charge of the group for one of its upcoming meetings?" In selecting this criterion the group would have important information available at such times when a choice for a leader needed to be made.

In selecting the criterion, the group should be informed that it may be possible to select more than one criterion. Time constraints may limit the options for additional criteria; however, it is a question which needs to be addressed at this time in the process. Having more than one criterion can demonstrate that group members make different choices depending on the activity implied in the criterion. It is important to keep referring back to what the group wishes to know about itself. (See Appendix II.)

Some Classifications of Criteria are: [11]

1. General versus Specific Criteria

    There are times when a group wants the protection that a general criterion appears to give. It is more comfortable to select a non-specific criterion. An example of the difference in general versus specific criteria is, "Whom do you choose to take a walk with after dinner?" and, "With whom do you choose to take a walk with after dinner in the unsafe section of the city?" The more specific the criterion the more clarity the group has of the meaning of the data. When general criteria are used it is important to analyze the reasons for choice and any hidden criteria implied in those reasons.

2. Actual versus hypothetical criteria

Hypothetical criteria concern future-projected roles and may imply actions or situations which have little likelihood of occurring. Actual criteria are reality-based and deal with the here and now role repertoire. An example of actual versus hypothetical criteria is, "Whom in the group do you choose to share your bomb shelter with in the case of nuclear attack?" and, "Whom in the group do you choose to invite to your home for a weekend visit?"

3. Action versus diagnostic criteria

Action criteria are criteria which are selected with the view in mind of carrying out the implied activity, either through assignment or simultaneous participation of group members. Diagnostic criteria are selected as criteria for investigation purposes only and are not proposed as criteria to be acted upon. Diagnostic criteria may be used to study the group's structure and to plan for activities which may re-structure the group.

4. Personal versus social criteria [12]

Helen Hall Jennings (1947) distinguished between psychetelic and sociotelic roles, psychetelic roles being those which are personal and private and involve leisure activities, and sociotelic roles being those which are social and public, involving work-related roles. Her hypothesis is that a person's choice-making process varies depending upon the nature of the role and the sphere in which it is encountered. Examples of personal versus social criteria are, "Whom do you choose to have as your partner in marriage?" and, "Whom do you choose to have as your partner in business?"

5. One-way versus two-way criteria [13]

Criteria may imply activity for which partners engage in the same role; or conversely, the criteria may imply one person is the recipient of the interaction from another. An example of a one-way criterion is, "Whom do you choose to teach you for one hour on a topic of their choice?" This is a one-way criterion in that one person is chosen to teach, and the chooser is the receiver of the action. A different one-way criterion is required to determine reciprocity of choice, i.e., "Whom in the group do you choose to teach on a topic of your choice?" A two-way criterion would be, "With whom do you choose to share a one-hour learning experience on a topic which you will jointly decide?"

A group which wants to be fully involved with the process of selecting the criteria may want to explore via discussion and consensus-taking, both the relevance of the criteria they are considering and the degree of the threat experienced when contemplating choosing others on the criteria. The reader is referred to Appendix IV, Ranking Criteria of Choice by Relevance, Threat and Type. A listing of criteria (to which others may be added) may be examined by the group and determinations made about the degree of relevance and threat they wish to explore. Additional space is given to determine willingness to risk exploring the various criteria.

There are times when the very discussion and vote for criteria becomes an action quasi-sociometric exploration. Persons who have a lot of influence in a group may attempt to persuade the group to choose criteria which will meet the needs of one individual or one sub-group. Majority rules as a process of selection may not be in the service of the group and certainly has a negative influence on the minority. The goal is to obtain unanimous consent to include others. Successful, unanimous participation of a group on a mildly threatening criterion for one exploration may encourage the more reluctant (threatened) group members to risk more in future sociometric tests.

The Wording of Criteria

In order that the activity implied in the criterion is clear, and that each participant can understand exactly where, when and what will be the basis of their choices, the group, or the investigator, gives particular attention to the wording of the criterion. The following guidelines have been extracted from the *Handbook of Social Psychology* (1954): [14]

1. Questions are future-oriented
2. Questions imply how the results are to be used. (If the criterion is to be acted upon, the group will need to know beforehand if small groups, pairs, etc., are to be formed as a result.)

3. Word questions in such a way as to use projection when using diagnostic or hypothetical criteria. (Ex., "If you could choose . . .")
4. The question should specify the boundaries of the group. (Ex., "Of the people in the group whom you have met for the first time . . .")
5. Word the question to fit the level of understanding of the members of the group.
6. Questions should always state the number of choices allowed if choices are limited.

Sociometric consciousness in groups requires the ability to recognize the criterion on which group members are making choices, from role to role and from moment to moment. This involves identifying the words which make the difference, especially qualifying words, words which identify the sub-groups. The more groups struggle with the selection of criteria the more opportunity they are having for learning this valuable aspect of sociometric consciousness.

Revealing Sociometric Data: Reasons to Keep the Data Private and Reasons to Make the Data Public

Groups need to decide about how the data from the sociometric test is be used and who has access to the data. It is common practice for group members to share the choices they have made for each other with the group, often sharing with each individual first, and then handing in their data sheets for quantifying, analysis and discussion. This practice is used in settings where the sociometric test is used as a tool for learning about group process and the individual's choice-making process. In instances where an outside investigator has been hired to study a group sociometrically, the group may negotiate for a sociometric test which is conducted confidentially. This would be the case when there is a mass testing situation or when the test is given only once with little follow-through. The data is preferred to be private in order to assure that those persons involved in the test have the option to choose to reveal their choices. Additional information on revealing sociometric data, and other options which affect the wording of the question, can be found in Chapter VI, p. 145-146.

Declaring Choices and Reasons for Choice

The process of declaring choices is briefly described for the first-time participant in Appendix III, p. 71. In accordance with Moreno's social atomic theory[15] the range of choice is given a valence, positive and negative.

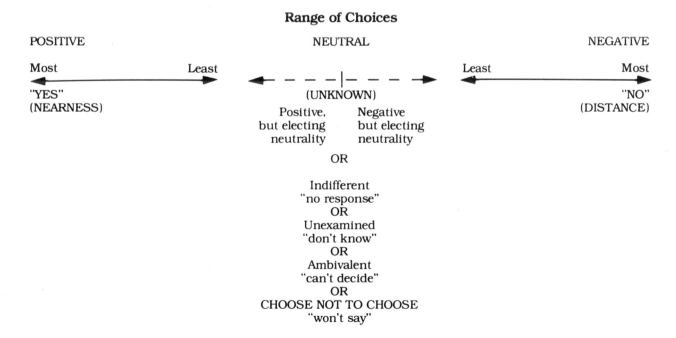

Figure 1. Range of choices.

Positive Choice (+)

A positive choice implies a choice to be near, to share space and to spend time with. There exists an attraction to another person. The positive choice evokes an image of a pleasurable, effective and/or desirable connection.

Negative Choice (-)

A negative choice means the person chooses to be at a distance from the other, not to share space or to spend time with the other person. There exists a repulsion for proximity to the other person. Negative choices evoke the image of interactions resulting in irritation, dislike and/or unpleasantness.

Neutral Choice (N)

The nearness and distance factor cannot be identified due to a number of factors:

A.   The person knows themself to be *positive,* but prefers to remain neutral on the basis of the criterion; or, the person knows themself to be *negative,* but prefers to remain neutral on the basis of the criterion. Electing this category of choice is identified by Zerka T. Moreno as "creative neutrality," choosing to set aside the positive or negative response in order to make alternative interactions possible; thereby creating a space and time for others to increase their experience of one another. [16]

B.   Indifference: Indifference responses are based on the lack of stimulation to choose. There is an absence of tele. If there is interest in the other person that interest is undifferentiated.

C.   Unexamined: The neutral choice is based on a lack of information and insufficient time to reflect and investigate the range of choice. This differs from the indifference category in that the person choosing has reflected and determined there is no response.

D.   Ambivalence: Positive and negative responses exist simultaneously thereby "neutralizing" the response. Ambivalent responses are more prevalent when criteria for selection are non-specific, allowing for varying interpretation and ambiguity. Ambivalence-motivated neutral choices may be due to the fact that a person is receiving two messages (positive and negative) or the person has two sets of responses when contemplating the consequences of acting on either the positive or negative choice.

E.   Choose Not To Choose: This category may be either due to a person refusing to partake in the sociometric test, or may be due to the person's desire to be isolated from the group.

Reasons for Choice

Participants are asked to give specific reasons for their choices, keeping in mind how these reasons relate to the question (criterion) and their underlying motivation to interact with the other person in the implied activity. The reasons are given as direct feedback *to* the person, rather than a more impersonal statement *about* the person.

It should be possible to determine from the statement whether the reason is based on tele, transference, or indifference and whether the reason is psychetelic or sociotelic. Some examples are:

tele—"I feel attracted to you, accepted by you for who I am; I feel seen by you, and respected."

transference—"Your anxious questioning annoys me. I am reminded of an old girlfriend and this puts me off."

indifference—"I don't have any sense of who you are, no strong feeling either way."

psychetelic reason—"You are expressive and natural with your body, therefore massage seems to be a wonderful means for communicating."

sociotelic reason—"I know you have trained in Aston patterning and therefore I'd learn a lot about massage from you."

Reasons given for sociotelic criteria tend to be statements about skill, ease in relating, intelligence, quickness or clarity of the person's style and honesty. ***Reasons given for psychetelic criteria*** tend to be statements about degree of comfortability, trust, sensitivity, enjoyment of contact and style of communicating.[17]

There are covert reasons for choice that often do not appear in objective data, but are alluded to on the perceptual data sheets. Also, an interviewer may be able to identify covert reasons if persons are encouraged to be candid. Covert reasons tend to result from a need to:

1. convey previously undisclosed material to the group, or aimed at revealing information to a specific person.

   Ex. "Ever since you told other people about me being gay I haven't trusted you."

2. undermine another person's connection to the group or to a specific person.

   Ex. "I'm strongly attracted to you." (Soliloquy: I'm sick of Bill getting all the girls. I couldn't care less if Sharon chooses me, but I'd sure like to cramp Bill's style. He seems to prefer her for some reason.)

3. hide one's real choice and prefer safer choices.

   Ex. "My first choice is Bill. I really trust you." (Soliloquy: I wish I had the nerve to choose Steve, but I know I could never get over my embarrassment if he didn't choose me, or even worse, if he put me down as negative. Oh, God!)

4. protect another person from exposure to choices received or level of choice.

   Ex. "My first choice is Sharon." (Soliloquy: I wish I could choose Carol, but she is so shy. She would probably be frightened to death if I put her on my list. Maybe I'll put her down as neutral, or fifth choice. Damn shame. But, I don't want her to be afraid of me.)

Making Perceptual Choices

Every individual in a group is able to sense where he or she seems to fit in a group with some degree of accuracy. The perception may be vague and tentatively offered; however, experience in making perceptual guesses strengthens the likelihood of accuracy of perception and builds trust in one's own intuitive system. At first, a person may begin to make guesses whether or not a person has chosen him or her in the "choose to" "choose not to" or "choose to remain neutral toward" category. Later, it may be possible for the person to distinguish the intensity of the choice, and whether he or she is ranked high as a preference, or low.

Several devices may be helpful to group members having difficulty making perceptual guesses. Have the group members mentally role reverse with another group member, and focus on what may be going on with that person as he or she is making choices. Suggest that they remember clues about earlier choices and what is likely to be the current response. If the perceptual guessing is distressing to the group member, have him or her write down the feelings which were present and share their reaction with the group during the sharing phase.

Have group members make perceptual guesses about the choices other group members are making for each of the other group members. This is similar to taking the sociomatrix and making a perceptual guess for each choice that is entered on the sociomatrix. This may be too time consuming and wearying; however, it is possible to select one or two group members and practice making perceptual guesses, "others for others" in addition to "others for self".

When making perceptual guesses the group members are also asked to give the reasons they have for forming this impression. This aspect of the exploration allows for group members to identify what they believe to be the source of the responses that others have for him or her. For example, a person may guess that John will choose him "Because John thinks it is wrong to publicly reject someone." This perception may be accurate, but included in the reason given is a message to John that "I know what you really feel about me, regardless of your principles about rejection." It is possible for group members to find the source of the projection which they may feel directed toward him or her as attempts are made to come into contact with a reason for a particular perception. "Joan will reject me because I remind her of her last boyfriend."

It is useful to remind group members that the more perceptual guesses they make, the more opportunities they will have to evaluate the areas in their perceptual system which require skill training. Often there are some aspects which will be more difficult than others. For example, it seems easier to perceive mutuality, than incongruity.

Revealing Choices in Face to Face Interaction

Once group members have made their choices they may be instructed to move to a previously designated area to begin sharing in dyads the following information:

> Category of choice and the reason for the choice
>
> Their perceptual guesses and reasons
>
> How they feel about the other's choice for them
>
> Where do they stand with each other in the here and now

Group members will need to be encouraged to limit their contact to the immediate task at hand. If additional time is required it should be arranged for after the sharing phase. People seem to have varying styles of relating on the verbal level. Some people will finish earlier than others. The sociometrist, or group, needs to allow for an adequate disclosure period, approximately five (5) minutes per person.

The group, and the person conducting the sociometric test, should be aware of the potential impact of disclosures on each individual, especially those persons likely to have the greatest discrepancy in their perceptual estimations, and/or the greatest discrepancy in choices desired and choices received. It helps to have each person identify a person in the group whom they could seek out if they feel in need of immediate support during the disclosure phase. Also, it is reassuring to persons to have a specific time to reassemble for sharing, support and assistance.

This interaction phase has enormous potential for connecting and reconnecting group members, even evoking a new set of responses. A rationale for this face to face stage in the sociometric test can be found in Leavitt and Mueller (1966) who have commented upon the effects of feedback on communication:

> . . . there is an
> 1. increase in accuracy with which information is transmitted
> 2. increase in confidence over accomplishment
> 3. cost of feedback is time
> 4. zero feedback engenders doubt, low confidence and hostility. Free feedback is accompanied by high confidence, amity and permits the learning of a mutual language which, once learned, may obviate the necessity for further feedback. [18]

The important task of the sociometrist/group leader is to monitor the process of disclosure sufficiently in order to assure that the effects are beneficial and contribute to increased awareness rather than harmful and impeding personal growth. [19]

The Sharing Phase

The sociometrist/group leader conducts a "reporting in" session following the exchange of feedback. The reader is referred to the flow chart for this aspect of the process (Appendix I.c., page 67) which provides a general guideline for this disclosure phase.

Group members will benefit from examining the impact of making and revealing choices on themselves and each other. There are occasions when the impact will still be felt and the group will need to facilitate the sharing of others. One of the major areas of the sharing phase is the comparison of the *expected outcome* with the *actual outcome.* This discussion can be the source of discomfort to some or can be the source of revelation and amazement. What is important is to have the group members identify aspects of their choice-making process which they find useful and wish to keep and aspects of their process which warrant change based on this experience.

When group members have identified the meaning of this experience for themselves personally, the next step in the exploration is to determine the meaning of the sociometric test collectively in terms of group structure. A break of an hour or so is often indicated before working with the quantifying of data, in order for persons to have informal sharing time and be more available for the exacting task of interpretation of the results.

The Analysis Phase

This phase in the sociometric test is largely determined by the original purpose for conducting the exploration. Whatever those intentions, the information via the choice-making questionnaire must be assembled in a way to be useful for study and interpretation.

Constructing the Sociomatrix

A sociomatrix is a graph on which the choices made in a sociometric test are recorded. (See Figure 2 for completed sociomatrix and Appendix VI for blank sociomatrix.) By charting the choices a person has made **across** the sociomatrix, it becomes possible, once all the choices of all the group members are recorded, to read **down** the sociomatrix and have information about choices made for a person. (Choices of, read across; choices for, read down.) It works in a similar way to mileage charts in a road atlas except that instead of using city names, the names of group members are used. An example of a sociomatrix is provided on the next page.

Ordering the names on a sociomatrix can provide access to information about sub-groups which are already known to exist, perhaps due to external factors. Names are listed in the same order down the left-hand column as across the top of the sociomatrix. In the example, the group wanted to look at the phenomenon of new group members' choices of the older, more experienced group members and wanted to look at the choices made for the opposite sex. By placing the names of all the older group members in the middle of the list, with the new males and new females on the periphery of the sociomatrix, it is possible to read the sociomatrix at a glance for the required information.

The ordering of the names on the sociomatrix in the example on the preceding page results in five smaller matrices:

    A. Males' choices for males.
    B. Males' choices for females.
    C. Females' choices for males.
    D. Females' choices for females.

Inner square: Old group members choices for old group members. By further compartmentalizing the reader can identify other groupings such as old male group member choices for new male group members, etc. The greatest clarity of sub-structures can be seen once sociograms are drawn.

SOCIOMATRIX

CRITERION: Whom do you choose to have as your partner in an hour-long trust exercise?

DATE: June 15, 1980

NAMES	1 MALE, NEW	2 MALE, NEW	3 MALE, NEW	4 MALE, OLD	5 MALE, OLD	6 FEMALE, OLD	7 FEMALE, OLD	8 FEMALE, OLD	9 FEMALE, NEW	10 FEMALE, NEW	11 FEMALE, NEW	12 FEMALE, NEW	Positive Choices Made	Negative Choices Made	Neutral Choices Made
1 MALE, NEW		①	②	③	3	1	4	2	·	④		5	5	④	2
2 MALE, NEW	①		3.	·	②	1.	2		4.			·	4	②	5
3 MALE, NEW				①			1.	·	6	5	3		6	①	4
4 MALE, OLD	1	4			2			③		②		4	③	4
5 MALE, OLD	②	5			2	①	3.		4				5	④	2
6 FEMALE, OLD	1.	4	①		3	2	5	②	4	③		6	③	2
7 FEMALE, OLD	4.	3		5.	2.		1.		6				6	0	5
8 FEMALE, OLD	5.	1	4.	7.	6.		2.		3	·		7	0	4
9 FEMALE, NEW	·	3.	·	2	1		4	5	①	6	·	6	①	4
10 FEMALE, NEW	①	②	③	5.	①		2	⑤		3	⑥	5	6	0
11 FEMALE, NEW	③	①	⑤	④		①	3	2		5.	4	5	⑤	1
12 FEMALE, NEW			①		·	·			2	①	8
13													Average Choices = 5.54	2.7	3.73
14															
15															
16															
17															
18															
19															
20															
Positive Choices Recd	1	6	5	3	5	7	10	9	2	3	6	4	61	30	41 = 132
Negative Choices Recd	⑤	③	④	③	⑤	①	0	0	③	④	0	③	30		
Neutral Choices Recd	5	2	2	5	1	3	1	2	7	4	5	4	41		
													132		
Positive Mutuals	1	4	3	1	3	4	5	6	1	2	4	0	34		
Negative Mutuals	③	②	0	②	②	①	0	0	①	④	0	0	16		
Neutral Mutuals	1	2	1	1	0	0	0	1	3	0	0	3	12	132	
Pos/Neg Incongruity	1	1	2	1	3	1	0	0	1	1	1	2	14		
Pos/Neut Incongruity	4	2	3	4	1	4	6	4	5	3	2	4	42		
Neg/Neut Incongruity	1	0	1	2	2	1	0	0	0	1	4	2	14		
WEIGHTING	5	36	15.5	13	10.5	43.5	47.5	52.5	12.5	24	19	12.5			

Figure 2.   Completed Sociomatrix

Once the names have been entered on the sociomatrix, follow this charting process:

1. **Arrange the objective data sheets** in the order in which the names appear on the sociomatrix.

2. **Chart the positive choices.**
   Scan the first objective data sheet and locate the first choice positive. Place a **1** under the name of the person who has been the first choice. Continue this process until the data sheet shows no further positive choices. When this has been completed there should be a listing horizontally across the page.

3. **Chart the negative choices.**
   Using a different colored pencil, or by circling the number, enter the "choose not to" preferences each person has made. Again, the choices of a person are entered under the name of the person chosen horizontally across the page.

4. **Neutral choices.**
   Leave a blank space for all the neutral choices. If research procedures require a symbol use an **N**.

5. **Total the positive expansiveness.**
   Enter the total number of positive choices made by a person under the column heading "Positive Choices Made." Since some persons may choose more than one person for a level of choice (say, three persons as 2nd choice) count the number of actual choices made.

6. **Total the negative expansiveness.**
   Total the number of negative choices and enter the number in the column indicated.

7. **Total the neutral choices.**
   Total the number of neutral choices made and enter the total in the column indicated.

   Note: When a person "chooses not to choose" and makes no indication of the level of choice (neither positive, negative or neutral) place a CNC in the space to differentiate it from neutral choice.

8. **Total positive choices received.**
   Reading down the column (vertically) the choices a person has received can be determined. Add the number of positive choices received and enter the total in the space provided.

9. **Total negative choices received.**
   Scanning down the column under each person's name, count the number of negative choices received and enter the total in the space provided.

10. **Total neutral choices received.**
    Scanning down the column under each person's name, count the number of blank spaces (or spaces with an **N**) and enter the total of neutral choices in the space provided.

11. **Total all choices made and received by group members.**
    Total the positive choices made by the group, and total the positive choices received by the group. The totals should result in the same number. Total the negative choices made and the negative choices received, the neutral choices made and the neutral choices received. If the totals do not match it will be necessary to recheck the totals or refer back to the objective data sheets.

12. **Weighting.**
    There are times when it becomes necessary to distinguish between one or more persons who are in the same or a similar position. Weighting the choices and placing value on mutuality will help to differentiate actual positions of group members, especially stars.

    a. Divide the total number of positive choices received by the number of persons in the group less one. (Ex: 61 positive choices received divided by 12 - 1 = 5.545.

       Value positive choices received as follows:
       1st choice—5
       2nd choice—4
       3rd choice—3
       4th choice—2
       5th choice—1
       6th, etc.—no value

b. Divide the total number of negative choices received by the number of persons who are in the group minus one. (Ex: 30 negative choices received divided by 12 - 1 = 2.72.)

Value negative choices received as follows:
1st choice — -3
2nd choice — -2
3rd choice — -1
4th, etc. — no value

c. Value neutral choices as equal to 0.

d. Total the number of all mutuals (positive, negative and neutral) and divide that number by the total number of group members. Divide that total by 2 (since mutuals involve 2 persons). (Ex: 34 + 16 + 12 = 62 divided by 12 = 5.16, divided by 2 = 2.58.) Value each mutual at 2.5.

Example: Using the values given above, the results of the sociometric choices weighted for person no. 1 would be:

```
     1  = -3
     N  =  0
     1  = -3                  -12
     2  = -2            +12.5 for 5 mutuals
     N  =  0                 ─────────
     N  =  0                   +0.5
     5  = +1
     N  =  0
     1  = -3
     2  = -2
     N  =  0
          ─────
     Total  -12
```

A discussion of weighting sociometric choices can be found in an article by Donald T. Campbell (1960).[20] Campbell's opinion is that differential weighting makes little difference; however, he offers a solution to those who wish to distinguish between level of choice.

Procedure for Determining Mutuality and Incongruity of Choice

In order to determine the connections between two persons, one must read the sociomatrix horizontally *and* vertically, matching *choices of* with *choices for*. This process is made simply by using a computing device[21] or the sociomatrix reader.[22]

To use the Sociomatrix Reader, place the uppermost triangle over the second black square in the line of squares which runs diagonally across the sociomatrix. Immediately to the left of the uppermost triangle on the reader and just above it are squares representing the choice male #2 has made for male #1 and vice versa. The diagonal lines on the reader connect *choices of* with *choices for*, allowing the sociometrist to determine whether the choices are reciprocal (positive-positive, negative-negative, neutral-neutral) or incongruous (positive-negative, positive-neutral, negative-neutral). It helps, when computing, if a small dot is placed on the sociomatrix when the choices have been identified as mutual. On the example below, male #1 has 3 negative mutuals, 1 positive mutual and 1 neutral mutual.

After completing one vertical row, slide the sociomatrix reader diagonally down and across to the next black square. Continue this process until the sociomatrix is completed.

(See Figure 3 for an example.)

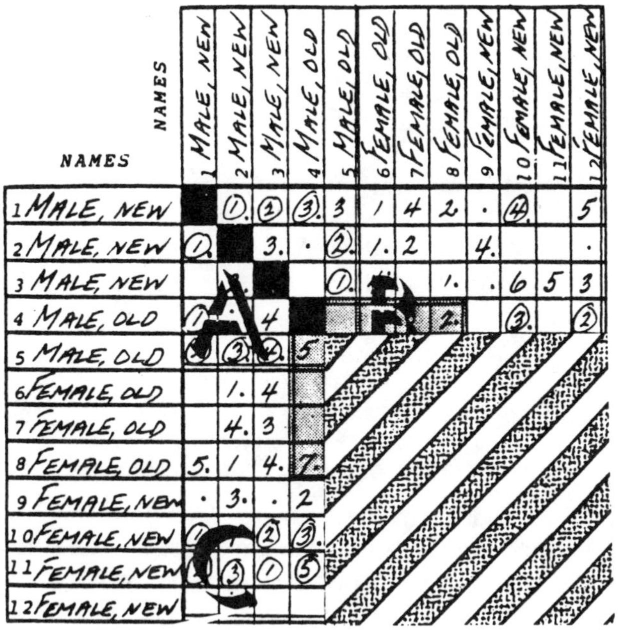

Figure 3. Placement of the Sociomatrix Reader (for determining mutuality or incongruity)

Determining a total of mutuals involves simply counting the number of dots entered on the sociomatrix. Determining incongruity is more time consuming. The following instructions may prove useful:

a. Subtract the number of mutuals the person has from the number of group members minus one. This number is the total number of incongruities that need to be identified.

b. Consult the example above. In this example the incongruities of male #4 are being identified. He has 4 mutuals, indicating that there need to be 7 incongruities identified. The sociomatrix reader is placed one column to the right of male #4's column looking vertically down the sociomatrix.

c. The incongruities from male #5 to female #12 can be identified by reading the sociomatrix and writing the kind of incongruity found on a piece of paper. To determine incongruities for Male #1-3, place the sociomatrix reader upside down with the triangle covering the third black triangle from the top, leaving exposed the entire line under the person's name. (See Figure 4 for an example.)

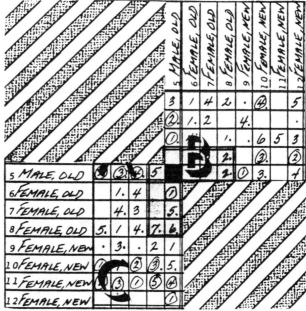

Figure 4. Placement of Two Sociomatrix Readers (for ease of reading one person's column)

d. In the example the incongruities are:

5 - blank	(positive-neutral)
blank - 1	(positive-neutral)
blank - 3	(positive-neutral)
a mutual	
2 - blank	(positive-neutral)
a mutual	
5 - blank	(negative-neutral)
blank - 2	(negative-neutral)

reading the upper square:

4 - blank	(positive-neutral)
a mutual	
a mutual	

e. Total mutuals and incongruities and place the total in the space provided on the sociomatrix.

Encourage group members to be involved in the charting of the data. When a person is actually involved in reading the identifying connections between persons on the sociomatrix, many subjective comments occur to a person. This is one way that sociometric consciousness can be raised. Questions and impressions arise which have pertinence for the whole group. Participation in this phase of the exploration is an important aspect of the role of co-researcher.

The Perceptual Sociomatrix

One of the primary purposes of obtaining perceptual data is to enable the group members to compare what they guessed would occur with what actually occurred in terms of choice-making. A separate sociomatrix can be used, or a computer program can be used to do this comparative phase; however, it is recommended that group members simply place a sheet of tracing paper over the objective sociomatrix, and quantify the perceptual data, placing the results onto the tracing paper in such a way as to see the other results.

The following process is employed for noting the perceptual data:

1. **Enter the names on the sociomatrix** in the same order as appears on the objective sociomatrix. (OR, place the tracing paper onto the sociomatrix in a way that leaves the names visible.)

2. **Enter the perceptual guesses a person has made** on the perceptual sociomatrix, by locating the person's name at the top of the sociomatrix and placing a + for positive choices and a - for negative choices in the spaces under the person's name, reading vertically down the sociomatrix. You are charting the perceptual guesses the person has about choices for him or her, and therefore the perceptual data must be compared with the data which is found in the vertical reading of the sociomatrix. For perceptual guesses about neutral choices, leave the space blank, or place an **N** in the space. Use NP for no perceptual guess.

3. **Total the perceived positive, negative and neutral expansiveness** of the group members. Once the perceptual guesses are recorded it is possible to identify a collective impression of how the group perceived each person would respond to the group members on the basis of criterion.

4. **Total the perceived positive, negative, and neutral choices received.** Add the number of pluses (+), minuses (-) and blanks each person received.

5. **Determine mutuality and incongruity of the perceived choices.** Using the same method as presented for determining mutuality of objective data (actual choices) determine the mutuality by using the sociomatrix reader.

6. **Total the number of perceived mutuals.**

7. **Total the number of perceived incongruities.**

8. Check any other perceptual guesses made against the actual choices and indicate on the perceptual data sheet whether those perceptions were accurate.

9. List all those mutuals which were actual and perceived mutuals. As well, list all those incongruities which were actual and perceived incongruities. (You may wish to shade with a lightly colored pencil

all choices which were accurately perceived. This way one can visibly notice if one sub-group is more accurate in perception than another.)

Sociogram Construction

A sociogram is a graphic representation of the results of a sociometric test (for example see Figure 5 below). The sociogram depicts sociometric structure, particularly nearness and distance of the inter-connections, cleavages, isolation and status. Sociograms can be drawn utilizing both objective (actual choices) and perceptual data, making it possible to graphically display the comparison of the two sets of data. The sociogram was first introduced by Moreno in the 1934 edition of *Who Shall Survive?* The intent of the sociogram is to cluster closely related persons and to thereby identify sub-groups, pivotal persons, and stars of the various groupings. Mary L. Northway introduced the *target sociogram* in 1940 as a way of depicting on a map of concentric circles the nearness and distance factor of several sociometric tests. This method may be particularly useful in instances where the group membership remains the same. The use of sectors can be added to the target sociogram allowing for a clearer reading of variables affecting choice.

Sociometrists may choose to depict all choices in the sociogram; however, in instances of large group explorations, the ease of reading the sociogram at a glance is considerably lessened. Since the purpose of the sociogram is to provide a visible picture of a group dynamic relating to choice, it is recommended that topical sociograms be drawn, highlighting one or two specific phenomena.

How to Draw a Sociogram

Assemble the necessary equipment: templates for circles and triangles, ruler, paper enough to accommodate the size of the group (8½x11 is large enough for a group of 8-12; 11x14 for groups 12-20; 14x17 for groups of 20-36). Other additional equipment would be colored pens, using the inks to differentiate from the categories of choice. Moreno used red for positive choices and black for negative choices. Have sociomatrix at hand.

1. Refer to the sociomatrix and identify the most highly chosen person. Place a circle (female) or triangle (male) to represent that person near the center of the piece of paper.

2. Identify the next most highly chosen person(s) and place them in proximity to the star. Placement is helped by (a) placing the circle or triangle in such a way as to decrease the necessity of intersecting lines, and (b) placing persons nearer to those persons with whom they have reciprocal relations.

3. Complete the placing of persons using the same principles as outlined in item #2.

4. Using the notational system outlined on the next page, draw the lines between persons, minimizing the intersecting lines wherever possible. Draw:

   a. Sociogram of positive mutuality
   b. Sociogram of negative mutuality
   c. Sociogram of neutral mutuality (use a color for neutral)
   d. Sociogram of positive-neutral incongruity
   e. Sociogram of negative-neutral incongruity
   f. Sociogram of positive-negative incongruity
   g. Individual sociogram of each person in the group

5. Other useful sociograms might be:
   a. Sociogram of first choice positive, first choice negative.
   b. Sociogram of star succession: For each person who has made a first choice for the star, identify their second choice. Draw a sociogram of all first choices for the non-star and all second choices of the persons choosing the star as their first choice. This will give an indication of whom in the group is likely to be star on this criterion in the absence of the star.
   c. Sociogram of choices for the same sex and for the opposite sex.
   d. Sociograms of choices for new members of the group and for old members of the group.

6. Perceptual sociograms.

Using the perceptual data as entered on the perceptual sociomatrix, identify the perceived star, and follow the same instructions for drawing sociograms as given for actual sociometric data. Compare these sociograms and draw lines on the page, or on a piece of tracing paper, which represent the perceptual data.

NOTATIONAL SYSTEM FOR SOCIOGRAM CONSTRUCTION

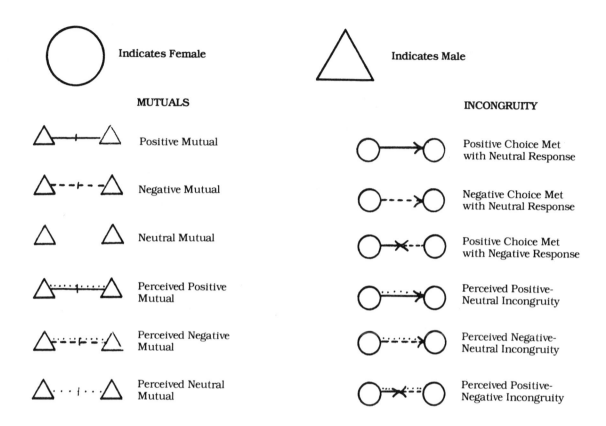

In instances when you want to indicate the preference shown (1st, 2nd choice, etc.) place a small number inside the circle or triangle showing the choice received:

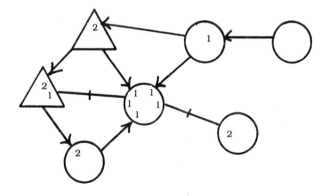

These symbols are used to indicate a choice for a person outside the group:

 Males   Females

Use a broken line to indicate a person who is absent or has died:

Figure 5. Notational System for Sociogram Construction

The Target Sociogram

The target sociogram provides a method of graphic presentation which makes it possible to depict longitudinal studies for research purposes, as well as offering ease in identifying sociometric configurations. The following instructions have been adapted from *The Primer of Sociometry*, by Mary L. Northway.[23]

1. Draw five concentric circles, the areas of each division being equal to one quarter of the whole target. These concentric circles have been used to represent significantly above chance, above chance, below chance and significantly below chance in studies where the choices were limited to a number smaller than the whole group. For an explanation of the formula required for computing chance expectancy and probability of choice see references.[24]

2. In sociometric explorations where persons are asked to make choices (positive, negative and neutral) for each person in the group, total the number of choices received (in all sociometric tests for this group) for each person. Identify the number of possible choices a person could receive, usually the number of tests times the number of persons in the group minus one. (For three tests with twelve persons: 3 x (N - 1) or 33. Next, divide the total space between the midpoint of the inner circle to the outer most edge of the concentric circles by the number (i.e. 33).

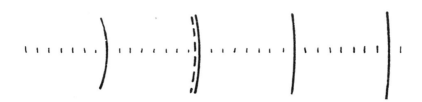

3. Next compute the average number of positive choices received for each of the sociometric tests. (For example, on one test the average positive choices received is 5.5, the next test 4.2 and the next test 6 is the average.) Add these together and the figure 15.7 is the average number of positive choices received. Find that space on the target sociogram and draw another concentric circle on the target. This makes it possible to notice at a glance those persons who are chosen above or below average.

4. Next identify two significant aspects about the group you wish to compare: For example, male and female English and non-English speaking group members, or Caucasian and non-Caucasian male and females. (It is possible to use only one aspect.) Now split the target according to the percentage of group members who have the characteristic selected.

5. Now place each person on the target sociogram (a circle for females or triangle for males) according to:
   a. the sub-group to which they belong, and
   b. the total number of positive choices received.

6. Draw lines between persons having a reciprocal relationship of positive choices. (If there is a large number of positive mutuals, it may be more meaningful to draw lines between all mutuals in the 1st, 2nd and 3rd choice range.)

7. The following is a sample target sociogram:[25]

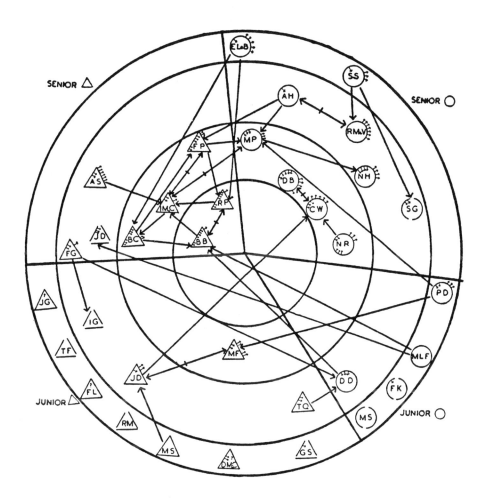

Figure 6. The Target Sociogram (Northway)

Analysis of Choices

Regardless of the size or the kind of group being investigated, the distribution of choices among group members will be uneven: one, or a few, persons will be highly chosen, a larger number of persons will receive an average number of choices, and a few will be significantly underchosen (neglected).[26] This phenomenon is termed *the sociodynamic law* by Moreno (1948) and is further explained by Zerka T. Moreno (1966):

> "In a given group, a percentage of individuals will be overchosen, obtaining more love than they can give or consummate (the sociometrically rich, sometimes referred to as the sociometric capitalists); another, larger percentage will represent the sociometric middle class, giving and receiving approximately an equal amount of choices, about as much as they can use productively; another percentage will represent the sociometric proletariat, the unwanted, unchosen or rejected individuals, who obtain and give far less love than they need for emotional growth and integration."[27]

The sociometrist will need to identify stars of acceptance and stars of rejection, isolates and isolated dyads, cliques or sub-groups, and persons in pivotal positions in order to effect an analysis of the group's structure.

The Sociometric Star

The sociometric star is the person, or persons, in the group who receives the largest number of choices. This can be determined by reading the sociomatrix and the choices received columns. The **star of acceptance** is the person receiving the highest number of choices that are positive. The **star of rejection** is the person receiving the highest number of negative choices. Reciprocity is a factor in the determination of the roles that stars play in a group. A star who is highly chosen and reciprocates those choices has a solid basis for interaction and support in the group based on the criterion for which the group has been making its choices. A star who is highly chosen who does not reciprocate those choices, or only partially does so, has a less secure position in the here and now. It is possible that this phenomenon is an indication of where the potential for leadership lies in the group. There is also a need at times to acknowledge the **star of incongruity.** This person has the highest number of unreciprocated relationships, and can therefore claim some of the focus of the group due to stress which results from choosing persons who don't choose you, and not choosing persons who do choose you. The impact is felt as disruption. Next, if the group is investigating itself on the basis of work-related criteria and leisure-related criteria, it becomes possible to determine the **sociotelic star** (persons highly chosen for their skills and intelligence) and the **psychetelic star** (highly chosen for personal attributes and subjective feelings).

Isolate and Isolated Dyads

The true isolate does not choose and is not chosen. He or she may choose others who are not members of the group, preferring to invest choice in persons not present. "They reduce cohesion in the group to a minimum, possibly leading to dissolution and death of the group."[28] An isolated dyad is a pair, who choose only each other, and remain apart from the other members of the group. They are unwilling to join activities in the group and unwilling to share with others. This has an impact of stopping the growth of the identity of the group when it attempts to include the isolates. The isolate's refusal to make choices stymies group members' attention to task.

Cliques and Sub-groups

Three or more individuals who mutually choose each other and/or include others in their group (which is less than the total number of the group) comprise a sub-group. The sub-group has the potential for exerting influence over the actions of the group, especially if they have a person in the sub-group who is identified as a star. Sub-groups have the capacity to split the group and divert group energies from task.

Pivotal Persons and Linkages

Persons who have a position in the group which link together key persons or sub-groups are termed pivotal persons. Identifying pivotal persons is usually accomplished by reviewing sociograms. They are visible by the fact that they are chosen by persons from both sub-groups, or chosen by both key persons. Pivotal persons often place value on both (or many) sides, and act as neutral ground for relating. Often there are several persons in the linkage, resulting in a sociometric configuration termed a *chain.* A chain is a line of persons each choosing in the same direction as indicated in the example below.

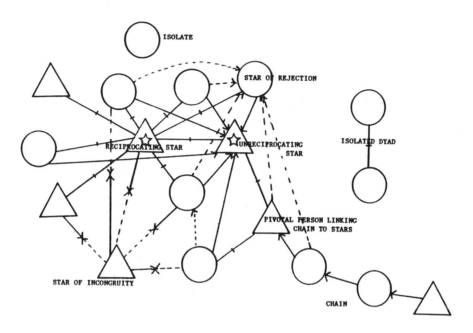

Figure 7. Sociogram Depicting Sociometric Configurations

Analysis and Interpretation of Sociometric Data

Interpreting the results of the sociometric test must be a function which relates directly to the original purposes for conducting the exploration. These reasons tend to fall into the general categories of (1) Diagnosis, of group structure, individual status, and interpersonal and intergroup conflict; (2) Comparison of sociometric data with other psychometric and sociometric data; (3) Sociometric consciousness raising via the study of choice-making processes; and (4) Planned social action via remedial sociometry and re-structuring of groups.

The body of knowledge which exists having to do with interpretation and analysis of sociometric data is enormous and requires sifting through many conclusive studies. The belief that in order to change something one must first understand it seems to have been a guiding principle for investigators. The major focus of the literature seems to be on establishing respectable quantitative methods for making and substantiating diagnostic efforts. However, sociometry as a therapeutic science has produced some hypotheses which assist group members in understanding and accounting for a number of the dynamics of the group and suggest ways for increasing sociometric wealth and flexibility.

Peter D. Mendelsson (1976) directs attention to the change in orientation of sociometric investigations.

> "In and of themselves sociometric methods could never change the world, even if they could contribute to understanding it better. Changing the world demanded action, but it was the fundamental actional orientation of sociometry from which the methods were divorced...Moreno himself recognized that the integrated character of his theory had begun to deteriorate within his own life; by the mid-1950's this was clear. And yet clear as it may have been, Moreno himself was unable to reverse this trend." [29]

The following questions which assist sociometrists in understanding the results of their explorations need to be actively engaged with the group, *and* have an action oriented followup. It is not enough for group members to become aware of the interpretations about their behavior and their choice-making processes. They require opportunities to experience the consequences of both and to practice the expansion of their interactive role repertoire.

Emotional expansiveness

Question: **"What seems to account for the positive expansiveness of a person?"**

The average number of positive choices group members make for others can be used to deduce which group members are more expansive in their positive choices and which group members are less expansive in their positive choices. The average number can be an indication of the collective or general response the group has to making positive choices for others on that particular criterion. If the average number is more than 50% of the choices allowed, in perhaps the 60-70% range, it can be assumed that the criterion poses little threat for group members, or that group members have sufficient knowledge of each other to make positive choices for large numbers of persons. Many factors enter into positive emotional expansiveness: (1) feelings of acceptance; (2) desire to positively identify oneself with specific persons or specific sub-groups by choosing them; (3) relevance of the criterion and the desire to connect with others on the basis of the implied activity; (4) risk-taking ability; (5) or, choosing others positively as a result of perceiving that they may choose oneself. Moreno states:

> "The test of emotional expansiveness measures the emotional energy of an individual which enables him to "hold" the affection of other individuals for a given period of time, in difference from social expansiveness which is merely the number of individuals with whom he is in social contact regardless of whether he is able to hold them or not." [30]

Persons who consistently over-choose others may be over-estimating the persons' actual positive position in the group. Over-choosers may be perceived as too eager to form a positive association with others and may be resented for declaring their acceptance on the basis of minimal contact. Persons who consistently under-choose others may be under-estimating the actual positive position of other group members and be resented for preventing opportunities for positive contact. Under-choosers may be perceived as arrogant or "too choosey." Under-choosers may have a very definite attitude toward making positive choices for others and prefer to limit the intensity of their interactions with the group.

Question: **"What seems to account for the negative expansiveness of a person?"**

Negative expansiveness in a group tends to increase in proportion to the degree of threat participants feel when contemplating having to act on the criterion of the exploration; or, the degree of unresolved interpersonal conflicts existant in the group. The average number of negative choices tends to be in the 15-25% range. The negative emotional expansiveness of a person can be the result of: (1) lack of the acceptance of the person in the implied role; (2) desire to be clear about the lack of readiness to engage in that role with the other person at this point in time; (3) desire to clearly disassociate oneself from a specific person or specific sub-group; (4) perceiving the non-acceptance of a person and desiring to "focus their animosities in the same direction" [31] as others.

Groups tend to under-choose negatively and yet over-estimate in their perceptual guesses the amount of negative choices made. This is often due to the unwillingness of persons to admit to negative feelings when either they do not want to invest in resolving any conflict which might arise from making the information public; or they perceive him or herself, the other person, or the group unable to deal effectively with conflict.

Question: **"What seems to account for the number of neutral choices made by a person?"**

Accounting for neutral choices is important due to the lack of preciseness about the meaning of that category of choice. The group is encouraged to investigate the various "reasons for choice" supplied on the objective data sheets, identifying any tendency to define neutral choice in a specific way. The neutral choice allows the group member the possibility of being clear about the numbers of persons they feel positive or negative toward on the basis of the criterion. Over-choosing in the neutral range may be accounted for as (1) the person being comfortable only when a small nucleus of interactors has been chosen; (2) the person's preference to declare choices only when he or she has a clear indication of positive or negative feelings; (3) an indication that the person has withdrawn from engaging with others, and particularly on this criterion; (4) the person having no clear indication of how others may be feeling about him or her.

Question: **"What seems to account for a person receiving a high number of positive choices?"**

Being highly chosen is an indication of wide acceptance by others in the implied role. The star of acceptance is perceived by others as having sufficient skill in the role and an ease in relating that others are comfortable with. The person behaves in a way others can identify with and support. Time should be given to determine how the person who is highly chosen feels about the role of star. There is quite a difference in feeling when the person who is a star on the criterion of his/her choice, and when they are chosen on a criterion about which he/she has mixed feelings. For example, when a child is chosen as the person with whom they would most like to study for an exam when he/she would rather be visible and highly chosen as the person you would most like to have on the baseball team, being highly chosen can be a disappointing experience. Every person needs to have the experience of being highly chosen on the criterion of his/her own choice. Groups may need to explore further in those instances when a person is highly chosen and not comfortable with such a high degree of acceptance. The person's own perception of him/herself may not allow for such a positive position; and while the group members may be able to account for the person being so highly chosen, the star may reject the position.

Question: "What seems to account for a person receiving a high number of negative choices?"

There is a tendency in groups to spread positive choices over a wider number of persons and reserve negative choices for only a few.[32] It appears to be safer (more acceptable) to reject persons whom the group has already tended to disapprove of, or persons perceived by several others as being inappropriate in their behavior, dress and appearance, or disliked for their hostility toward others. The rejected individual has a great deal to teach the group about itself, the norms which have developed and the restrictions that these norms place on the behavior of the minority. Northway and Wigdor (1947) found that persons with a low sociometric status tend to be the most seriously disturbed. "They show less ability to control their emotions and seem more egocentric, moody and impulsive as a group."[33]

The highly rejected person(s) tend to require facilitation in having the expectations that they have of the group met and respected. The negative star's lack of skill in relating to the group is felt by others as an irritant. It is also possible to account for a high number of negative responses in instances where a person has withheld something that the group needs. For example, the group may need for a person to remain present to what is going on in the group, to invest in what is going on, even when what is happening does not immediately appear to be productive. When a person fails to attend to the group process and be direct about the feelings he or she may be having in response to what is going on, choosing to sit back and close their eyes, the group may reject the person for their lack of commitment. The reasons persons give for their negative responses to others need to be explored and responded to by the person receiving the negative response.

Question: "What seems to account for a person receiving a high number of neutral choices?"

A high number of neutral choices could indicate that: (1) group members acknowledge that a person has a small social atom and can relate to only a small nucleus of persons; (2) group members have very little information about the person on which to base choices; (3) the group members may wish to allow a person who has had considerable focus (either positively or negatively) time to have a low-profile; (4) it is not known whether or not the person would reciprocate a positive or negative choice. On some criteria, such as "Whom in the group do you wish to encounter?", to receive a neutral choice is an active statement of lack of interest, a rejection by default. As discussed earlier in this chapter, neutrality can be a creative act of resisting a first response and giving a person time to change or grow into a role. For someone who is used to being the negative star, to be highly chosen in the neutral category can be interpreted as a statement of support.

Mutuality and Incongruity of Choice

There can be mutuality of choice category and incongruity within the choice category, and there can be mutuality in the reasons given for a choice and incongruity of category of choice. For example: Mary and Joan have been lifelong friends. On a sociometric test, with the criterion "Whom do you choose to have as your partner in a trust exercise?" Mary may reject Joan with the reason, "I trust you so completely. I want to do this with people I don't know as well." Joan may choose Mary as her first choice, "I trust you so completely." Also, Moreno considered the valence of the choice in computing incongruity. For instance, a first choice positive is incongruous when compared with a fifth choice positive. Both are positive, but the intensity is not comparable. In determining mutuality and incongruity it may involve reconsideration of the reasons for choice as stated on the objective data sheets.

Question: "What seems to account for the degree of mutuality in the group?"

Mutuality implies that the choice one has made is reciprocated. A pair or dyad results. Each person in the pair has made a choice to relate to each other in the same or similar way. There is agreement at least in the way each has chosen the other. A high degree of mutuality in a group can be accounted for as: (1) a direct result of clear communication; (2) clear understanding of the criterion and choice-making process; (3) agreement about the goals and expectations of others; (4) willingness to involve oneself with others in a reciprocal way. The higher the degree of positive mutuality in a group the higher the cohesiveness of the group. However, the mutuality needs to be perceived mutuality to assure cohesiveness.

Question: "What seems to account for the degree of incongruity in a group?"

Incongruity of choice results when there is a lack of clear signals between persons about their responses to each other as potential interactors. Or, in the case of clear communication, incongruity can be a clear decision on the part of the persons to not reciprocate the choice (choices) of the other. Incongruity can result when: (1) one party rejects the advances or positive choice of another; (2) a person has changed in the response that he or she has had toward another person; (3) a person grows tired of a role or a particular position in the group and refuses to reciprocate choices which result in having to remain in an old role; (4) influx of new members results in access to new roles and a change in the patterns of communication; (5) loss of group members results in access to new roles and a change in the patterns of communication; (6) group members develop new skills for relating which result in a change in their responses to other group members. Group members tend to rely upon a certain degree of mutuality to exist in order for them to feel the support necessary to deal with change and disturbances in sociostasis. A high degree of incongruity (50% or higher) results in increased caution and increased dissatisfaction with persons with whom one has become accustomed to having a reciprocal relationship. A group will need to give time to interpersonal and socioemotional needs before returning to a focus when there is a high degree of incongruity present in the group.

Perceptual Data and Self and Other Ratings

Various studies (Schiff, Tagiuri, Ausubel, Criswell) have undertaken to test out the effect of accurate or inaccurate perception of self and/or other on interpersonal relationships and specific group phenomena, especially leadership.

> "Awareness of own and others' status and of others' attitudes or traits may be influenced by tendencies in an individual: (a) to make constant errors of prediction or estimation (i.e., consistent under- or overestimation of self or others), (b) to reciprocate his own expectations, and (c) to perceive himself as more or less accepting of others than other individuals in the group are. These influences in part will determine an individual's ability to accurately predict the relative degree of acceptance or rejection accorded the component members of the group (including himself) by the other group members..."[34]

Schiff found that persons who underestimate their own status in a group also overestimate the status of others. One can infer that underestimaters have a low self-regard. When the composite findings of the group's perceptions result in frequent underestimation of choices others are making for oneself, it will be important for the group to focus on ways to improve self-esteem and to be clearer in the communication of positive feelings. Persons who overestimate the acceptance others may have for him or herself also perceive themselves as highly accepting to others. This overestimation could be an indication of the status a person wishes to achieve; and their behavior may be ambitious, independent and highly visible. If the findings of the investigation of the group's perceptions result in consistent overestimation, it is likely that a competitive atmosphere exists, with group members in need of clear, firm and honest communication. "The perceptual or judgemental set is distorted by strong ego needs for success and for acceptance by others."[35]

Persons in the mid-range, neither under- nor overestimating the status of self or others, have a clear picture of the group norms concerning acceptance and rejection and apply this norm to their perceptual sets. "The extreme groups are presumably more independent and less group-suggestible than the middle group is in their affective responses to associates."[36]

Of greatest value to the group will be the combined effect of the feedback session following the making of choices and perceptual guesses. Each group member will, at that time, make an interpersonal accounting of accuracy and inaccuracy of perception, identifying misinterpreted cues, false assumptions and changes in feeling as the cause of actual misperception.

Cleavage

One of the reasons that groups investigate their sociometric structure is to find out if there are sub-groupings that appear with frequency regardless of the variation in the criterion for exploration. The adage, "Birds of a feather flock together," may hold some truth for the group. Often there is already a suspicion that a sub-group exists. What a sociometric exploration can confirm is the nature of those sub-groups, the existence of cleavages and point to those persons in the group who are in a position to assist with regrouping and integration of persons into a more cohesive unit.

A number of factors contribute to cleavage: sex, sexual preference, lifestyle, propinquity, kinship, job training, education, intelligence, ethnic background, religion, socioeconomic status, physical characteristics, language.

One way to identify cleavage is to ask the group to form two (or more) informal groups to accomplish a task which is one of those tasks for which the group formed. Have the groups account for the groupings which were made. Also, the sociometrist can have the group divide into some of the many external structures on the basis of the factors identified above. Have the group identify the sub-groups which are familiar and operative based on these characteristics.

Identifying Leaders

The sociometric test can be used to identify where the potential for leadership lies in a group. The major writer and investigator of leadership, in addition to J.L. Moreno, is Helen Hall Jennings. Beliefs about what produces leaders have undergone several changes over the centuries. Born leaders at one time commanded countries by divine right. This was followed by a belief that leaders had certain traits or innate characteristics that prompted others to follow. Other believed that a situation, being in the right place at the right time, produced leaders, or that it wasn't *who* a person was that mattered, but *what* the person did that is powerful. Jennings' writings (see the bibliography) focus the sociometrist on two kinds of leaders: *leaders of sociogroups* (groups that have a work-related focus) and *leaders of psychegroups* (groups formed for pleasure or leisure-related activities).

Jennings' writings support a functional view of leadership with leaders being chosen because they have attributes which will support the role of leader. "An analysis of their ways of behaving (depending upon toward whom) shows the leadership they exert to be definable as *a manner of interacting with others.*. . . . It is as if these individuals recognize and think more of the needs of others than others think of their own needs. The leader-individuals often take actions in behalf of others whom they do not choose and who do not know of the effort made for them."[37]

There may be persons in the group who wish to have, or exert, influence over the person chosen to be in the role of leader. One way to trace leadership, especially in the instance of hidden leadership, or leadership channels, is to identify who has influence over whom.

> "The aristo-tele position, so called by Moreno because the individual in it could exert influence all out of proportion to its sociometric prominence, may be thought of as "feeders-to-leaders" since he is an individual who receives a high degree of tele preference from individuals who **do** receive a great number of choices from the population as a whole. Such feeder leaders, however, are not and should not be thought of as in actual positions of leadership from a sociometric standpoint. They are **given** influence at the discretion of those in leadership positions . . ."[38]

In studying the results of a sociometric test designed to identify the potential or actual leadership of a group, this occurrence of feeder-leader might occur in the cases of (1) a former leader who has asked for role relief but who still wishes to appoint, or encourage, the identification of his/her replacement; and (2) a person who has no desire for the role but has a strong interest in the identification of a leader who can be the leader in such a way as to meet his/her own approval.

Jennings found that, "In the sociogram, it is noted, the newcomer often chooses the over-chosen leader-individuals. For psychegroup affiliation, he seldom does. It is as if the individual could find compatibility in his psychegroup best with individuals *psychologically located* more nearly like himself, but in the sociogroup selects individuals who can importantly create a milieu benefiting many members."[39]

In discussing what accounts for a person being identified as leader in a group it will be important for group members to be clear about what the role of leader is to be, what characteristics they want in their leaders and what style of leadership they prefer. Often leaders have the responsibility to censure and to praise others. Leaders protect the interests of the minority and assure that rejected individuals are responded to. A paragraph from *Words of the Father* gives the sociometrist a clue about the relationship of the leader to the minority:

> THE TREE OF LIFE IS AILING.
> TO HEAL IT,
> START FROM THE TOP.
> THE TOP IS NEARER THE ROOT
> THAN THE MIDDLE. [40]

A Note on the Reliability of Sociometric Data[41] and Test Re-Test Results

Sociometrists will need to address the question of reliability of the information which is made available to them by sociometric testing. Group members should be encouraged to raise issues and make comments about any factors or events which result in questions about the validity of responses and test procedures. Some of these factors will be obvious. For example, the effect of change in membership in the group, changes in the test situation, lack of clarity about the meaning of the criterion for choice, or inadequate information about what would be done with the test results. The role of participant as co-researcher is important in this phase of the process. Group members will need to account for the degree of change or non-change in their sociometric choice-making or in their sociometric position on the basis of re-testing.

It is possible that the relevance or significance of change in sociometric position can be determined through quantitative analysis. A number of published studies have had reliability as a major focus. "Product-moment and rank-difference correlations are the methods which have been employed most frequently to compute reliability coefficients. Since the distribution of choices is highly skewed it is doubtful that the conditions for applying these methods are sufficiently satisfied in sociometric type data."[42]

The factors which affect the degree of change in choice are: "extent of acquaintance, the relevance of the choice criterion to the activity of the group, the age of the subjects, the technique of choosing and the time interval between test and retest."[43]

Sociometric Intervention Phase

By the time a group has reached this stage many interactions between group members will have taken place, both *a deux* and within the group. The data will seem old; the group members will remark that the group has changed. A new awareness of choice-making (evident in some of the humor going around) and a heightened sensitivity to others will often occur, especially in groups where an active regard for others has been employed. There may be a reluctance to continue working with the data. The reluctance can be overcome if group members realize that this phase offers opportunities for them to be active: explore new possibilities for relating, experience the consequences of choice by following up the criterion in action, and identifying directions for change in one's sociometric set.

The following activities provide that active focus: the action sociogram, with improvisation; making of assignments to test choices in action; regrouping; identifying criteria on which persons would like to be highly chosen; role training; conflict resolution; sculpting the group metaphor; and, identifying new criteria for future sociometric explorations.

Enacting the Group Sociogram

Discuss the sociograms which the group has drawn. Select a sociogram that seems to be important to explore in action; perhaps a sociogram which depicts an area of unfinished group business.

1. In a space identified as "the group," have each person position themselves in the space according to their position in the sociogram.
2. Ask group members to soliloquise about the place they have in the group.
3. Offer group members an opportunity to reverse roles with other group members and report how it

feels to have that position in the group. Have the group member identify what would have to happen in this group in order for him or her to be in this position. Check out with other group members.

4. Have group members generate ideas for what this sociogram feels like by having them pick a metaphor for the group. Examples could be: for chains, a daisy chain, or waiting in line at the airport; wheels for a cart, a metaphor given once when there were several stars; the ocean, some people being waves and others being sand carried away.

5. Have group members maintain the position they had in the sociogram, get in touch with the feelings that position evokes, and begin to take on a role which fits the metaphor. Interact with others from that role. The group leader may call "Stop Action!" and have persons say what was evoked by being in action.

6. Have group members choose a metaphor which represents how they want the group to be in the future. Examples have included: a porch swing, used car lot, auction at an antique store, and Cinderella.

Making Assignments to Test Sociometric Choices in Action

In the warm-up phase of the sociometric test, participants choose the ways in which the data will be utilized. Therefore, they know beforehand that they will be assigned a partner for those activities indicated in the criterion for which they made choices for another person; or, they will be assigned to a group on the basis of a criterion selected with the making of small groups. There are certain basic principles that are followed when making assignments using sociometric data.

1. Provide optimal satisfaction for the entire group. The assignments must have a therapeutic impact that is good for the whole of the group.

2. Persons in a weaker sociometric position tend to have fewer reciprocated choices. Find the strongest, positive link they have in the group and begin the assignments with these persons.

3. Share the sociometric wealth.

Assignment of Pairs:

1. Identify the strongest mutually positive relationship each person has in the group. The descending order is as follows: 1:1, 1:2, 1:3, 1:4, 2:2, 2:3, 3:3, etc.

2. If a person has no mutual, assign them to the highest choice they made that is met with a neutral response.

3. If none of a person's choices are met with a positive or a neutral response, assign them to a person who has chosen him or her the highest choice.

4. In some instances there is no way to satisfy everyone without giving a person (usually a star) more than one assignment. Avoid this whenever possible. It may be helpful to point out that if the assignments were being made on the spot, it would be likely that fewer persons would have optimal satisfying reciprocal partners.

Followup of Pairing:

1. Have the persons discuss, after their involvement in the activity, ways in which the experience confirmed or disaffirmed the initial reason for choice.

2. Have group members identify other group members (whom they chose to remain neutral toward or whom they rejected on this criterion) with whom they would be willing to try out relating on this activity.

Assignments into Small Groups

Usually the criterion is worded in such a way as to imply that a small group would be formed from the results. Persons would make several choices for fellow group members. Again, positive mutuality is the basis for membership whenever possible.

1. Weighting of choices may prove useful in making group assignments; therefore, have available the relative weighting of each person's position.

2. Depending upon the number of small groups desired (in some instances the number of small groups depends upon the interconnections of group members and not upon some external factor [number

of seats in a car, beds in a room, etc.]), identify persons in the group who have a low sociometric status figure. Perhaps there are three or four. Determine if any of these persons has a strong reciprocal connection to any of the other three. If so, it may warrant these persons being in the same group. Keep it in mind as a possibility.

3. Place the name of each person at the head of a column, and place the sociometric weighting in a column to the right of each person's name.

4. Locate the persons to whom each has a reciprocal relation. Place a second name in each column, the name of a person with whom the first is connected in some positive way. Keep track of the weighting of each group.

5. Continue adding persons, making attempts wherever possible to avoid placing negatively connected persons in the same group. Shift and change the groupings until there exist small groups having a similar number of members and a similar sociometric value.

6. Draw a sociogram of each group to check the interconnections. Identify what are likely to be issues with which the small group will have to deal.

Criteria Selection for Identifying Act Hunger

Now that each person has experienced being chosen on a criterion designed to focus the group on the collective structure of the group, it is possible for group members to use the same approach toward identifying (1) the criteria on which each person would most like to be highly chosen, and (2) identifying what has to happen to make that a possibility. The exercise "Group Exploration of Act Hunger for Roles of High Value" (Appendix I, Chapter VI), helps to provide this future projected focus.

Role Training

During the feedback sessions and dialogue, group members will be identifying skills, behaviors and attitudes they may wish to explore, change and practice. A role training session follows a specific format, as follows:

1. Have the person identify the role they wish to develop, or a situation in which the desired change in behavior may occur.

2. Have the person produce the scene where the failure occurs or is likely to occur.

3. Bring the person out of the scene and have them watch the action taking place while a double mirrors the actions of the protagonist.

4. Interview the protagonist about possible changes they could make in the action which would bring about a change in the outcome.

5. Test out any of these suggestions by instructing the protagonist to provide the new behavior which is designed to result in a change. See if it works. If so, conclude the role training session by having the protagonist make a few closure statements to oneself in the empty chair.

6. If the suggestions that the protagonist makes do not produce the desired results, have the protagonist reverse roles with the significant interactor in the scene. Then instruct group members to come from the audience and provide in action suggested changes in behavior. This is participant modeling.

7. The protagonist in the role of the other is in a position to gauge the impact of the changes on other people and evaluate the success of the suggestions that are provided by the audience. Have several persons offer suggestions in action. Each experience will give the protagonist opportunities to role reverse and to experience a wider role repertoire.

8. Have the protagonist select an example from the suggestions made, and practice the interaction. Replace the original auxiliary ego.

9. Have the protagonist continue the training in the role until there is adequate comfort with the role or change in behavior.

Identifying New Criteria for Sociometric Explorations

The sociometric test in which the group has recently involved itself may have clarified group concerns. Also, group members will have identified criteria on which they would like to be chosen. These criteria result from needs to be seen or involved in a way in the group which is satisfying. The majority of sociometric issues depend upon accessibility to roles. Discuss with the group other sociometric criteria and procedures which may benefit the group at this point in time.

QUASI OR NEAR SOCIOMETRY

"Any study which tries to disclose with less than maximum possible participation of the individuals in the group the feelings which they have in regard to one another is **near sociometric.**"[44] The terms "near sociometry" and "quasi sociometric" are interchangeable, and generally mean that the method which has been used has been adapted or altered in some way which produces data which has specific limitations, or which produces data upon which it would be difficult to act. Moreno also uses the term near sociometric in instances where the test situation does not provide sufficient motivation for persons to make choices.[45] This would be true in cases where the participant's attitude is, "Nothing is going to be done with this information, so I might as well not worry too much about whom I choose."

There is an aspect of the quasi-sociometric exploration which can be fascinating and which can lead to sociodramatic sessions. This is the sociometric test which is conducted using hypothetical criteria. (See Chapter III, p. 34.) This kind of exploration can give an indication of what the choices of group members might be under certain conditions. Fantasy sociometry can be considered to be in this category. The famous example of this kind of sociometric test (so famous that it has become part of the collective bag of tricks) is the "Life Boat" exercise. A group is placed in a life boat following a ship disaster. Conditions for survival become worse and worse. Group members are instructed to have a person go overboard. Another disaster occurs, and another person is to go overboard, and so on, until only one person remains in the boat. Of course, the original ideal of the exercise is to explore the ways that groups have of negotiating and making decisions together. However, the negotiating does involve making choices (for oneself and for others) on a hypothetical-yet-made-real criterion.

The following is a listing of hypothetical criteria which may be useful for sociometric explorations:

If I become frightened in the middle of the night, whom would I choose to wake to comfort me?

If I was to go on a vacation to Hawaii, whom would I choose to accompany me?

If I was on an airplane that had been highjacked, whom in this group would I want to head up the negotiating team that is seeking the release of hostages?

If I broke up my current love relationship, with whom in the group would I seek a more intimate relationship?

If my usual co-trainer had to cancel working with me for a week-long psychodrama training seminar, whom in this group would I choose to have as a co-trainer replacement?

Short-cuts and Trade-offs

Every sociometrist needs to learn what the consequences will be to a group when short-cuts in the classical form of sociometric procedure are made. The weighing of advantages and disadvantages rests with the sociometrist in those cases when the group members are not co-researchers. Or, when the group members are in the beginning stages of familiarity with the methods, they may need to be advised of the consequences of taking a short-cut. Some of the typical short-cuts are:

Working only with positive choices

Limiting the number of choices made

Not making perceptual choices

Eliminating ranking choices according to preference

Focusing only on reciprocated choices

Observing sociometric choices, not asking for them

Declaring choices directly onto the sociomatrix; no reasons given

No feedback sessions

No neutral choices solicited

An index to various sociometric studies can be found in The Sociometry Reader (1960) in an article by Mouton, Blake and Fruchter.[46] A table is provided which identifies key aspects of the various sociometric procedures which can act as a guide to further research on the effects of short-cuts on reliability or validity of the results.

CHAPTER III

FOOTNOTES

1. Lindzey, Gardner and Edgar F. Borgatta, "Sociometric Measurement," Chapter 11, in *Handbook of Social Psychology*, Edited by Gardner Lindzey, Cambridge, Mass., Addison Wesley, 1954, p. 405.

2. Moreno, J.L., et. al, *The Sociometry Reader*, Part III, Glencoe, Ill., Free Press, 1960, pp. 401-704 contains an example of various applications.

3. Hollander, Carl E., *An Introduction to Sociogram Construction*, Denver, Colo., Snow Lion Press, 1978, pp. 2-3.

4. Moreno, J.L., *Who Shall Survive?*, Foundations of Sociometry, Group Psychotherapy and Sociodrama, Beacon, N.Y., Beacon House, 1953, p. 61.

5. *Ibid.*, p. 95.

6. *Ibid.*, p. 94.

7. Hale, Ann E., "Warm-up to a Sociometric Exploration," *Group Psychotherapy and Psychodrama*, Vol. 27, no. 1-4 (1974), pp. 157-172.

8. *Op. Cit.*, p. 110.

9. *Ibid.*, p. 3.

10. See pages 111-116 for a Conflict Resolution Facilitator Training Model.

    Additional Reading for the Warming-up Phase of the Sociometric Test:

    Gibb, Jack R., "Climate for Trust Formation" in *T-Group Theory and Laboratory Method*, edited by Leland P. Bradford, Jack R. Gibb and Kenneth D. Benne, New York: John Wiley and Sons, 1964, pp. 279-309. Particular attention should be given to "persuasive" and "participative" models of group decision-making and interaction.

    Moreno, J.L., *Who Shall Survive?*, pp. 94-95, 99, 101-103.

11. Hart, Joseph W., "Constructing the Sociometric Questionnaire," Unpublished Material, Little Rock, Arkansas, n.d., pp. 44-65.

12. Jennings, Helen Hall, "Sociometric Differentiation of the Psychegroup and the Sociogroup," *Sociometry*, vol. 10, no. 1 (February, 1947), pp. 71-79.

13. Criswell, Joan H., "Measurement of Reciprocation Under Multiple Choice Criteria" in *The Sociometry Reader*, Glencoe, Ill., Free Press, 1960, pp. 307-308.

14. Lindzey, Gardner and Edgar F. Borgatta, "Sociometric Measurement," in *Handbook of Social Psychology*, pp. 407-408.

15. Moreno, J.L., "The Atomic Theory of the Social Sciences," *Sociometry, Experimental Method and the Science of Society*, Beacon, N.Y., Beacon House, 1951, pp. 57-64.

16. Moreno, Zerka Toeman, "Sociodrama," a lecture delivered July 24, 1974, Moreno Institute, Beacon, New York.

17. Hale, Ann E., and Carolyn Gerhards-Gagnon, "Advanced Sociometry Training Group: A Sociometric Analysis and Comprehensive Report of a Week-long Residential Workshop," Roanoke, Va., Unpublished Material. 1980.

18. Leavitt, Harold J. and Ronald A.H. Mueller, "Some Effects of Feedback on Communication," in *Small Group Studies in Social Interaction*, Edited by A. Paul Hare, Edgar F. Borgatta and Robert F. Bales, New York: Alfred Knopf, 1966, pp. 434-443.

19. Zeleny, Leslie D., "Table III. Sample Responses of Students to Personalized Sociometric Guidance," *Sociometry*, Vol. 13, no. 4 (November, 1951), pp. 326-327.

20. Campbell, Donald T., "A Rationale for Weighting First, Second and Third Sociometric Choices," in *The Sociometric Reader*, Edited by J.L. Moreno, et. al, Glencoe, Illinois: Free Press, 1960, pp. 137-138.

21. Computers have been used to assist with quantifying sociometric data and even providing sociograms. See Naugher (1975).

22. The Sociomatrix Reader, designed by Ann E. Hale, has been inserted in this manual.

23. Northway, Mary L., *The Primer of Sociometry*, Toronto, Canada, University of Toronto Press, 1953.

24. Bronfenbrenner, Urie, "A Constant Frame of Reference for Sociometric Research," *Sociometry*, Vol. 6, No. 4 (November 1943), pp. 363-397. Specifically note pp. 372-386.

25. *Op. Cit.*, p. 29.

26. Moreno, J.L., "The Three Branches of Sociometry: A Postscript," *Sociometry*, Vol. 11, no. 1-2 (February-May, 1948), pp. 125-127.

27. Moreno, Zerka T., "Sociogenesis of Individuals and Groups," in the *International Handbook of Group Psychotherapy*, Edited by J.L. Moreno, et. al, New York: Philosophical Library, 1966, pp. 223-234.

28. Moreno, J.L., "Address of the Honorary President of the Fourth International Congress of Group Psychotherapy," *Group Psychotherapy,* Vol. 21, No. 2-3 (June-September, 1968), p. 96.

29. Mendelsson, Peter Dean, *Rethinking Sociometry: Toward the Reunification of Theory, Philosophy, Methodology and Praxis.* (Dissertation, Ph.D.), St. Louis, Missouri: Washington University, 1976, p. 20.

30. Moreno, J.L., *Who Shall Survive?,* p. 285.

31. Smucker, Ogden, "Measurement of Group Tension through the Use of Negative Sociometric Data," *Sociometry,* Vol. 10, No. 4 (November, 1947), p. 380.

32. *Ibid.,* p. 379.

33. Northway, Mary L. and Blossom T. Wigdor, "Rorschach Patterns Related to the Sociometric Status of School Children," *Sociometry,* Vol. 10, No. 2 (May 1947), p. 194.

34. Schiff, Herbert, "Judgemental Response Sets in the Perception of Sociometric Status," *Sociometry,* Vol 17, No. 3 (August 1954), p. 207.

35. *Ibid.,* p. 218.

36. *Ibid.,* p. 217.

37. Jennings, Helen Hall, "Leadership and Sociometric Choice," in *Sociometry Reader,* Edited by J.L. Moreno, et. al, p. 447.

38. *Ibid.,* p 451.

39. *Ibid.,* pp. 452-453.

40. Moreno, J.L., *Words of the Father,* New York: Beacon House, 1941, p. 150.

41. Mouton, Jane Srygley, Robert R. Blake and Benjamin Fructer, "The Reliability of Sociometric Measures," in *The Sociometry Reader,* Edited by J.L. Moreno, et. al, pp. 320-361.

42. *Ibid.,* p. 326.

43. *Ibid.,* p. 343.

44. J.L. Moreno, *Who Shall Survive?,* p. 102.

45. *Ibid.*

46. Mouton, Jane Srygley, Robert R. Blake and Benjamin Fructer, "The Validity of Sociometric Responses," in *The Sociometry Reader,* Edited by J.L. Moreno, et al., Glencoe, Illinois, The Free Press, 1960, pp. 362-387.

CHAPTER III

BIBLIOGRAPHY

Ausubel, David P. "Reciprocity and Assumed Reciprocity of Acceptance Among Adolescents: A Sociometric Study," *Sociometry,* Vol. 16, no. 4 (November, 1953), pp. 339-348.

Barbour, Alton. "Sociometric Meaning in Interpersonal Relationships," *Group Psychotherapy,* Vol. 21, no. 4 (December, 1968), pp. 193-201.

Beum, Corli O. and Joan H. Criswell. "Application of Machine Tabulation Methods to Sociometric Data,"*Sociometry,* Vol. 10, no. 3 (August, 1947), pp. 227-348.

Bonney, Merl E. and Seth A. Fessenden. *Bonney-Fessenden Sociograph.* Los Angeles, Calif. California Test Bureau, 1955.

Borgatta, Edgar F. "Analysis of Social Interaction and Sociometric Perception," *Sociometry,* Vol. 17, no. 1 (February, 1954), pp. 7-32.

Bradford, Leland P., Jack R. Gibb and Kenneth D. Benne. *T-Group Theory and Laboratory Method.* New York: John Wiley and Sons, 1964.

Bronfenbrenner, Urie. "The Graphic Representation of Sociometric Data," *Sociometry,* Vol. 7, no. 3 (August, 1944), pp. 283-289.

———. "The Constant Frame of Reference for Sociometric Research," *Sociometry,* Vol. 6, no. 4 (November, 1943), pp. 363-397.

Campbell, Donald T. "A Rationale for Weighting First, Second and Third Sociometric Choices" in *The Sociometry Reader,* edited by J.L. Moreno, et. al. Glencoe, Ill., The Free Press, 1960, pp. 137-138.

Criswell, Joan H. "Sociometric Methods of Measuring Group Preferences," *Sociometry,* Vol. 6, no. 4 (November, 1943), pp. 398-408.

Danielsson, Clare. *The Intimate Community Experience: an Experiment in Social Reorganisation Based Upon Sociometry and Christian Tradition.* (Ph.D. Dissertation) New Paltz, New York, 1979.

Gibb, Jack R. "Climate for Trust Formation," in *T-Group Theory and Laboratory Method,* edited by Leland P. Bradford, Jack R. Gibb and Kenneth R. Benne. New York: John Wiley and Sons, 1964, pp. 279-309.

Hale, Ann E. "Warm-up to a Sociometric Exploration," *Group Psychotherapy and Psychodrama,* Vol. 27, no. 1-4 (1974), pp. 157-172.

Hale, Ann E. and Carolyn Gerhards-Gagnon. *Advanced Sociometry Training Group: A Sociometric Analysis and Comprehensive Report of a Week-long Residential Training Workshop.* Roanoke, Virginia, unpublished manuscript, 1980.

Hart, Joseph W. *Constructing the Sociometric Questionnaire.* Unpublished material. Little Rock, Arkansas, n.d.

Hart, Joseph W. and Raghu Nath. "Sociometry in Business and Industry: New Developments in Historical Perspective," *Group Psychotherapy, Psychodrama and Sociometry,* Vol. 32 (1979), pp. 128-149.

Hare, A. Paul, Edgar F. Borgatta and Robert F. Bales, Eds. *Small Group Studies in Social Interaction.* New York: Alfred Knopf, 1966.

Hollander, Carl E. *An Introduction to Sociogram Construction.* Denver, Colo., Snow Lion Press, 1978.

Hollander, Carl E. and Sharon Leman. "Sociometry," *Sensorsheet* (a co-publication of the Environmental Studies Project and the Earth Science Teacher Preparation Project), Winter, 1973.

Jahoda, Marie, M. Deutsch and S.W. Cook. *Research Methods in Social Relations,* Part II. New York: Dryden Press, 1951.

Jennings, Helen Hall. "Sociometric Differentiation of the Psychegroup and the Sociogroup," *Sociometry,* Vol. 10, no. 1 (February, 1947), pp. 71-79.

———. *Sociometry of Leadership.* (Sociometry monograph, no. 14) Beacon, New York: Beacon House, 1947.

Katz, L. and J.H. Powell. "A Proposed Index of the Conformity of One Sociometric Measure With Another," *Psychometrika,* Vol. 18 (1953), pp. 249-256.

Leavitt, Harold J. and Ronald A.H. Mueller. "Some Effects of Feedback on Communication," in *Small Groups Studies in Social Interaction,* edited by A. Paul Hare, Edgar F. Borgatta and Robert F. Bales. New York: Alfred Knopf, 1966, pp. 434-443.

Levy, Ronald B. *Human Relations—A Conceptual Approach.* New York: International Textbook Co., 1969.

Lindzey, Gardner and Edgar F. Borgatta. "Sociometric Measurement," in *Handbook of Social Psychology,* edited by Gardner Lindzey. Cambridge, Mass., Addison-Wesley Publishing Co., 1954, pp. 405-448.

Loomis, Charles and Harold P. Pepinsky. *Sociometry: 1937-1947 Theory and Methods.* (Sociometry monograph, no. 20), Beacon, N.Y.: Beacon House, 1949.

Loomis, Charles and Charles Proctor. "The Relationship between Choice Status and Economic Status in Social Systems," *Sociometry,* Vol. 13, no. 4 (November, 1950), pp. 307-313.

Moreno, J.L. "Address of the Honorary President of the Fourth International Congress of Group Psychotherapy," *Group Psychotherapy,* Vol. 21, no. 2-3 (June-September, 1968), p. 96.

———. "Sociometric Theory of Leadership and Isolates," in *Who Shall Survive?* Comments on F. Stuart Chapin's article, "Sociometric Stars as Isolates," *Sociometry,* Vol. 13, no. 4 (November, 1950), p. 383.

———. *Sociometry, Experimental Method and the Science of Society.* Beacon, N.Y.: Beacon House, 1951.

———, et al. *The Sociometry Reader.* Glencoe, Ill.: Free Press, 1960.

———. *Who Shall Survive? Foundations in Sociometry, Group Psychotherapy and Sociodrama.* Beacon, N.Y.: Beacon House, 1953 ed.

———. *Words of the Father.* Beacon, N.Y.: Beacon House, 1941.

Naugher, Jimmie R. *A System for the Collection and Computer Analysis of Sociometric Data for Research and Classroom Purposes.* (Ph.D. Dissertation, North Texas State Univ., 1975) Ann Arbor, Michigan: University Microfilms, 1980.

Northway, Mary L. *A Primer of Sociometry.* Toronto, University of Toronto Press, 1952.

———. *Sociometric Testing: A Guide for Teachers.* Toronto: University of Toronto Press, 1957.

——— and Blossom T. Wigdor. "Rorschach Patterns Related to the Status of School Children," *Sociometry,* Vol. 10, no. 2 (May, 1947), pp. 186-199.

Proctor, C.H. and Charles P. Loomis. "Analysis of Sociometric Data," in *Research Methods in Social Relationships,* edited by Marie Jahoda, M. Deutsch and S.W. Cook. New York: Dryden Press, 1951, pp. 561-585.

Schiff, Herbert. "Judgemental Response Sets in the Perception of Sociometric Status," *Sociometry,* Vol. 17, no. 3 (August, 1954), pp. 207-227.

Smucker, Ogden. "Measurement of Group Tension Through the Use of Negative Sociometric Data," *Sociometry,* Vol. 10, no. 4 (November, 1947), pp. 376-383.

Sociogram Techniques. University of Kentucky, Center for Interdisciplinary Education in Allied Health (Strategies for Evaluation, no. 5), 1979.

Tagiuri, Renato, Nathan Kogan and Jerome S. Brunner. "The Transparency of Interpersonal Choice," in *The Sociometry Reader,* edited by J.L. Moreno, et al. Glencoe, Ill.: The Free Press, 1960, pp. 672-683.

Wolff, Kurt H. *The Sociometry of Georg Simmel.* New York: Free Press, 1950.

WARM-UP PHASE

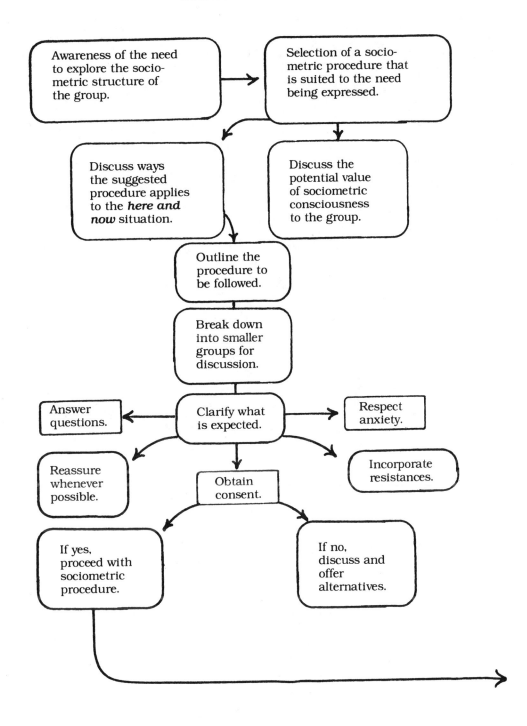

ACTION PHASE

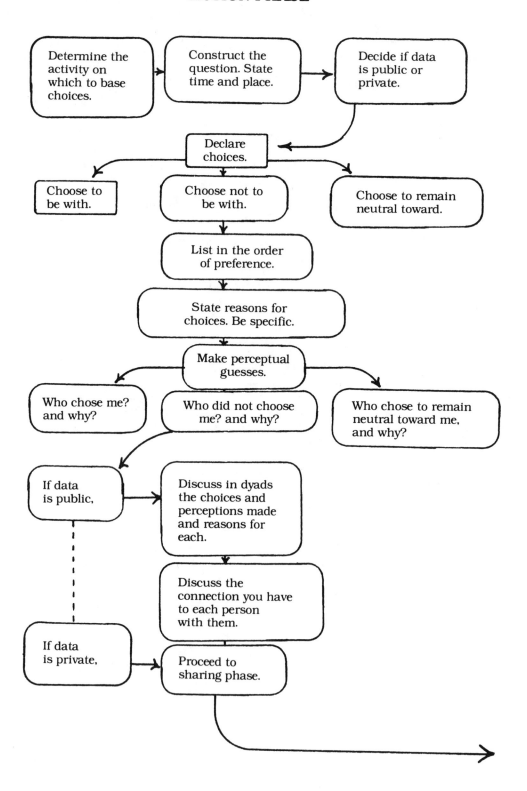

Determine the activity on which to base choices.

Construct the question. State time and place.

Decide if data is public or private.

Declare choices.

Choose to be with.

Choose not to be with.

Choose to remain neutral toward.

List in the order of preference.

State reasons for choices. Be specific.

Make perceptual guesses.

Who chose me? and why?

Who did not choose me? and why?

Who chose to remain neutral toward me, and why?

If data is public,

Discuss in dyads the choices and perceptions made and reasons for each.

Discuss the connection you have to each person with them.

If data is private,

Proceed to sharing phase.

SHARING PHASE

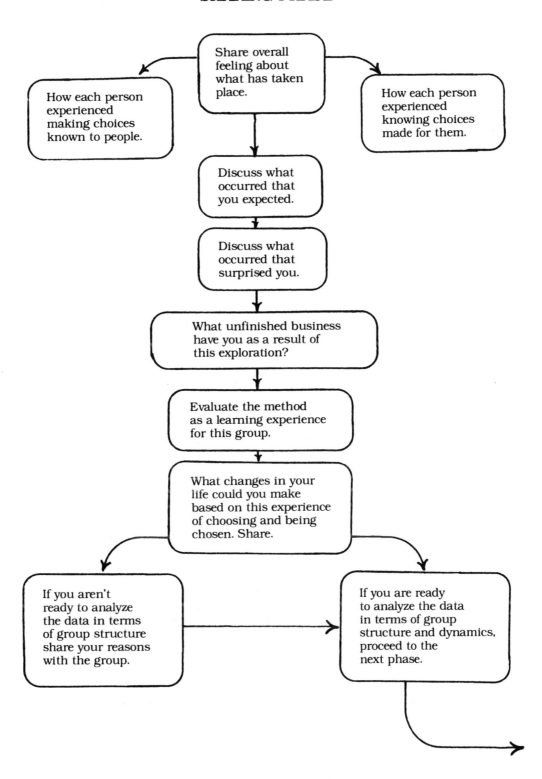

ANALYSIS PHASE

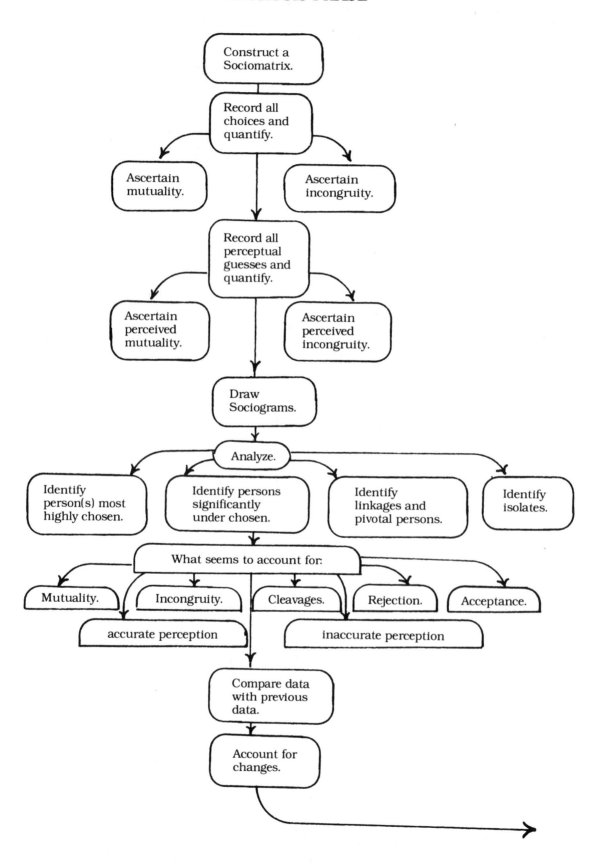

INTERVENTION AND FUTURE PROJECTIONS

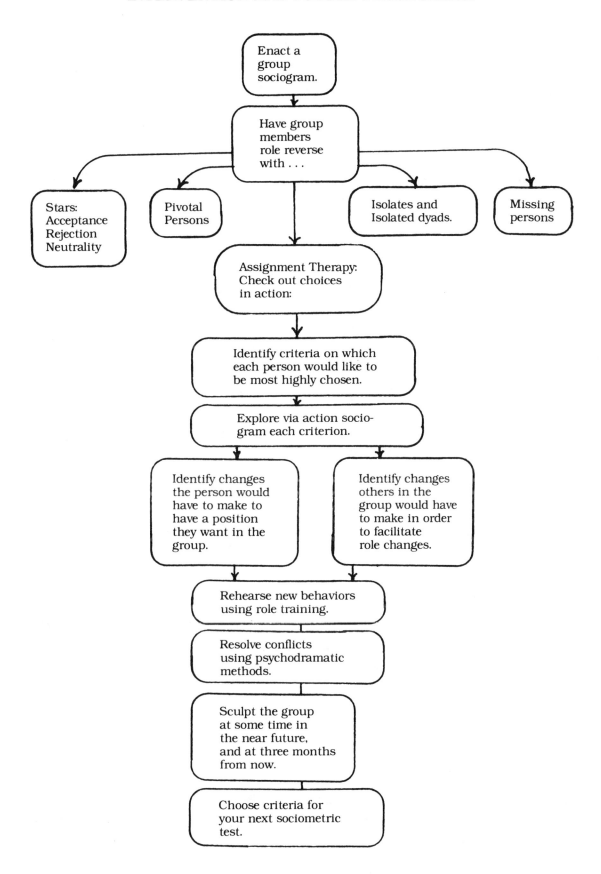

STAGES IN A GROUP'S DEVELOPMENT WHEN THE SOCIOMETRIC TEST WOULD BE A CHOICE

There are certain stages in a group's development when the group could benefit from a sociometric test. There are cues which indicate a need for such an exploration, and the sociometrist can develop this sensitivity in him or herself and pass this awareness on to the group. The following are guidelines which have been provided to help identify these stages (or moods).

A. **The newly formed group**

Reasons:
1. The sociometric test makes visible and concrete preexisting connections and group structure.
2. Identifies telic connections as well as transference and empathic connections.
3. Diagnoses issues of inclusion and suggests intervention possibilities.
4. Clarifies level of risk-taking in the group.
5. Provides a task and focuses central concern.

B. **A blocked group**

Reasons:
1. Provides vehicle for expressing feelings in a collective, directed and focused manner.
2. Motivates group members to examine ways to involve themselves with group members less known to them.
3. Stimulates imagination and expands perceptions.
4. Identifies the stultifying group structure and focuses on existant act hunger.
5. Identifies persons carrying the heaviest loads of projection in the group and can provide role relief.

C. **A hostile group**

Reasons:
1. Reduces anger due to "nothing being done about a situation" by providing a focused alternative and a structured vehicle for expressing feelings and choices.
2. Provides relief of tension which may be due to the "invisibility" of dynamics producing hostility, by making group structure visible.
3. Identifies possibilities for alternative group structures.
4. Clarifies areas where group members have to take responsibility for their impact on others when motivations for choice are explored.
5. Focuses on fear which exists in the group and can suggest focus on supportive and confrontive role development.

D. **A risking group**

Reasons:
1. Makes visible changes in group members' positions in a group.
2. Provides practice in being open, firm, clear, and honest about one's responses and choices for others.
3. Provides an experience in facing the fear of rejection, and the fear of rejecting.
4. Provides information on group dynamics which are supportive of risk-taking which can be applied to groups less open and in need of skills.

E. **A terminating group**

Reasons:
1. Focuses on issues to be resolved in the group which are preventing adequate closure.
2. Highlights role development needs of group members (act hunger) not yet met by the group as it has currently structured itself.
3. Identifies areas of group and change for the group which can be the focus of evaluation.
4. Can clarify the end or continuance of relationships.

DESCRIPTION OF THE SOCIOMETRIC TEST
FOR THE FIRST-TIME PARTICIPANT

The sociometric test is a procedure designed by Jacob L. Moreno, M.D., to determine the connections which exist between persons in a group, from time to time and from role to role. Moreno wrote in **Words of the Father** (1920): [1]

> "All Creators Are Alone
> Until Their Love of Creating
> Forms a World Around Them."

In this instance, the "world" is one's own group, which has a structure which can be identified, studied, and "formed" by the group to meet their expectations. A group's structure is complex and its dynamics involving. Therefore, group members need to develop skills for influencing and changing groups.

The sociometric test which is described below is not a test in the same way one takes an exam and derives a grade, but it is a test in the sense of a laboratory exploration. The following is a brief description of how the sociometric test is conducted.

First, the group picks a criterion for the evaluation. For example, the criterion might be "Who would I choose to take a half-hour walk with after lunch?" or, "Who would I choose to share with the three things I am most ashamed of in my life." Once the criterion is picked, each person in the group is asked to choose among the other members: (1) those he or she would prefer to interact with; (2) those he or she is neutral toward, and (3) those he or she would prefer **not** to interact with, on the basis of the chosen criteria. Each person writes down his choices, and wherever possible, gives a reason for each choice. The results are shared, with each person spending a few minutes of time with each person, discussing their choices for each other. The data sheets are collected, quantified, and depicted in the form of charts, a sociomatrix and sociograms. Naturally a person's choices of others will vary depending on the criterion, thus the first criterion given in the example above might produce many more positive choices than the second one.

In addition to choosing others, each group member is asked to make guesses as to which other members have chosen him or her, remained neutral toward him or her, or have chosen not to interact with him or her. In this way each person creates his or her own "perceptual sociogram". Later, these perceptions can be checked out against the data generated by the group and depicted on the sociomatrix. Thus a group member can discover how accurate he or she is in assessing how others in the group react to him or her.

The finished sociogram will illustrate who is chosen by whom, how often the choices are mutual, who is chosen infrequently or isolated from the group, and who is rejected by other group members. From the sociometric data, assignments will be made so that each person will carry out the activity implied in the criterion with someone of his or her choice.

The sociometric exploration provides focus on a question which often goes unasked in groups: "Where do I fit in this group?" This is a threatening question, but an important one. By confronting "the need to know" and the "fear of knowing" about oneself in relation to others, the group member can gain freedom from these needs and fears, and become more effective as a group member, group leader and self-therapist.

The Criterion

The group's choice of criterion will reflect the unique features of that group. It is important that all group members give input into this choice. Be sure that the activity has relevance for you. Feel free to speak out and offer suggestions, and look for criteria which will provide a "stretch" in your risk-taking ability.

Choosing

Once the criterion has been selected each group member works independently. The following information may help you in making choices. Every group member is to be placed in one of three categories:

choose to, choose not to, choose to be neutral towards. There is no limit, however, to the number of persons within each category. For example, if the criterion is "choose to go nude bathing with" you might put everyone in the "choose not to" category (or conversely you might choose to put them all in the "choose to" category!). In any case, list both your positive and negative choices in order of preference. (The neutral choices, of course, have no order of preference, otherwise they would not really be neutral.) It may be helpful to first make a list under each category and then place the number of your preference in the margin. If you cannot distinguish between two or more persons in the order of preference, they may be given the same number.

If you have difficulty making your choices, close your eyes and imagine yourself engaged in the activity specified with each person in the group. What feelings does this evoke? Make your choices on the basis of those feelings.

Report as accurately as possible the specific reasons for making each choice. Others will be struggling with putting their feelings into words. It is not an easy task. Verbalizing your feelings will help you better understand yourself as well as enable you to give constructive feedback to others. Write your reasons as if you are speaking to the person, not about them. This makes the reason more personal.

Be aware of the feelings you have about the process of choosing and rejecting others. Respect your anxiety. It is possible to learn from it. Remember that this choosing process goes on all the time (beneath the surface) during our daily contact with people. This group is a relatively safe, controlled "laboratory" situation where you can look carefully and honestly at this process, and come to understand yourself better. If you still find it difficult to be "completely honest" especially with people you choose not to interact with, you may find it helpful to fill out two data sheets: one you hand in, giving only the data you can share openly, and another which you keep, which reveals choices and reasons you would give if you were completely comfortable.

When you get to the part of the procedure that asks for perceptual guesses you may find it helpful to put yourself in each person's place (role reverse) in order to get in touch with the choices they might have made. Note what you are using as a clue to their choice. The more perceptual guesses you make, the greater the opportunity for learning about and sharpening your perceptual skills.

Summary

There are many different kinds of learning which come from the sociometric test. The most obvious question which it addresses is about group structure: "Where do I fit in this group?" "Where is the potential for leadership within the group and how may I make a contribution?" "What aspects of my personality cause people to choose me? to reject me?"

The procedure also helps each individual to look at his own choice process: "What are my needs, my fears, my anxieties surrounding the choice process?" "Am I able to make choices based on the fullest range of positive and negative feelings, and be responsible for acting on these choices?" After someone has participated in several explorations with different groups, he or she may begin to look at the factors involved in what kind of group (size, age, sex, culture, temperament, etc.) allows him or her the greatest degree of expansiveness, creativity and productivity.

All of the above questions look on the sociometric test as a measuring device (i.e. a method of assessing what is). But it is more than a means of measurement. It is also an agent of change. The process of carefully looking at relationships changes those relationships. This spin-off may occur in many ways, and happen immediately or over time. People who are mutual positive choices may get together quicker once they have acknowledged each other. Often in the process of writing down the reasons for a negative choice, a group member will realize that the person reminds him or her of someone else in the past who was a negative influence. That realization often releases the group member from some of the transference and allows him or her to establish a here and now relationship.

It is particularly useful to understanding social interactions if the group will redo the sociometric test later in the history of the group. Choices at this point will be based less on first impressions and transference, and more on mutually shared experience. The test can indicate growth and change and the degree to which a person has been able to "form a world around them."

---

[1] Moreno, J.L. **Words of the Father.** New York: Beacon House, 1941, p. 138.

CHAPTER 3   **APPENDIX IV**

RANKING CRITERIA OF CHOICE BY RELEVANCE, THREAT & TYPE

In the columns indicated below rank the following criteria using the scale as itemized.

THREAT

1 = No threat
2 = Mildly threatening
3 = Threatening
4 = Very threatening
5 = Overwhelmingly
      threatening

RELEVANCE

1 = No relevance
2 = Some relevance
3 = Very relevant

TYPE

P = Psychetelic
S = Sociotelic

DECISION

1 = I would urge others
      to use it as well.
2 = I would use it.
3 = I'm neutral about
      using it.
4 = I could be persuaded
      to use it.
5 = I won't use it.

THREAT	RELEVANCE	TYPE	DECISION	CRITERIA
				Whom do I choose to hold me when I need to cry?
				Whom do I choose to be a confrontive double in my psychodrama?
				Whom would I allow to practice psychodrama directing on me?
				Whom would I choose to tell about a distressing sexual incident?
				Whom do I choose to advise me about a current decision?
				With whom do I choose to take a nap?
				With whom do I choose to share a room?
				Whom do I choose to wrestle?
				Whom do I choose to spend leisure time with?
				From who do I choose to borrow notes?
				Whom do I choose to have over to my house after class (after session)?
				Of the people who are a risk for me to encounter about my angry feelings toward them, whom do I choose to encounter?
				Of the people who are a risk for me to let them know I am sexually attracted to them, whom do I choose to spend a hour with being open and direct?
				Whom do I choose to have as my partner for analyzing the data from this sociometric test?
				With whom do I choose to share the impact this sociometric test has had on me?
				Whom do I choose to tell about my first impressions of the other group members?
				With whom do I choose to draw sociograms?
				Whom do I choose to advise me about my physical appearance?
				Whom do I choose to have on my volleyball team?
				Whom do I choose to lead the group in a guided fantasy?
				Whom do I choose to lend my car to?
				Whom in the group do I choose to ask for a loan of money (over $20, less than $50)?
				Whom do I choose to dance with, to slow music, when the lights are down?
				With whom do I choose to share a weakness?
				Of the people in the group whom it would be a risk for me to have them hold me, whom do I choose to hold me for five minutes in order for me to check my perceptions?
				With whom do I choose to design a sociometric exploration for use in my work setting?
				With whom do I choose to share a massage?

APPENDIX IV, *continued*

THREAT	RELEVANCE	TYPE	DECISION	CRITERIA
				To whom would I go for comfort if I find myself distressed in the middle of the night?
				Whom do I choose to support me if I should be encountered in this group?
				Whom do I choose to sit across from in group sessions?
				Whom do I choose to spend an hour with exchanging feedback?
				Of the people in the group whom I know least well, whom do I choose to spend time with on the break?
				Whom do I choose to have as members of my support group?
				OTHER:

CHAPTER 3
APPENDIX V.a

OBJECTIVE DATA SHEET
FOR
THE SOCIOMETRIC TEST

Name _____ Date _____

1. Whom in the group do I choose to _____
   List in the order of preference.
   NAME   REASON FOR THIS CHOICE

2. Whom in the group do I choose not to _____
   List in the order of least preference.

   NAME   REASON FOR THIS CHOICE

3. Whom in the group do I choose to remain neutral toward on the basis of this criterion. It is not necessary to list in any particular order.

CHAPTER 3   **APPENDIX V.b**

PERCEPTUAL DATA SHEET
FOR
THE SOCIOMETRIC TEST

Name: _____   Date: _____

Criterion: _____

A. 1. Whom in the group do I perceive will choose me?

   NAME   REASON FOR THIS PERCEPTION

   2. Whom in the group do I perceive will place me in the "choose not to" category?

   NAME   REASON FOR THIS PERCEPTION

   3. Whom in the group do I perceive will choose to remain neutral toward me on the basis of this criterion?

   NAME   REASON FOR THIS PERCEPTION

B. I have chosen to make perceptual guesses about the choices of _____ .

   HE/SHE CHOSE: HE/SHE DID NOT CHOOSE: HE/SHE WAS NEUTRAL TOWARD:

SOCIOMATRIX

CRITERION   DATE:

NAMES	1	2	3	4	5	6	7	8	9	10	11	12	13	14	15	16	17	18	19	20	Positive Choices Made	Negative Choices Made	Neutral Choices Made
1																							
2																							
3																							
4																							
5																							
6																							
7																							
8																							
9																							
10																							
11																							
12																							
13																							
14																							
15																							
16																							
17																							
18																							
19																							
20																							
Positive Choices Rec'd.																							
Negative Choices Rec'd.																							
Neutral Choices Rec'd.																							
Positive Mutuals																							
Negative Mutuals																							
Neutral Mutuals																							
Pos./Neg. Incongruity																							
Pos./Neut. Incongruity																							
Neg./Neut. Incongruity																							
WEIGHTING																							

NAMES

EXPLORING YOUR SOCIOMETRIC SET

A **sociometric set** is a determination a person makes over time and via exploration of the number and quality of relationships. A person who has grown used to "Two's company, three's a crowd." and organizes his/her life around being in dyads, most likely has a set number of two in his/her psychological social atom. Helen Hall Jennings, who studied and reported on this phenomenon stated: "As the individual invests his affection in others, the extent and quality of these individuals appear by early childhood to be stabilized into what can be called his *emotional repertoire.*"[*]

To explore your sociometric set and begin to determine what kind and number of persons you need to feel secure, happy, productive, even creative and spontaneous, you will need to investigate the patterns which emerge as you engage in a process of recorded choice-making, the sociometric test. What is provided here is a set of structured questions designed to focus attention on key elements in your warm-up (preparation) for making choices, the impact of making public your choices for others, and the evaluation you make of your choices after following through in action. The last page is a cumulative record of data from sociometric tests which will make it possible for you to review the choice-making experiences you have had and account for the impact of the relevance of the criterion on your choices, the frequency of your choices for persons of the same sex or opposite sex, the frequency of reciprocated choices, the kind of incongruous choice-making which appears most often, and the usual position you have in a group.

The following is an outline of the process and questions:

1. Take part in a sociometric test.

2. Answer questions in Part A.

3. Quantify the data and draw sociograms.

4. Answer questions in Part B.

5. Make assignments on the basis of the choices persons have made for each other. Carry out the assignment.

6. Answer questions in Part C.

7. Fill in the Cumulative Data Sheet

8. Make comparisons between this test and other sociometric tests.

[*]Helen Hall Jennings, "Sociometric Choice Process in Personality and Group Formation" in The Sociometry Reader, Edited by J.L. Moreno, et. al. Glencoe, Illinois: The Free Press, 1060, p. 88. The term is also used by Edgar F. Borgatta: "It is characteristic of persons that they constantly assess each other as desirable or undesirable according to some frame of reference (or set)." p. 272.

CHAPTER 3   **APPENDIX VII.a**

EXPLORING YOUR SOCIOMETRIC SET:
QUESTIONS RELATING TO THE SOCIOMETRIC TEST (A)

Your Name: _____ Date: _____

Criterion: _____

A. Complete this set of questions once you have made your objective and perceptual choices.

1. Is this sociometric test a new experience for you? _____ Yes _____ No

2. Have you participated in a sociometric test using this criterion before? _____ Yes _____ No

   If yes, what was your response to this criterion: And, was it relevant to you then?

3. What is your present response to this criterion? Comment in terms of the nature of the activity, the
   time specified and the space indicated.

4. Rate the relevance of this criterion for you on a 1-5 scale: _____
   (1) Extremely irrelevant; (2) Not very relevant; (3) Not clear; (4) Occasionally relevant;
   (5) Extremely relevant.

5. Please summarize your reaction to placing persons in the "choose to" category.

6. Did you find yourself comfortable, anxious, unable to, reluctant to (circle one) place people in the
   "choose not" category? Please summarize your reactions.

7. Summarize your reactions to placing persons in the "choose to remain neutral toward" category.

8. In your choices were you prevented from declaring a choice for someone for any of the following reasons?

    a. **Unfinished business with a person.** If so, what reason did you give for placing the person in the category you did choose? How does this relate to the choice you would have liked to have made for this person? What is preventing the resolution of the unfinished business, and whom is likely to initiate the resolution?

    b. **Fear of rejection.** From whom? How would this rejection manifest itself? Under what kinds of conditions would you be able to discuss your fears with this person?

    c. **Unable to commit yourself to the responsibility of relating at this point in time.** What factors have prevented you from being clear and candid about your choices?

    d. **Unsure of your feelings.** For whom? What do you believe that you need to know about your feelings, or about the other person, before you can declare your choices?

9. Are you aware of your choices being motivated by a tele response, or emphatic or transference reaction? Please identify.

CHAPTER 3   **APPENDIX VII.b**

EXPLORING YOUR SOCIOMETRIC SET:
QUESTIONS RELATING TO THE SOCIOMETRIC TEST (B)

Your Name: _____ Date: _____

Criterion: _____

B. Complete this set of questions once the data about persons' choices has been entered on the socio-matrix and sociograms have been drawn.

1. In your choices have you given higher preference to:

   _____ Women; _____ Men.

   _____ Women near your age; _____ Women Older; _____ Women Younger.

   _____ Men near your age; _____ Men Older; _____ Men Younger.

   _____ Persons known to you; _____ Persons new to you.

   _____ Persons whom you perceived would choose you.

   _____ Persons in a sociometric position more positive than yours.

   _____ Persons in a sociometric position less positive than yours.

   _____ Persons having a similar background or lifestyle.

   _____ Persons who had the most to teach you.

2. In making perceptual guesses which did you perceive more accurately:

   _____ Choices made of you; _____ Choices made of persons other than you.

   _____ Mutual choices; _____ Incongruous choices.

   _____ Positive choices; _____ Negative choices; _____ Neutral choices.

   _____ Choices concerning sociometric stars; _____ Choices concerning isolates.

   _____ Choices persons of the same sex made for other persons of the same sex.

   _____ Choices persons of the opposite sex made for persons of the opposite sex.

   _____ Choices persons of the same sex made for persons of the opposite sex.

   _____ Choices persons of the opposite sex made for persons of the same sex.

   _____ Choices made by persons of the same background.

   _____ Choices made by persons having a different background or lifestyle.

EXPLORING YOUR SOCIOMETRIC SET:
QUESTIONS RELATING TO THE SOCIOMETRIC TEST (C)

Your Name: _____ Date: _____

Criterion: _____

C. Complete this set of questions once you have carried out the assignment of acting on the criterion. (For use in sociometric tests for partners.)

1. I chose _____ , who was my _____ choice for this reason:

_____

2. _____ chose me as his/her _____ choice for this reason:

_____

3. Who initiated the arrangements for the completion of the assignment? What feelings did this evoke in you?

4. Compare the response you have had to relating to the person you chose to the original reasons you gave for choosing this person. Comment.

5. What additions, or corrections to your original perceptions would you like to make now, on the basis of this experience.

6. Has the criterion the same relevance for you now as before? Identify any changes in your opinion of the criterion.

7. On the basis of this experience, are there any persons you rejected or felt neutral toward, whom you could now engage on this criterion, for the purposes of learning? Explain.

9. Summarize what you have learned from this experience which has not been included elsewhere. (Use the back of the page if necessary.)

10. How do you experience **knowing** your position in the group based upon the choices others made for you on this criterion?

11. How do **you** evaluate your position in the group?

12. Where would you like to be?

13. What must happen in you, or in the group, for you to have the position in this group that you would most like to have?

14. If this group would explore another criterion, what would you like that criterion to be?

15. Enter the data from the sociomatrix onto the **Cumulative Data Sheet.**
    a. Compare positive, negative and neutral expansiveness from previous sociometric tests with the data from this test. Account for any similarities or differences.
    b. Compare the mutuality from previous sociometric tests with the mutuality of your position in this sociometric test. Account for any similarities or differences.
    c. Compare the incongruity of choices from past sociometric tests and the kind of incongruity which existed in this sociometric test. Account for any similarities or differences.
    d. Does the size of the group seem to be a factor affecting your sociometric set.
    e. What configuration of persons (number and quality of relations) seems to appear with frequency? Draw a sample sociogram:

EXPLORING YOUR SOCIOMETRIC SET:
INSTRUCTIONS FOR THE CUMULATIVE DATA SHEET

Date:							
Date Group Formed:							
Criterion:							
Relevance scale:							
Group Size:	SS						
	OS						
Positive expan-	SS						
siveness:	OS						
Negative expan-	SS						
siveness:	OS						
Neutral expan-	SS						
siveness:	OS						
Positive choices	SS						
received:	OS						
Negative choices	SS						
received:	OS						
Neutral choices	SS						
received:	OS						
Positive	SS						
mutuals:	OS						
Negative	SS						
mutuals:	OS						
Neutral	SS						
mutuals:	OS						
Pos/Neg	SS						
Incongruity:	OS						
Pos/Neutral	SS						
Incongruity:	OS						
Neg/Neutral	SS						
Incongruity:	OS						
Pos. Mutuals	SS						
Perceived:	OS						
Neg. Mutuals	SS						
Perceived:	OS						
Neutral Mutuals	SS						
Perceived:	OS						
Pos/Neg Incon-	SS						
gruity perceived:	OS						
Pos/Neut Incon-	SS						
gruity perceived:	OS						
Neg/Neut Incon-	SS						
gruity perceived:	OS						

SS = Same Sex
OS = Opposite Sex

Relevance Scale:
1 = Extremely irrelevant
2 = Not very relevant
3 = Not clear
4 = Occasionally relevant
5 = Extremely relevant

LEISURE ROLE CLUSTER EXPLORATION

Your Name: _____ Date: _____

A. The following list of leisure roles (non-work related activities) are roles in which I like to be engaged because they relax me, or provide a change in focus from my work related activities.

THESE I LIKE TO DO BY MYSELF   THESE I PREFER A PARTNER FOR

B. List the names of persons in this group. In the column beside their name indicate some leisure time activities that you could imagine yourself engaged in with this person. Be sure to include some that are within the realm of possibility in this setting. Include everyone in the listing. Use the above named leisure roles as a guide; however, you do not have to limit yourself to these roles. This information will be shared with each person.

NAME   IMAGINED LEISURE ACTIVITY

SOCIOMETRIC TEST OF THE LEISURE ROLE CLUSTER

Your Name: _____   Date: _____

C. Of the leisure time activities I like, I would most like to be engaged in the following activity during my stay here:

_____

(Choose an activity which would involve a partner, or partners.)

1. With whom in this group do I choose to interact on this criterion? (List in the order of preference)

NAME   REASON FOR THIS CHOICE

2. Whom do I choose not to interact with on this criterion? (List in order of least preference.)

NAME   REASON FOR THIS CHOICE

3. Toward whom in this group do I choose to remain neutral on the basis of this criterion?

NAME   REASON FOR THIS CHOICE

STAFF ROLE EXPLORATION

This exploration gives attention to self-evaluation of role performance and the perceptions you may have in the areas of your work which could be developed or changed in some way.

1. In terms of your own estimation of your performance, state and describe the roles in which you are engaged (often or occasionally) about which you feel the most negative. Explain.

2. In terms of your own estimation of your performance, state and describe the roles in which you are engaged (often or occasionally) about which you feel the most positive. Explain.

3. What roles do you feel you have not yet had an opportunity to develop? What and/or whom prevents you?

4. What dynamics, or factors, leave you feeling isolated from roles which would bring you into closer contact with the rest of the staff?

5. Speaking as specifically as possible, what behaviors do you have which you perceive the staff would most like you to change?

Share with the other staff members what you have experienced while taking part in this exploration. Pair off and share with each person the answers you have given to the above questions.

CHAPTER 3   APPENDIX VIII.d

STAFF ENCOUNTER EXPLORATION

Name: _____ Date: _____

1. In terms of **interpersonal unfinished business** list the staff members with whom you feel you have the most (to the least) to deal with at present.

    NAME   NATURE OF THE UNFINISHED BUSINESS

2. When you consider the possibility of a positive outcome (understanding to eventual resolution) with whom are you the most hopeful (to least hopeful) of dealing with the issues between you?

    NAME   EXPLANATION

3. Based on this information choose three persons you wish to encounter in the group:

    NAME   STATE REASON FOR THIS CHOICE

    1)

    2)

    3)

CHAPTER 3   **APPENDIX VIII.e**

SOCIOMETRIC CHOICE FOR CENTRAL ROLES

Name: _____ Date: _____

This exploration focuses the group on whom is likely to be highly chosen for specific key auxiliary ego roles, and on the basis of this, who may be carrying the heaviest load of projection for a particular role. It is suggested that the group form action sociograms as a way to share the information with the group. Allow time for group members to tell the persons they have chosen the reason for the choice. Allow at least one and a half hours.

1. Whom in the group would I choose to play the role of my Mother as she used to be? List in the order of preference.

    NAME   REASON FOR THIS CHOICE

2. Whom in the group would I choose to play the role of my Father as he used to be? List in the order of preference.

    NAME   REASON FOR THIS CHOICE

3. Whom in the group is most like me? What role would I choose them to play in relation to me?

    NAME   ROLE   REASON FOR THIS CHOICE

4. Whom in the group is least like me? What role would I choose them to play in relation to me?

    NAME   ROLE   REASON FOR THIS CHOICE

5. Excluding my Mother and Father, the person with whom I have the most unfinished business, who is not a member of this group, is: _____
    Whom in the group would I choose to play the role in a psychodrama session?

    NAME   REASON FOR THIS CHOICE

6. Identify other central roles and continue making choices in action.

CHAPTER IV
ENCOUNTERING MORENO-STYLE

"...eye to eye,
face to face"
J.L. MORENO

"A MEETING OF TWO: EYE TO EYE, FACE TO FACE,
AND WHEN YOU ARE NEAR, I WILL TEAR YOUR EYES OUT
AND PLACE THEM INSTEAD OF MINE,
AND YOU WILL TEAR MY EYES OUT
AND WILL PLACE THEM INSTEAD OF YOURS,
THEN I WILL LOOK AT YOU WITH YOUR EYES
AND YOU WILL LOOK AT ME WITH MINE.

THUS EVEN THE COMMON THING SERVES THE SILENCE AND
OUR MEETING REMAINS THE CHAINLESS GOAL:
THE UNDETERMINED PLACE, AT AN UNDETERMINED TIME,
THE UNDETERMINED WORD TO THE UNDETERMINED MAN."

Translated from *"Einladung zu einer Begegung,"* by
J.L. Moreno, Vienna: Anzengruber Verlag, 1914, p. 3

ENCOUNTERING MORENO-STYLE

Introduction

Moreno's conception of encounter is of a meeting whereby both persons begin to become known to each other through the reciprocal process of role reversal. The phrase, ". . . and when you are near" implies proximity—being near to see, hear and experience the other person. Moreno forewarns that the act of seeing can produce pain. The desire to know another person and have them know you has to be strong enough to warrant, if necessary, the "tearing out of eyes": ". . . and I will look at you with your eyes and you will look at me with mine."

This poetic and inspiring description is supported by a practical, therapeutic procedure developed by Moreno, the **role reversal.** When role reversing, each person sheds his or her own identity and takes on the identity of the other person. This enables him or her to broaden the awareness of the other person's world, to know firsthand the feelings, responses and experiences of the other person, *including* ways in which that person experiences the very person taking his or her role. The process of role reversing provides a whole new set of information.

Role reversal is a process which can be learned. This chapter will provide ways to assist others in role reversing. The most difficult time to role reverse is when the feelings we have in our own role prevent us from being aware of the other person. It becomes necessary to have facilitation. This chapter offers exercises which are designed to assist persons in establishing a connection with each other and a conflict resolution facilitator training model to help group leaders, psychodramatists and sociometrists develop the skills required to facilitate encounters and assist with role reversal.

Role Reversal

"As the term implies, role reversal means an exchange of roles, an exchange of positions; conceptually, role reversal means transcendence of self or self-component; in practice, role reversal is a gradual, cautious technique of outsight training."[1]

Most persons have developed a way of "putting themselves in the other's place." We think of it as "trying to understand," remaining in our own role and mentally working out what it must be like to be that other person. Moreno wanted to bring life, depth and accuracy to that mental process by providing a place where the role reversal takes place in action, the psychodramatic stage. As with most psychodramatic action, some warming-up to the task is required. When first taking the role of another person, the participants may experience anxiety and difficulty which cloud their sensory resources and block their spontaneity. The following guide has been prepared to assist with training in role reversal.

ROLE REVERSAL TRAINING TIPS

When first taking the role of another, it helps to:

A. **Approximate the person physically**
   1. Imagine what it feels like to wear this person's clothing and to have his or her physical appearance. If the person's clothing is tight and binding, adjust your own clothing until you can feel that tightness. Let yourself put on their physical appearance.

   2. Mirror the body stance and facial expression.

(Note: Some persons may find it difficult or painful to mirror another person's actions, or to be mirrored. The process of doing so can evoke memories of crude characterization or mimicking, the intention of which was humiliating another person. Or, the person(s) involved may experience performance anxiety, block, and be unable to effectively recall. A way to minimize these problems is to have each person teach the other person how to be in his or her role, by first accepting the other person as his or her double. Figure 1 below describes a doubling training exercise helpful also in role reversal training.)

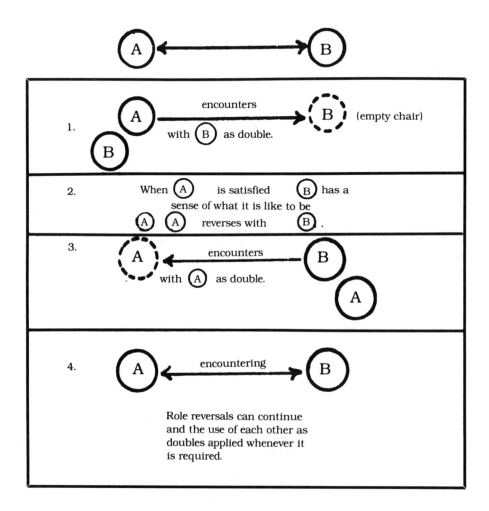

Figure 1. Double-bonding (paradoxical) role reversal: In situ training the double in role reversal.

B. **Repeat the verbal dialogue, mirroring and incorporating:** (1) gestures, (2) tone of voice, and (3) mode of expression.

C. **Deepen the experience internally.**
   Allow yourself to make contact with the feelings in the role of the other, to experience the reverberations which occur in the person as he or she interacts with you. As the other person takes your role, **interact** with the person playing you, rather than simply **observing** him or her. Take in what it feels like to relate to yourself from the other person's internal, private, personal place. Interact from that place.

D. **Risk in the role of the other,** putting the insights you have from being that person **into action.** Make statements to yourself from the role of the other.

E. **Reverse back into your own role.**
   Allow yourself to respond to the content of the interactions as well as the process of role reversal. Correct any misperceptions of you as produced by the other person. Make additions or deletions where necessary. Share with each other the experience you had being in his or her role.

REFLECTIVE LISTENING

Reflective listening is a structured process engaged in by a **sender** with a message and a **receiver** who listens reflectively. Many interpersonal difficulties result from poor communication: the message sent is received in ways other than intended; and, once compounded, it becomes difficult to trust in the process of communication between persons. Reflective listening is designed to provide interactors with a success experience in sending and receiving messages, teaching a valuable skill and restoring trust for relating in the future.

The Reflective Listening Process

A person (A) has something to say which they wish to have heard by the other person (B) who is asked to listen reflectively. Each person selects another person, familiar with the reflective listening process, to facilitate him or her in the case of difficulty. (A) begins speaking to (B).

> "When the 'receiver' (B) is listening reflectively, he will signify to the 'sender' that what he just said was heard, accepted and understood. He does this by repeating, rephrasing and by including in the feedback the feelings that are being expressed . . . trying to stay within (the sender's) frame of reference and without in any way trying to defend himself." [2]

During this process the facilitators assist the sender, or the listener, in being clear in their communication and connected to the same frame of reference. The same process applies should the receiver desire the role of sender.

This training is helpful for persons having difficulty with role reversal.

WARM-UP TO ENCOUNTER IN A GROUP SETTING

The word "encounter" bothers some people. In the group therapy field it became identified with an "honest at all costs" dynamic: "Encounter is most popularly identified with what we call the attack approach, or intense, aggressive confrontation between group members." [3] Even within the psychodrama community encounter has come to imply a conflict situation and the use of a specific format for resolution. The broader view of encounter as envisioned by Moreno is:

> "The encounter is extemporaneous, unstructured, unplanned, unrehearsed—it occurs on the spur of the moment . . . it is the experience of identity and total reciprocity; but above all, psychodrama is the essence of encounter." [4]

Unplanned and unrehearsed as encounter may be, developing and creating an atmosphere where encounter with self and others can emerge is the task of the group leader/sociometrist. Achieving an atmosphere of trust, openness, honesty and cohesion is the subject of hundreds of books—books which have been written from other persons' **experience** of groups and leading them. Nothing which is written in this book, or any other, can take the place of the learning in action; however, encounter can be taught and learned. The following text has been designed to provide assistance in gaining the skills and outlook which is helpful in that learning process.

In the early stages of a group, when there is a certain wariness present, group members are more focused on the identity, attitudes, personality and healing philosophies of the other group members than on techniques and methods. It is a time of beginning, and starting fresh, despite all the burdens people bring with them. It is important for groups to build a collective identity, to co-produce the reality of what it means to be in that particular group, to identify their own ground rules in terms of the expectations of members, and consequently to create their own definition of encounter. A sociometrist who remains open, philosophically and methodologically, assists in this process of developing "total reciprocity" by removing the clutter of conserves, if not in entirety, then by acknowledging the here and now as having as much value as past learnings. The word encounter can be a good place to start.

According to Carl Hollander (1968) encounter is the first step in any warm-up.[5] It involves noticing, awareness, examination, and exploration of oneself (or others) in relation to something else. Then, it can involve deciding what to do about it. In Chapter III the sociometric test was presented as a method of exploration. Encounter is moving into action with the results. There is a greater likelihood of having positive results from encounter when group members are able to identify the presence of constructive communicative relationships. The following principles developed by Dean C. Barnlund (1968) clarify those relationships.

Constructive Communicative Relationships

1. **"A constructive communicative relationship is likely when there is willingness to become involved with the other person.** When students who are graduating from high school or college are asked to identify the best teachers they had, they often identify teachers who were available or accessible to them. The willingness to become involved with another person can be more important at times than the quality of the interaction itself. Knowing that someone who is important to you cares enough about you to devote time to the relationship and to focus on matters of mutual interest can make quite a difference.

2. **A constructive communicative relationship is likely when one or both persons convey positive regard for the other.** Positive regard for another person is expressed not so much by the specific content of our remarks when we interact as it is by the general way we treat that person. If we are manipulative, if we attempt to control or to coerce the other person, if we prevent the other person from saying or doing things that displease us, then we are not displaying positive regard. Positive regard for another can be said to exist when we treat that person with a basic respect and as a person of integrity regardless of the specific things that person says or does.

3. **A constructive communicative relationship is likely when a permissive psychological climate develops.** A permissive psychological climate is not necessarily one in which individuals agree with and praise everything that everyone says or does. However, it is one in which the emphasis is on understanding rather than on judging the behavior of others. Furthermore, a permissive climate is one in which the love that we have for others and the acceptance that we show them are not withdrawn whenever their behavior displeases us.

4. **A constructive communicative relationship is likely when there is the desire and the capacity to listen.** Listening is not a passive process. It requires commitment and the capacity to focus on many of the things that the speaker is saying with his words, inflections, voice, facial expressions, and the like. Effective listening requires that we respond to the content of the message and the metacommunication, or the information about the message, as well. Furthermore, constructive listening includes responding to the other person with words and nonverbal expressions that demonstrate to the other person that he or she was understood.

5. **A constructive communicative relationship is likely when empathic understanding is communicated.** The reflection of empathic understanding was alluded to in our discussion of principle four when we stressed the importance, during the listening process, of conveying to the other person that he or she was understood. Empathy involves the ability to "know" what the other person is thinking and feeling. Empathy is difficult to achieve—not only because our perceptive ability is limited but because we are often so wrapped up in our own thoughts and concerns that it becomes difficult to focus our attention on the communication of others.

6. **A constructive communicative relationship is likely when there is accurate reflection and clarification of feeling.** There is a tendency to respond more to the content of what others say—the

ideas, thoughts, opinions, and attitudes conveyed—than to the feelings that others are expressing. Feelings are harder to respond to because most of us in our culture have had less experience responding to feelings than to ideas, and a response to feelings may require more of a commitment on our part to the interpersonal relationship than we are willing to give. Nevertheless, the accurate reflection and understanding of feeling is an essential part of the constructive interpersonal relationship.

7. **A constructive communicative relationship is likely when the communicators are genuine and congruent.** We are not as likely to develop a good relationship with others if we communicate in a false and misleading way. Facades are difficult to maintain and ultimately not very attractive. A constructive relationship is one in which the participants respond to each other in an honest and genuine manner. Our communication is congruent when the things that we do and say accurately reflect (are congruent with) our real thoughts and feelings."[6]

It will be possible to identify the constructive aspects of the interpersonal relationships in a group by engaging in activities designed to involve group members with each other. The following warm-ups (structured exercises) include numerous opportunities for group members to encounter one another.

Warm-ups to Encounter

A. **See Me, Outside and In**
   1. Ask group members to choose a partner whom they do not know well.
   2. Instruct each person to stand facing their partner, and take a few moments to thoroughly study the other person's appearance.
   3. Have the persons turn around with their backs to each other. Ask each person to change three things about his/her appearance. At a given signal, the partners turn around and face each other again.
   4. Ask the partners to identify the changes in the appearance of the other person.

   Inside:
   5. Have the partners turn their backs again. This time each person is asked to get in touch with a mood, or feeling state which has been problematic for him/her in the recent past, and which they would like to change.
   6. The leader briefly checks with each person to find out if each person has identified a feeling state. Then, have the persons turn around and face their partner.
   7. Ask each person to stay in touch with what they are feeling, yet notice what the partner is feeling. Share with the partner what it is that you see in him/her.
   8. Have each person, in turn, ask for three things from their partner which would help to change the feeling state. The partner may accommodate the request, but only does so when it feels genuine and congruent.
   9. Share what has been experienced with each other and with the group.

B. **Drum Warm-up**
Doug Warner described this warm-up to me which he saw Eya Branham of Taos, New Mexico, do at her psychodrama center. It seems to me to be an excellent way to eliminate words, facilitate ventilation and relieve tension. (Other percussion instruments may be used in lieu of drums.)
   1. Two parties wishing to encounter each other position themselves at a drum, each having their own drum.
   2. They begin, engage and conclude the encounter with the sounds they make on the drums.
   3. Later, a dialogue may clarify where they feel themselves to be with each other.

C. **Valentine Warm-up**
(This warm-up is designed for a group which has been experiencing difficulty being direct about their feelings of caring and dissatisfaction with each other.)
   1. Buy a bag of Valentine candies which have colored hearts with short messages printed on them.
   2. Pour the hearts out onto a tray and place in an area within convenient reach of the group members.
   3. Instruct group members to find hearts to give people in the group which have messages printed on them which feel appropriate to the person. (Messages range from "You're Sweet," "Too Cool" to "Drop Dead" and "Not Now".) Each person should only give to the persons they specifically want to give a message to.
   4. Have the group members stop after awhile and spend at least 15 minutes sharing and clarifying with the group **OR** proceed to this optional extension of the exercise:
   5. Have group members turn the candy hearts over to the unprinted side and imagine a short, two-word message on the heart. One at a time, in the group, the hearts are given and the message spoken to the person. (Messages in groups I have been in have been like, "Sorry Now," "Love Me," "Hands Off" and "Quit Dope," etc.)
   6. The messages may lead to encounter which may need facilitation, or group members may wish to clarify any unfinished business.

D. **Withholds**
"This training group exercise is helpful in 'clearing the decks' of group process 'jetsam' so that the group can get back to work. Each member is allowed to ask any other member in turn the single question 'What have you withheld from me?' When he gets his answer, the interrogator can only respond with 'Thank you' or 'Can you be more specific?' This is a good exercise for learning to accept information non-defensively." [7]

If this exercise leads to the need for more clarification or resolution the reflective listening and/or role reversal experience may be helpful.

E. Tell Me Something

"This structured experience which is a variant of Withholds, generates a lot of information about the people in your group and gives group members a chance to express things which have been left unsaid. It is most appropriately used midway in a personal growth or training weekend. It can be done in dyads, small groups or with the whole group depending on the needs of the group. One member goes to another and, in rapid alternation (for, say, three minutes) makes these two demands: 'Tell me something you would like to tell me'; and after the response, 'Tell me something you would not like to tell me.' Since the information seeker is not allowed to go beyond these two statements, he has to take in whatever information is given him non-defensively. After all participants have the opportunity (if they wish to take it) to experience both roles, the experience is open for processing and any kind of checking out group members may wish to do."[8]

F. Tough-Tight-Tender

This exercise was first described to me by Bob and Ildri Ginn at the Moreno Institute in 1972. It has been written up in Warner's *Psychodrama Training Tips* (1974).

"This exercise is best utilized in a group in which members have been together for a reasonable length of time. The members know each other by name and have a fair knowledge of each other. The entire group may be involved. The group leader should be aware that considerable time is involved in the performance of this exercise."[9]

1. Group members are given a 3x5 card and a pencil.
2. Group members make three headings on their paper: Tough-Tight-Tender.
3. The leader explains the headings:
   TOUGH: Someone with whom you are angry, impatient, irritated, etc.
   TIGHT: Someone with whom you feel tense, nervous, uptight.
   TENDER: Someone with whom you would like to share tender, understanding feelings.
4. Group members are asked to look around the group and list the names of persons toward whom they have these feelings, and write the names under the appropriate heading. (The group can choose to restrict each heading to one name.)
5. Group members are asked to form an action sociogram by placing their right hand on the person whom they choose for each category.
6. Group members are asked to meet with each person they chose, and share the category and the feeling of TOUGH, TIGHT or TENDER, whichever applies.
7. A space in the room is designated as a "Waiting Room" where people gather to wait for time to speak to the person on their list who may be otherwise engaged. Persons in the "Waiting Room" use the time to become better acquainted and to clear up any unfinished business.
8. The group reconvenes once the exercise has been completed, and group members share what each experienced during the exercise.

G. Similarities and Differences

It aids cohesion in groups when group members encounter and respect the commonalities and the differences of its members. Various modes of creative expression can be used to facilitate pairs coming into contact with these facts:

1. Dance and movement—Have two persons move to music, having been given the instruction to identify and express their differences and similarities.
2. Poetry—Have two persons write a poem which expresses in form, style and content their similarities and differences.
3. Art—Have two persons create a painting or drawing of their relationship in such a way as to focus on their similarities and differences.
4. Music—Two persons, seated at a piano, improvise a piece of music which is inspired by their similarities and their differences.
5. Sculpture—Two persons take two auxiliaries and sculpt them into a statement about their similarities and their differences.
6. Drama—One person stands in front of the other, each free to move in any way except at the feet. Together they improvise a way to make dramatic their similarities and their differences.

H. **CONFLICT WARMUP,** a paper and pencil exercise

  1. Conflicts can be with people whom:
    a. we like a lot:

    (Whom?) _____ (About) _____

    b. we dislike a lot:

    (Whom?) _____ (About) _____

    c. we are neutral toward:

    (Whom?) _____ (About) _____

    Think of a conflict you have with someone who fits each category.

  2. Conflicts can be over:

    small issues   to   big issues

    Think of a conflict going on in this group which is over a:

    a. small issue: _____

    b. big issue: _____

  3. If you were in conflict in this group would it be with persons having:

    a. _____ Less power,   _____ Same power   _____ More power
              Influence

    b. _____ Less skill   _____ Same skill   _____ More skill

    c. _____ Less self esteem _____ Same self esteem   _____ More self esteem

  4. Some conflicts seem unresolved and leave a person feeling as if the solution to it has been postponed. Can you identify a time when that has happened in this group?

  5. Some conflicts seem best avoided as there appears to be little likelihood of resolution. Identify a conflict which feels this way to you.

  6. In your opinion what does this group need to do in order to handle the conflicts that arise?

  7. List the names of the members of this group and identify the resources you believe they have for dealing with conflict.

    NAME   **THEIR RESOURCES**

This warmup is based upon the theories of Morton Deutsch as conveyed in "A Theory of Cooperation and Competition," **Human Relations,** 2 (1949), pp. 120-151.

Conflict Resolution

An extension of the role of sociometric and of psychodrama director is the role of facilitator of encounters between persons experiencing conflict. Recommended reading for this aspect of encounter is the chapter, "Intervention Principles and Practices" by Joyce Hocker Frost and William W. Wilmot in their book, *Interpersonal Conflict* (1978).[10] Offered here is a role diagram of the role of facilitator (third party) and a Conflict Resolution Facilitator Training Model.

The Role Diagram of Facilitator in Conflict Situations (p. 101-104)

"Any effective interventionist, whether a friend of the disputants or someone in an official role as conflict manager, must have at least three major sources of strength. The person must have sufficient analytical ability to understand processes of conflict, must manifest a communication style that can be used effectively in the interventionist role and must have some tactical choices available that will facilitate the management of the conflict."[11]

The various roles implied above can be categorized under the role cluster name of Analyzer, Communicator and Manager. A Bilateral Role Diagram has been chosen because it can be used to depict the self-evaluation of the facilitator in relation to each of the parties in the conflict, as well as depict the feedback about the facilitator from each party.

Analyzer Function

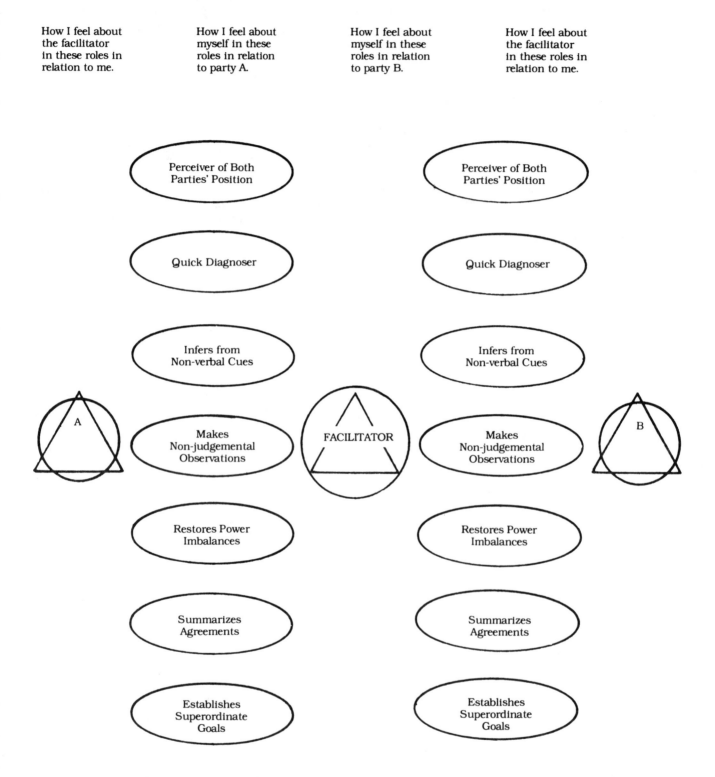

How I feel about the facilitator in these roles in relation to me.

How I feel about myself in these roles in relation to party A.

How I feel about myself in these roles in relation to party B.

How I feel about the facilitator in these roles in relation to me.

(See page 129 for the notational system for role diagrams)

Figure 2. Bilateral Role Diagram: The Role of Facilitator

Communicator Function

How I feel about the facilitator in these roles in relation to me.

How I feel about myself in these roles in relation to party A.

How I feel about myself in these roles in relation to party B.

How I feel about the facilitator in these roles in relation to me.

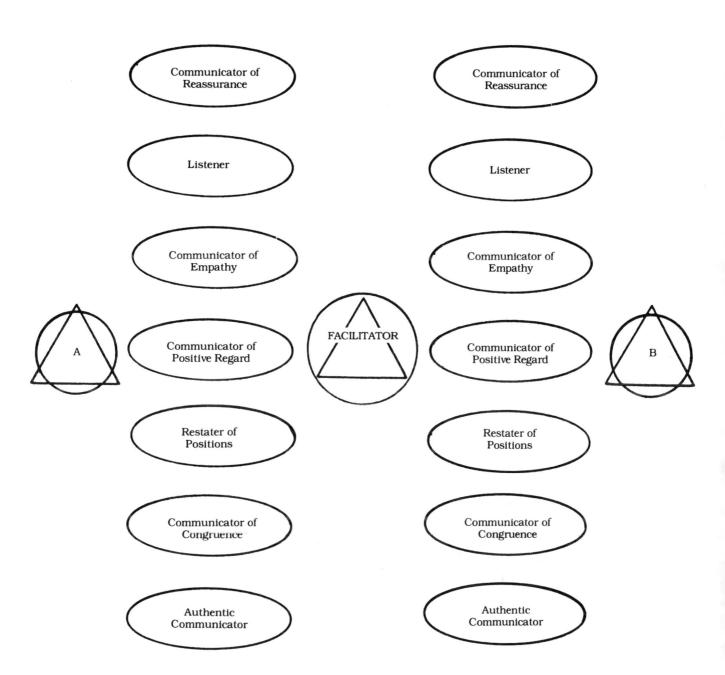

(See page 129 for the notational system for role diagrams)

Figure 3. Bilateral Role Diagram: The Role of Facilitator

Conflict Manager Function

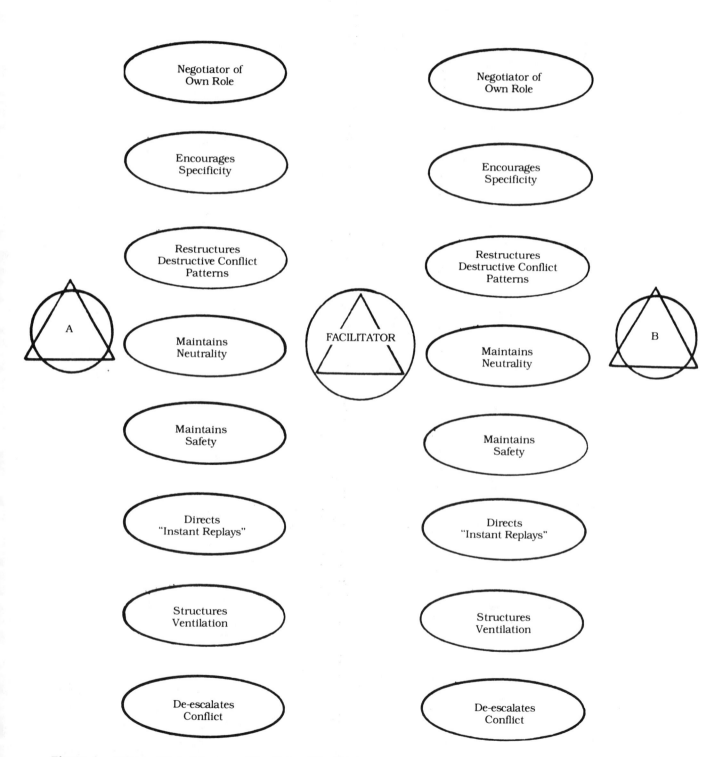

How I feel about the facilitator in these roles in relation to me.

How I feel about myself in these roles in relation to party A.

How I feel about myself in these roles in relation to party B.

How I feel about the facilitator in these roles in relation to me.

Negotiator of Own Role

Encourages Specificity

Restructures Destructive Conflict Patterns

A

FACILITATOR

Maintains Neutrality

B

Maintains Safety

Directs "Instant Replays"

Structures Ventilation

De-escalates Conflict

Figure 4.   Bilateral Role Diagram: The Role of Facilitator

CONFLICT RESOLUTION FACILITATOR TRAINING MODEL (HALE)

This model is presented as a process which assists persons in developing the role of facilitator in conflict resolution situations. It is abstracted from psychodramatic method and provides for the application of action methods in a sequence of events which may occur, one after the other, or, interspersed throughout the exercise. Of importance is not so much the order of events but rather an increasing recognition of the elements which affect the potential for resolution. This model is not a "how to" for conducting encounters, although there may be confrontations which may benefit from the method which is implied here.

The model is best used by first practicing the role in interpersonal conflicts with the significant other **absent.** Once the facilitator-in-training is comfortable with the model, then he/she may begin facilitating encounters with both parties present, progressing to intergroup and multiple-protagonist sessions when fluent with the method.

The Facilitator Training Model

1. **Person states his/her position** in the conflict directly to the other person. (An empty chair is used in the case of the absent other.) The position is stated:
   a. Clearly
   b. Firmly
   c. Honestly

2. **Person is encouraged to ventilate** pent up tension and emotions evoked by the conflict, the other person, and/or their behavior. Ventilate:
   a. Freely
   b. Loudly and physically
   c. Maximally

3. **Person identifies the interference** resulting in barriers to communication, resistance to change, and inability to affect a resolution. Interferences may involve:
   a. Ghosts—persons from his/her past having the same or similar impact; a transference figure.
   b. Parental Injunctions—a tape, script, or life stance which has a strong influence on his/her behavior and may need to be re-examined in light of this conflict situation.
   c. Physical and Socioeconomic Realities—here and now constraints or "facts of life" which need to be acknowledged or re-examined.
   d. Third parties—persons directly involved in the conflict, who may even be primary causes of the conflict, and who have either an interest in the outcome of the conflict, or in the continuation of it.

4. **Role reversal**
   (When directing a conflict resolution with significant other absent have the person reverse roles with the absent other and repeat steps 1, 2 and 3 as outlined above.)
   The subject of role reversal is frequently the future of the relationship based on new information.
   Double-bonding role reversal is useful at this point. (See Figure 1, p. 94 for graphic.)
   a. Ask one person to reverse roles and become the double of the other person while he/she remains in his/her own role.
   b. Place an empty chair to represent the person who is now being a double.
   c. Direct the person, and their double, to make clear statements about:
      (1) feelings being experienced in the here and now
      (2) ways to relate to each other and the issue in the future
      (3) a possible contract
   d. Help the double to stay in role by coaching him/her, using an echo, and taking a similar body stance.
   e. Once the process has been completed, repeat it with the other person taking the role of double. If the significant other is absent, simply role reverse.
   f. Have the person being doubled reply to the statement of feelings and the prospective contract, with his/her own feelings, and his/her own suggestions for resolution.

5. When each person is back in his/her own role, they **finalize the contract,** reach an agreement, how they will deal with this conflict situation in the future.

6. **Persons rehearse new behaviors** which they have agreed upon in the contract. A role training session can be introduced in a supportive environment.

7. If additional group members are present they may wish to **respond to the persons by sharing** what was evoked in them as the conflict situation progressed.

The Role of the Facilitator/Director

The facilitator role requires alertness, objectivity (neutrality), firmness within flexibility, and the ability to maintain the integrity of the process. Other than creating an equitable atmosphere in which to explore the conflict, the facilitator can have no vested interest in the outcome of the conflict. The facilitator negotiates his/her role, explaining that a model is being used which will give him/her practice in the role of facilitator. The facilitator explains that he/she is engaged in a process of learning and that it may be necessary to stop the action and receive help from the training director.

Often, one party in the conflict will be more skilled at asserting him/herself, or, have more power, self-esteem. The facilitator seeks to effect equity of warm-up, rather than equity of "air time". When one party requires assistance in being articulate, direct, or clear, the facilitator restores the balance of power by providing on-the-spot skill training.

The facilitator allows the person(s) to begin at the point where there is access to the most spontaneity. If they attempt to make clear, firm, honest statements of their position, and are unable to do so because of increasing pressure to allow feelings to emerge, have the person move into ventilation. Once the pent up tensions and emotions have been released there will be more "room" psychically to return to the statement of position phase.

The facilitator observes nonverbal cues and has the person(s) expand these as a way to facilitate maximal ventilation. Some props may be necessary. Encounter bats (batacas) are useful for bringing home emphatic points and for hitting. Cardboard boxes can be torn up if the person wants to rip into something. Stacks of pillows may be useful for the person wishing to throw things. An auxiliary, or twin-sized mattress may be used for the person who needs to "shake some sense into you." Whatever the mode of expression, the facilitator provides props which will protect the safety of the participants. Once expressed, the ventilation phase automatically de-escalates. The facilitator finds ways to monitor the further expression of ventilation and prevents destructive lashing out from contaminating subsequent stages in the encounter restructuring the destructive conflict patterns. An example of doing this would be by remarking, "When he does that just ignore it and focus on what is really important right now," or "I am not comfortable with you doing that right now. You stated that you had felt the ventilation to be complete. It certainly seemed that way to me as well. Have you a fear of this next phase in the encounter? What can I do that would be helpful to your right now?"

There is considerable information about interferences which is shouted out in the heat of the ventilation phase. As the spontaneous actor emerges the observer falls away.[12] Therefore, it becomes necessary for the facilitator to observe, listen and recall for the participants information which will provide clues for identification of interferences. For example, a person may be quite angry with the other person's behavior and be shouting "For Christ's sake, I had enough of that from my first husband without having to take it from you!" (Ghost); or, "That was a despicable, sneaky thing to do! It doesn't matter whose paycheck it was. Money that either of us makes belongs to both of us. That's what marriage means!" (Injunction/life stance); or, "I'm sick of you going around afraid to take your next breath in case you drop over with a heart attack. The doctor said for you to let up on jogging. He didn't say permanent bed rest!" (Physical realities); or "You promised your daughter a fancy wedding with all the trimmings. Now she tells me you want to shorten the guest list. What am I supposed to say to that? You never do what you say you are going to do." (Third party). If videotape is available participants can take advantage of immediate replay and identify the interferences for themselves.

The role reversal phase includes the use of the double as a way to promote connectedness and to provide the person(s) with the opportunity to demonstrate their availability to cooperation via an active form of understanding. "Studies show that persons who successfully carry out this effort at understanding increase their level of cooperation when their positions are ultimately compatible or can be made so by relatively minor compromise or change of position. However, the drawback of this tactic is that if the positions are basically incompatible either because the resources are indeed so scarce that no accommodation is possible or because the parties are not interdependent enough to have to come to resolution together, then the level of competition is actually **increased** by the role reversal technique (Johnson, 1967). Thus the tactic is no panacea and can be used quite naively by the untrained leader. No tactics are sure-fire cures for destructive conflict: only the participants involved in the conflict can make the final decision to cooperate."[13] The reader is referred to the description of this form of role reversal on page 94 of this chapter. The participants may be unable to act as doubles. In this case there are several options: (1) have the person who is to be the double sit slightly to the right and behind the person, using the time to reflect silently. The person continues to address the empty chair; or (2) have a double from the audience be a double for both parties; or, (3) move on to the contract negotiation stage, thereby eliminating this stage.

The facilitator refrains from giving the participants solutions to their problem. The facilitator may provide opportunities for the persons to engage the interferences which they have identified and direct the contract-making to involve decisions about how these interferences can be handled in the future. The role of the facilitator at this point is primarily that of offering non-judgemental observations and giving concise, clear information. Stay out of the decision-making process and avoid advice-giving. To do so allows the participants to experience being successful in reaching conclusions jointly.

Many persons using this model will be doing so in the framework of a psychodrama training group. There may be a tendency to move into the more familiar, personal psychodrama. The intrapsychic factors, which become apparent and which may warrant further exploration and catharsis, will tempt the facilitator to move from the encounter into a psychodrama. For the purposes of learning to direct conflict resolution situations, it is recommended to remain with the model which was part of the original contract. It is allowable for the facilitator to "tag" the debilitating factors at the moment of discovery and to assist the person in feeling and acknowledging the warm-up which is present. If immediately explored, and the other person is allowed to leave the conflict resolution contract without resolution, the person making the discovery may be left feeling they had the "problem" all along, when in fact the situation was co-produced. Deciding what to do about the unfinished personal constraints can be part of the contracting phase. Another reason to stay with the model despite temptations to work in a protagonist-centered mode is that this provides a containment experience for both the participants and the facilitator.

The facilitator may want to provide auxiliary egos and doubles. It is true that the help of therapeutic assistants can increase the effectiveness of the process. However, for training purposes, it is recommended that the facilitator work without assistance, thereby increasing the opportunities for the facilitator in training to connect with the participants and provide for a complete, unassisted role reversal experience. The elimination of the auxiliaries more closely resembles many therapy situations when clients come as couples to see one individual. This model can be used as a training method for the use of psychodramatic techniques in one-to-one therapy.

When using this model for conflict resolution when both parties are present, the facilitator decides which is more helpful: (1) to have the persons freely interacting with one another in steps 1, 2 or 3, or (2) to have each person complete separately the first three steps of the process. As a guideline, if the participants appear to be familiar with the content and the emotions displayed, and it is clear that this is "old territory," prefer the more structured approach. By observing, and not interacting, the person observing may learn something, and the person involved in the action may feel freer to produce new material. Conversely, if this appears to be providing the disputants with a "new" experience in relating, do not interrupt the flow of the interaction until it becomes clear that more structure is warranted.

If the encounter has been taking place in a group setting, the facilitator assists the participants in reentry into the group. This may be accomplished by having the group express non-verbally and spontaneously their feelings for one, or both, of the participants or having the group respond to them in some way that is comfortable. Persons having advice, questions and negative statements should be assisted by the facilitator in identifying the projection.

The Role of Training Director

It is recommended that the training director, or the person presenting the model to others, describe the steps involved in the model and then demonstrate the method in a conflict situation with an absent other. A "stop action" procedure can be employed to allow students to ask pertinent questions and get immediate information.

The training director can also use the "stop action" procedure while the facilitator-in-training is working with a client. It is useful to have the facilitator identify his/her own soliloquy at key choice points, or at moments of difficulty. If it appears that the facilitator is losing the neutral stance or is making judgements which inhibit the persons in conflict the training director can assist the facilitator in identifying his/her own projection and facilitate the facilitator's reentry in the process.

Once the facilitators-in-training have practiced the model with absent others, the training director can demonstrate the model as used with both parties present.

Conclusion

The model, while being flexible, is just that—a model. The spontaneity of facilitators, their own personal experience being on the receiving end of their own encounters, and the courage to come face to face with the persons in conflict is the best learning experience. The anxiety over "what do I do if nothing works to resolve the conflict?" diminishes as the facilitators develop confidence and belief in the people with whom they work. No positive outcome is an outcome. Trust that it leads the person to their "next step" with each other.

CHAPTER IV
FOOTNOTES

1. Brind, Anna B. and Nah Brind, "Role Reversal," *Group Psychotherapy,* Vol. 20, no. 3-4 (September-December, 1967), p. 176.

2. Warner, G. Douglas, *Psychodrama Training Tips,* Hagerstown, Md., Maryland Psychodrama Institute, 1974, pp. 104-106.

3. Siroka, Robert W. et al. Editor, *Sensitivity Training and Group Encounter,* New York, Grosset and Dunlap, 1971, p. 83.

4. Moreno, J.L., "The Viennese Origins of the Encounter Movement . . ." *Group Psychotherapy,* Vol. 22, no. 1-2 (1969), p. 9.

5. Hollander, Carl, "A Blueprint for a Psychodrama Program," *Group Psychotherapy,* Vol. 21, no. 4 (December, 1968), p. 227.

6. Barbour, Alton and Alvin A. Goldberg, *Interpersonal Communication: Teaching Strategies and Resources.* Urbana, Ill., ERIC Clearinghouse on Reading and Communication Skills, 1974.

7. Warner, G. Douglas, *Psychodrama Training Tips,* p. 89.

8. *Ibid.*

9. *Ibid.*

10. Frost, Joyce Hocker and William W. Wilmot, *Interpersonal Conflict,* Dubuque, Iowa, Wm. C. Brown, Co., 1978, pp. 144-177.

12. Moreno, J.L., *Psychodrama,* Volume I, Beacon, N.Y.: Beacon House, 1946, p. 205.

13. Frost, *Op. Cit.,* pp. 164-165, referring to Johnson, David W., "Use of Role Reversal in Intergroup Competition," *Journal of Personality and Social Psychology,* Vol. 7 (1967), pp. 135-141.

BIBLIOGRAPHY

Barbour, Alton and Alvin A. Goldberg. *Interpersonal Communication: Teaching Strategies and Resources.* Urbana, Ill., ERIC Clearinghouse on Reading and Communication Skills, 1974.

Bradford, Leland P., Jack R. Gibb and Kenneth D. Benne. *T-Group Therapy and Laboratory Method: Innovation in Re-education.* New York: John Wiley & Sons, 1964.

Brind, Anna B. and Nah Brind. "Role Reversal," *Group Psychotherapy,* Vol. 20, no. 3-4 (September-December, 1967), pp. 173-177.

Deutsch, Morton. "Conflicts: Productive and Destructive," in *Conflict Resolution Through Communication,* edited by Fred E. Jandt, New York: Harper and Row, 1973, pp. 155-177.

Deutsch, Morton and R.M. Krauss. *Theories in Social Psychology.* New York: Basic Books, 1965.

Frost, Joyce Hocker and William W. Wilmot. *Interpersonal Conflict.* Dubuque, Iowa: Wm. C. Brown Co. Publishers, 1978.

Gendlin, Eugene T. and John Beebe. "Experiential Groups," in *Innovations to Group Psychotherapy,* edited by George M. Gazda. Springfield, Ill.: Charles C. Thomas, 1968.

Hollander, Carl. "Blueprint for a Psychodrama Program," *Group Psychotherapy,* Vol. 21, no. 4 (December, 1968), p. 223-228. Now available in another edition and known as *The Hollander Psychodrama Curve.* Denver, Colorado: Snow Lion Press, 1978.

Johnson, David W. "Use of Role Reversal in Intergroup Competition," *Journal of Personality and Social Psychology,* Vol. 7 (1967), p. 137-141.

Moreno, J.L. *Psychodrama.* Volume I. Beacon, N.Y.: Beacon House, 1946.

————. "The Viennese Origins of the Encounter Movement, Paving the Way for Existentialism, Group Psychotherapy and Psychodrama," *Group Psychotherapy,* Vol. 22, no. 1-2 (1969), pp. 7-16.

Siroka, Robert W., Ellen K. Siroka and Gilbert A. Schloss. *Sensitivity Training and Group Encounter.* New York: Grosset and Dunlap, 1971.

Warner, G. Douglas. *Psychodrama Training Tips.* Hagerstown, Maryland, The Maryland Psychodrama Institute, 1974.

Watzlawick, Paul, Janet Helmick Beavin and Don D. Jackson. *Pragmatics of Human Communication: A Study of Interactional Patterns, Pathologies and Paradoxes.* New York: W.W. Norton, 1967.

CHAPTER V
THE ROLE DIAGRAM EXPANDED

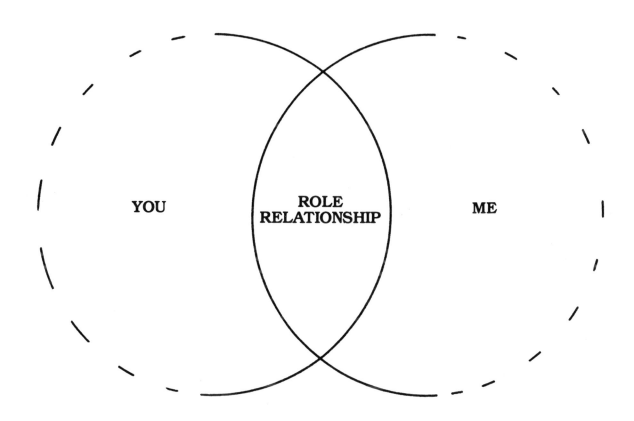

YOU   ROLE RELATIONSHIP   ME

"What would you be
If I were not?
What would I be
If you were not?"

From *Words of the Father*, No. 101
By J.L. Moreno

THE ROLE DIAGRAM EXPANDED

J.L. Moreno, the originator of the role diagram, postulated that the self emerged from the roles a person has (has had, or seeks).[1] As a person begins to relate to others the personality becomes defined; however, not only has each person in the relationship a personality, but the relationship itself produces its own reality—a meeting and merging of role perceptions and role expectations which result in actions ranging from submersion of the self to the highest degree of freedom and creativity in relating. Moreno had found that two healthy people could produce an unhealthy relationship and that two "sick" people could produce a healthy relationship. In order to understand this phenomenon and to treat patients with personality or other mental disorders Moreno began to explore the patient's relationship with significant others. His early research led him to develop a role theory of personality.[2]

Of the many sociometric procedures developed by Moreno, the role diagram is designed to represent visually the role construction of a particular relationship at a specified point in time, space and reality. As a diagnostic instrument the role diagram focuses upon the role interaction of two or more individuals and the degree to which they are complementary or incongruous. It directs the persons involved, or their therapist, to aspects of the relationship which would benefit from psychodramatic or other kinds of therapeutic intervention.

A role diagram is constructed by first compiling a list of roles which represent the interactions in the relationship. In the simplest form of role diagram each person indicates how they feel about the other person in each role in relation to him or herself. Participants may choose to use data from different periods in the history of the relationship, possibly illustrating how critical choices or events have influenced the structure of the role interactions. A future projected, ideal, or fantasy role diagram can be drawn to focus on the role expansion needs or other goals of the relationship. The expanded forms of the role diagram make it possible to view how roles outside the relationship (extramural roles) affect role interactions. Other expanded forms, such as role diagrams of bilateral and multilateral relationships, are especially useful in working with non-traditional role constructions found in group marriages and extended families. Role diagrams also have wide applicability in traditional settings such as social groups, organizations and most work settings.

The sociometrist is urged to view this chapter as a guide to the use of the role diagram and encouraged to experiment and expand the format. As has so often been exclaimed by therapists, "Insight is not enough." This method evolved out of a **science of action**[3] and has a practical and active application. Included here are some strategies for the use of the results of the role diagram as well as some action means for dealing with role conflicts. Again, these comments are given only as a rough guide. A good starting place for discovering the use of this procedure is with oneself.

BASIC ROLE DIAGRAM CONSTRUCTION

To begin a role diagram the participants decide upon which aspect of their relating they wish to explore (often that area for which they have sought outside help). Regardless of the role relationship to be explored, certain key elements require clarification by the sociometrist/therapist. The *Role Diagram Data Sheet* and *Instructions to Participants in a Role Diagram Exploration* are included in this chapter as aids to be reviewed with clients. (See pages 127-128.)

Compiling the List of Roles

A role is an observable unit of conserved behavior recognizable by the actions involved.[4] Every role is influenced by biological, psychological and socio/cultural factors which affect the perception of the role and consequently the enactment of the role. These factors influence the actual definition of the role and the selection of the role name. When working with clients, it is best to assist them in translating what they do in their relationship into role names they will recognize as their own.

The list of roles can reflect roles in ascendence, roles in descendence, dead roles, future projected roles, ideal roles, fantasy roles, or combinations of these. The roles may be somatic, psychodramatic or socio/cultural in origin. The sociometrist/therapist helps the clients to select roles most central to their relationship and the issues affecting them. As the sociometrist works with various relationships (husband/wife, co-workers, manager/staff, etc.) he/she develops expertise in the role definition process. It is helpful to keep lists of roles for use as examples or guides; however, clients should be urged to generate a listing of roles which reflect the **uniqueness** of their relationship.

The following is an example of an interview in which the roles are being defined:

Susan: What would you call it, Jerry? When we talk about things that have happened to us. You know, deep things?

Jerry: I know what you mean. When we confide in one another, but it is more than that. It's being there for each other.

Therapist: Sounds like a role cluster to me, involving both sharing and comforting.

Susan: Yes, but I like confiding better. Listening is O.K., but comforting gets confused. I like to cry and be held, but Jerry won't let me hold him. Jerry, you know how you like me to just leave you alone for awhile.

Therapist: For now you could leave it as a broad category of comforter, and then try out various actions later in psychodrama. One thing I'd like to point out is that you have been talking of these roles, confidant, comforter, listener in terms of sharing emotions which are painful. These same roles apply to expressions of anger, joy, resentment, embarrassment, etc. Get the idea? You may want to draw a role diagram which relates primarily to emotional support.

Jerry: Good point. I know I'm great at holding Susan when she's sad, but I don't listen very well when she's mad.

There are some excellent sources of role names which are especially useful when compiling the role names for your clients. Consult job descriptions and books which professionals have written about their activities.

Choosing the Point in Time

The role diagram can reflect the role construction of the past, the present and the future. Key periods in the development of a person, relationship or group are (1) its beginning; (2) when new persons are introduced into the social atom; (3) when critical events occur; (4) when key decisions are made or will be in effect; (5) when persons or relationships die; and other time frames determined to be vital.

The present is a good starting place for any initial role diagram. Diagramming current interactions has the effect of anchoring the relationship in reality, making it possible to have a basis of comparison. Clues to other important time points are statements such as: "Think what it could have been like, if only . . ." and "What are we going to do when . . ." The sociometrist becomes adept at picking up these clues and involving clients in explorations which change, add to, or confirm their perceptions of the relationship they have here and now.

A future role diagram reveals changes in role interactions due to decisions the person or group makes. These include the development and expansion of new roles; retiring old roles; areas for **role creating**[5] and alternatives to current role constructions. A role diagram of a future point in time is indicated when the persons involved are finding the relationship (or job) too routine, flat, unimaginative and confining. A future role diagram is also useful in defining the goals for the future.

A role diagram set in the past can provide insight into the history of the relationship and reveal the degree of change in the relationship from period to period. These diagrams can be a gauge for the amount of role death sustained; the demands placed upon the persons for role taking, role playing and role creating; and the proportion of time spent in roles perceived as relevant or irrelevant. It is also possible to draw an ancestral role diagram.[6] By using one's perception of how things "were" a person can compare their role relationships with that of their parents.

Selecting the Role Diagram Format

Factors influencing the choice of role diagram format become more apparent with continued use of the method. Some general guidelines, as well as a description of the various diagrams, are included here. Also provided are combinations and variations of the diagram format.

Role Diagram (Intrapersonal)

Internal dynamics, role perception, and role expectation are more in focus in this form of diagram. Each person indicates how they feel about themself as an **interactor** in each role in relation to the other person(s). The perceptual aspect is achieved by having each person state how they perceive other persons may feel about him or herself in each role in relation to him or her. Note: This diagram can be drawn on tracing paper and laid over the interpersonal role diagram for comparison of the two diagrams.

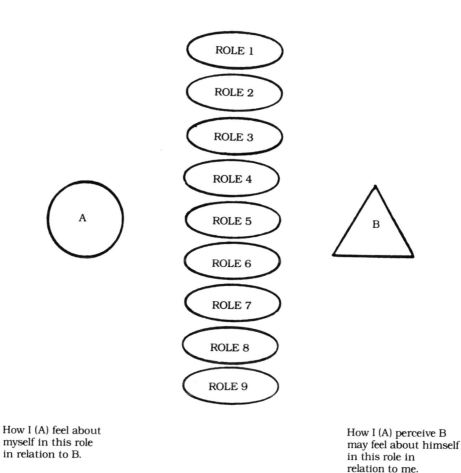

How I (A) feel about myself in this role in relation to B.

How I (A) perceive B may feel about himself in this role in relation to me.

ROLE DIAGRAM
(INTRAPERSONAL)

In this form of role diagram **A** states how she feels about herself in each role in relation to **B**, and then makes perceptual guesses about how **B** may feel about himself in each role in relation to her. **B** (if available) completes the diagram using the same format. To forego the perceptual aspect each person completes the side of the diagram referring to him or her.

Figure 1. Role Diagram (Intrapersonal)

Role Diagram (Interpersonal)

This diagram focuses on the role **interaction** between two or more persons. A statement is made by each person about how they feel about each other in the roles in relation to him or herself. It is also possible to include the perceptual aspect: have each person state how they **perceive** each other person may feel about him or herself in each role. Once each person has done this the perceptual data is checked against the objective data for correction and confirmation. It is recommended that clients begin with this format before using the expanded forms.

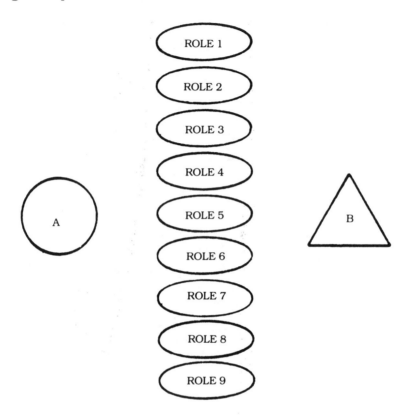

How I (A) feel about
B in this role in
relation to me.

How I (A) perceive
B may feel about me
in this role in
relation to him.

ROLE DIAGRAM
(INTERPERSONAL)

In this form of role diagram **A** states how she feels about **B** in each role in relation to her and then makes perceptual guesses about how **B** may feel in each role in relation to her. **B** (if available) completes the role diagram using the same format. To forego the perceptual aspect each person completes the side of the diagram referring to him or her.

Figure 2. Role Diagram (Interpersonal)

Combined Interpersonal and Intrapersonal Role Diagram

This combination depicts more completely the dynamics of role interaction as described in the above diagrams. It is possible to eliminate this format by using the overlay of the interpersonal role diagram as noted above.

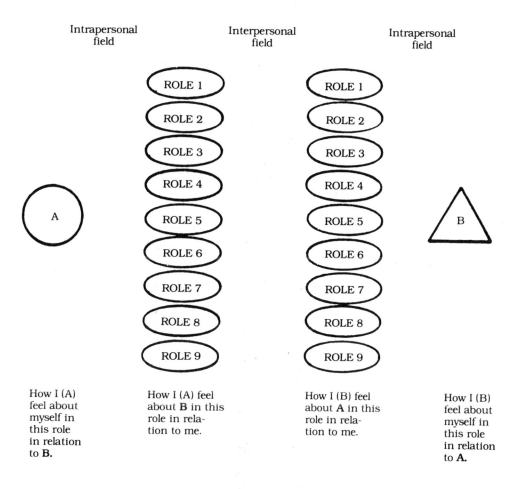

Intrapersonal field   Interpersonal field   Intrapersonal field

How I (A) feel about myself in this role in relation to **B.**

How I (A) feel about **B** in this role in relation to me.

How I (B) feel about **A** in this role in relation to me.

How I (B) feel about myself in this role in relation to **A.**

ROLE DIAGRAM
(INTERPERSONAL AND INTRAPERSONAL)

In this form of role diagram **A** and **B** each state how they feel about themself and the other person in each role. The perceptual aspect can be included by having each person complete the other half of the role diagram by making perceptual guesses. The two efforts are then compared with the objective data from each person.

Figure 3. Role Diagram (Interpersonal and Intrapersonal)

Role Diagram Expanded (Extramural Roles)

Often the roles a person has outside a relationship affect the amount of shared time, space and energy devoted to the relationship. This example shows the combination of interpersonal, intrapersonal and extramural aspects. It is possible to use a format allowing for just extramural roles. Each person states how he or she feels about each other person in the extramural role and how he or she feels about their own extramural role repertoire. It is also possible to include the perceptual aspect by having each person make perceptual guesses about how the other person may be feeling about him/herself in each extramural role.

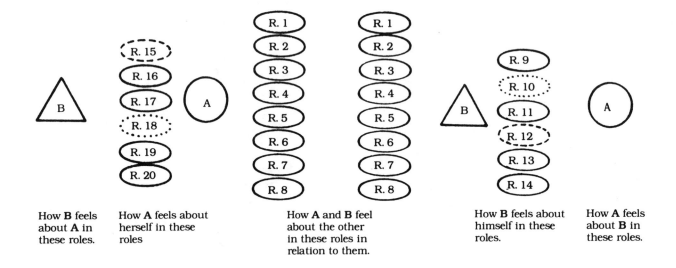

| How **B** feels about **A** in these roles. | How **A** feels about herself in these roles | How **A** and **B** feel about the other in these roles in relation to them. | How **B** feels about himself in these roles. | How **A** feels about **B** in these roles. |

ROLE DIAGRAM EXPANDED
(INCLUDES EXTRAMURAL ROLES)

This form of role diagram includes both the interpersonal and the intrapersonal fields as well as the expansion of the diagram to include roles engaged in by each person outside of the relationship (extramural roles). The perceptual data may be obtained by having each person complete the diagram by making perceptual guesses about how the other person may feel in each role. The two efforts are then compared with the objective data from each diagram.

Figure 4.   Role Diagram Expanded (Includes Extramural Roles)

Bilateral Role Diagram

This diagram illustrates the relationship one person has with two other persons involving the same or similar role construction. This diagram is most often used to depict the role interaction between a child and two parents. The role construction is generally complementary, i.e., provider and recipient, rather than mutual or reciprocal. In the bilateral role diagram the central person indicates how he/she feels about each of the others in relation to him/herself. Each of the other persons involved indicates how they feel about themself in the role in relation to the central person. The bilateral role diagram can be expanded to include the comments each person has about the other in each role. An additional line of roles drawn to the right and left of the two outside persons. An example of a use of the bilateral role diagram can be found in Chapter IV, p. 102-104.

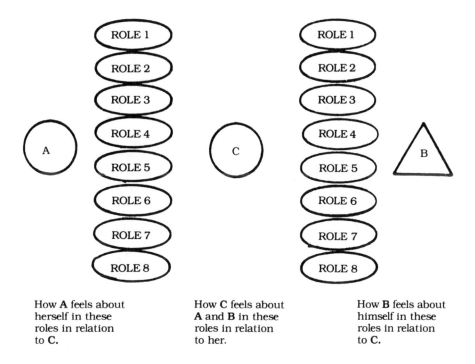

How **A** feels about herself in these roles in relation to **C**.

How **C** feels about **A** and **B** in these roles in relation to her.

How **B** feels about himself in these roles in relation to **C**.

BILATERAL ROLE DIAGRAM
(ONE PERSON, TWO INTERACTORS)
SAME ROLE CONSTRUCTION

This role diagram, most often used to diagram the role interaction between a child and two parents, is the format for any bilateral relationship. In the above example the parents (A & B) each indicate how they feel in each of the parental roles, and the child (C) indicates how she experiences each parent in those roles. This diagram can be expanded further to show how each parent feels about the other in each of the roles. Role 1-8 would be drawn in columns to the left of **A** and to the right of **B**. Then each would draw lines to indicate how they feel about each other in these roles.

Figure 5. Bilateral Role Diagram (One Person, Two Interactors)

Multilateral Role Diagram

This format is used to diagram the role interactions of three or more persons involved in the same or similar role construction. Each person indicates how they feel about the others in each role in relation to him/herself. Intrapersonal and extramural aspects can be included; however, as with any device, it may become increasingly complex in proportion to the number of persons and the variety of roles introduced. When plotting, if the data becomes unwieldy and unreadable it is time to seek other sociometric devices. For large group interactions involving the same or similar roles, the target sociogram which can result from a composite of sociometric tests is usually preferable.[7]

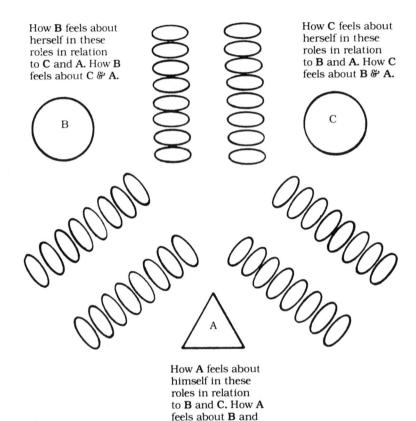

How **B** feels about herself in these roles in relation to **C** and **A**. How **B** feels about C & A.

How **C** feels about herself in these roles in relation to **B** and **A**. How **C** feels about B & A.

How **A** feels about himself in these roles in relation to **B** and **C**. How **A** feels about **B** and **C** in these roles.

MULTILATERAL ROLE DIAGRAM
(THREE INTERACTORS)
SAME ROLE CONSTRUCTION

This form of role diagram is used for three or more persons interacting with each other in the same or similar role construction (Eg. three adults sharing a house, or having the same job description). The above diagram includes both the interpersonal and the intrapersonal field.

Figure 6. Multilateral Role Diagram (Three Interactors)

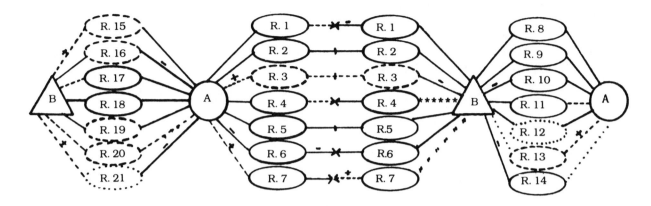

SAMPLE EXPANDED ROLE DIAGRAM
(INCLUDING EXTRAMURAL ROLES)

This form of role diagram includes both the interpersonal and the intra-personal fields of exploration as well as roles **A** and **B** have outside of the relationship. The key to the notation can be found in Appendix III.

R. 1 - Managing finances
R. 2 - Providing income
R. 3 - Lover
R. 4 - Household chores
R. 5 - Dinner companion
R. 6 - Sports fan
R. 7 - Comforter

R. 8 - Gymnast
R. 9 - Tennis
R. 10 - Professor
R. 11 - Politician
R. 12 - Traveler
R. 13 - Ex-husband
R. 14 - Friend to Jean

R. 15 - Student (Grad. School)
R. 15 - Hospital Aide
R. 17 - Poet
R. 18 - Daughter to parents
R. 19 - Arts Council President
R. 20 - Companion to Stuart
R. 21 - Divorcee

Figure 7. Sample Expanded Role Diagram (Including Extramural Roles)

Indicating Responses to Roles and Role Interaction

Once the role names and the oval shaped spaces for the roles of each person have been placed on a sheet of paper according to the chosen format, the participants are ready to indicate, using the notational system, the feelings they have in each role. As a reminder, the statement beginning "How I feel . . ." is shown on each format. Consult Appendix III, this chapter, p. 129 for a system of notation which is fairly simple to use. Various colors are given for indicating the various responses. Some clients may find it useful to use their own system and meanings, even giving it their own phrasing.

The following comments and suggestions from role diagram explorations may be helpful in guiding clients in this particular aspect of role diagram construction.

Question

"I feel like there are two responses to each of these roles. I don't know what to put down. If Jerry is away on a trip things seem to fall apart. I'd put down something different for when he is around."

Reply: Ambivalent Responses

Absence of a significant person is a factor which influences the **sociostasis** of all the individuals involved. If the participant finds that certain recognizable events, moods, and circumstances make it difficult to indicate a general response, it is suggested that additional role diagrams be drawn to illustrate the impact of these varying circumstances. Examples of times when this might apply are:

a. Parental roles when partner is present and when partner is absent.
b. Emotional supportive roles when person is tired as opposed to when the person is relaxed and rested.
c. Office interactions when meeting a deadline as opposed to normal office functioning.
d. Student roles at the beginning of the semester and at the end of the school year.

Question

"If I gave my most honest response to these things we do together I could hurt her very much. In the long run it doesn't matter all that much compared with her feeling hurt and possibly resentful."

Reply: Fear of Rejecting and Being Rejected

Another factor in **sociostasis** is the amount of emotional support a person has available when confronted with painful personal data such as inadequacy and weakness. To deliberately uncover all the hidden hurts and faults is not the purpose of this exploration. Encourage the participants to trust their own intuitions regarding how much and when to confront the other person(s) honestly. The ability to see beyond the truth with acceptance for the other person is a valuable part of relating in a meaningful way; however, help the participants to assess the impact of withholding critical remarks on the growth potential of both persons and their relationship.

When sparing another person's feelings is of primary interest to one (or more) participants it is suggested that the exploration begin with a **perceptual** focus. This provides information about the degree of rejection or inadequacy anticipated by a participant. It is equally possible that resentment can be caused by withholding negative responses because one is thought not to have the strength of character for dealing with the truth. It is suggested that this be the first topic of discussion before proceeding with role diagramming, as it may reveal the degree of commitment the persons have to problem areas and eventual solutions.

Question

"I couldn't begin to guess what Jerry may feel about me in this role. I wouldn't even know where to start."

Reply: Fear of Failure and/or Fear of Knowing

A significant number of people I have encountered have a fear of failure, especially when it involves making perceptual guesses about the preferences and reactions of someone closely related. Have each person reverse roles with the other person(s). After warming-up the participants to the role of another, have the participants produce the perceptual guesses in non-threatening areas. Allow time for correction of perception. If this proves to be a reassuring experience proceed with the role diagram.

Question

"When trying to say how I feel about myself in these roles, I have conflicting responses. I keep flashing on what my Mother says about me. I have never thought much about how I feel."

Reply: Ambivalent Self-Concept

The experience of measuring up to someone else's expectations is a common one. Sometimes even the derivation of these expectations becomes obscure, and yet they persist. It is suggested that the participants note on their Role Diagram Data Sheet the origin(s) of their role perception, or the role model they have had for a particular role. If the role model seems to appear consistently it may be useful to draw a role diagram of that relationship. An ancestral role diagram may give insight into scripted role interactions. As a person's perception of him or herself is separated from the perceptions others have of him or her, the intrapersonal role diagram will reflect more accurate information about the client's self-concept.

Question

"As I begin to focus on these roles I begin to remember other roles or parts of roles I hadn't thought of when making out the list. What should I do when this happens?"

Reply: Hidden or Masked Roles

The process of defining roles uncovers many unconscious or masked roles which influence unknowingly the interactions with others. Role diagramming, as with other sociometric procedures, is designed to heighten sociometric consciousness, especially in the areas of role perception and role expectation. The conserved role, the more rigidly defined role and the role allowing for the least spontaneity is more frequently a masked role. The masked roles do not always become apparent when making out the list of roles for the exploration. They emerge at varying points throughout the exploration. Have the participants jot down any flashes they have regarding emerging roles in their notes, or, on the diagram itself. These insights may prove helpful in role therapy.

INTERPRETING THE ROLE DIAGRAM AND MOVING INTO ACTION

The process of role diagramming requires a high degree of self-disclosure on the part of the participants. When the diagramming is completed the sociometrist or therapist is advised to assess the impact of the exploration on the clients and to provide an opportunity for sharing immediately following the experience. The sharing can be guided by the following questions:

1. What information have you given on the role diagram that makes you feel the most anxious? Why?
2. Whose role diagram, or what role interaction, are you the most eager to see? Why?
3. Whose role diagram, or what role interaction, are you the most reluctant to see? Why?
4. What conclusion have you already drawn from this exploration? Are there any sweeping statements you would like to make?
5. Have you any specific feelings about how we should proceed with this exploration in action?

Once this part of the exploration is completed, go over the completed diagrams with the participants. They will need to compare their perceptions of the data each person has supplied and to understand how each has produced the responses which they have. The clients may wish to compare their role diagram to one conducted previously.

Short psychodramatic scenes can be used to help clarify or present in action how a particular perception was formed. Have the persons choose the place, the time, and identify what is going on in the scene to be staged. The therapist/director will be directing a scene in which the actual participants take their own roles, and it may be necessary for the director to have each person present the action according to his/her own perception as he/she experienced it. Whenever possible role reversal and auxiliary egos trained in the use of mirroring can be used in order to enhance the observation and awareness skills of the participants.

Role therapy usually includes the following *in situ* and psychodramatic intervention:

1. Encounter with self and others
2. Un-learning and deconserving roles
3. Role training
4. Future projection (which includes role testing)

The original purpose of the exploration determines the way to proceed in action, as well as consideration of the setting in which the therapy is taking place, and the level of skill the therapist has with action methods. The following guidelines are briefly described here as a reminder of the application of the psychodramatic method. Additional sources can be found by consulting the bibliography.

Encounter with Self and Other

The process of encounter is described in Chapter IV, where one may also find a description of role reversal. A summary of encounter is included here: Have the protagonist (using an auxiliary ego, if available, for absent significant others or to represent a part of the self) sit across from the person they wish to encounter. Have each person express their feelings and responses to each other in the here and now. Especially seek a statement from each participant about the commitment he or she may have to the positive outcome to the encounter. It is often helpful if the therapist will give both (all) parties an opportunity to maximize their feelings in order to accomplish a ventilation of feelings which may be inhibiting adequate role reversal and comprehension of the interaction.

It may not be possible to reconcile the differences between two or more persons until some previous scene between them has been enacted and corrected. In this case have the protagonists enact the scene as they remember it. Have each person soliloquize about what they are not doing or saying. Redo the scene as they would have liked it to have happened. Once ventilation has occurred it will be possible for protagonists to state or describe in action the changes they would like to see take place in their interaction.

Unlearning and De-conserving Roles

It is very normal and comfortable to have habits of interaction. These habits help to save time and energy given to the decision making processes between people. However, relationships can become flat and unimaginative, especially when the persons involved are stuck in roles tied to a history which no longer is viable for the relationship *here and now.* Conserved roles are those which are inherited from or defined by someone other than the person enacting the role. The actor is working from a script which does not allow for his or her own spontaneity.

To de-conserve roles, have the protagonist(s) stage the scene in which the prescribed behavior occurs. The protagonists are encouraged to confront the role model which is made psychodramatically present in the scene. This representation can be either by having an auxiliary ego take the role or by having the protagonists create a sculpture to represent the influence another person or group has had on their role perception. A confrontation with the role model could include: (1) how the protagonists experience the confines of the role; (2) how changing their enactment of the role could affect the feelings they have for the role model; (3) how the role is dysfunctional; and (4) the ways in which they anticipate changing in the future.

A follow-up scene could involve having the role models watch the new enactment of the role. This provides practice, confidence and an opportunity to role test the changes in the presence of critical observers.

Role Training

Clients may need to practice new roles in a supportive setting before confronting the roles in everyday life. Awkwardness, or an overwhelming feeling of inadequacy associated with a particular role, may prevent a person from carrying out their "good intentions"; therefore, it may also be necessary to train the partner(s) in the necessary supportive roles while they are learning this new behavior.

A scene involving the enactment of the new role can be concretely presented using the psychodramatic method. Once the scene is staged, the clients rehearse the interactions which are likely to occur when the new role is in evidence. The interaction can be mirrored, if there are trained auxiliary egos present, in order that the persons may view the interaction objectively. Audio-visual equipment can also be used for this purpose. It may also be useful to have members of the audience or group supply alternative enactments of the situation so that the spontaneity of the group can be utilized as a way of sharing. (See page 59 for additional description.)

Future Projection (Including Role Testing)

Testing out desired or anticipated events in action provides an opportunity for participants to reorder their life **here and now** in response to their perceptions of the future.[8] A couple may wish to test out in action their perceptions of how they will be in the future, i.e., in the role of parents after a child is born. Having participants deal with fears they have concerning unknown roles or unknown consequences of roles may prepare them for the future. Once anxiety around particular roles has a chance for expression, the client will be freer to enact the role with more spontaneity.

Of course the real role test is the one which happens **in situ** (in the situation). Many of your clients will be ready to move from insight into action without further preparation or rehearsal. This process will be enhanced if they agree upon a period of time to experiment. Many will want to take the role diagram home to guide them in their "homework." The role therapy should consequently include reviewing the changes in interaction which take place and facilitating the self-therapist in each participant.

CHAPTER V
FOOTNOTES

1. In *Who Shall Survive?* (1953 ed.) Moreno states (pp. 75-76): "The tangible aspects of what is known as 'ego' are the roles in which it operates. Roles and relationships between roles are the most significant development within any specific culture. Working with the role as a point of reference appears to be a methodological advantage as compared with 'personality' and 'ego'. Role emergence is prior to the emergence of the self. Roles do not emerge from the self, but the self may emerge from roles."

2. Moreno as a personality theorist is (examined in) Bischof, Ledford J., *Interpreting Personality Theories*, New York: Harper and Row, 1964, pp. 355-420.

3. *Ibid.*, p. 73.

4. *Ibid.*, pp. 688-691.

5. *Ibid.*, p. 85.

6. For more information on ancestral roles in social atom repairwork see Danielsson (1972).

7. See "A Method for Depicting Social Relationships Obtained by Sociometric Testing," by Mary L. Northway, *Sociometry*, Vol. III (April, 1940).

8. Yablonsky, Lewis, "Future Projection Techniques," in *Psychodrama Theory and Practice*, edited by Ira A. Greenberg, New York: Behavioral Publications, 1974, pp. 341-344.

BIBLIOGRAPHY

Armstrong, Renate G. and David Schur, "Warm-up Techniques in a Marriage Couples Group," *Group Psychotherapy and Psychodrama*, Vol. 25, No. 3 (1972), pp. 92-101.

Bischof, Ledford J., "Moreno," *Interpreting Personality Theories*. New York: Harper and Row, 1964, pp. 335-420.

Danielsson, Clare, "Redemptive Encounter: Its Use in Psychodrama, Ancestral Sociodrama and Community Building," *Group Psychotherapy and Psychodrama*, Vol. 25, No. 4 (1972), pp. 170-181.

Haskell, Martin, *Socioanalysis: Self-Direction through Sociometry and Psychodrama*. Long Beach, Calif.: Role Training Associates, 1975.

Kerstetter, Leona, "Role Testing for Marriage Prediction," *Sociatry*, Vol. 1, no. 2 (June, 1947), pp. 220-224.

Lawlor, Gerald W., "Role Therapy," *Sociatry*, Vol. 1, no. 1 (March, 1947), pp. 51-55.

Moreno, Florence B. and J.L. Moreno, "Role Tests and Role Diagrams of Children" in *Group Psychotherapy: a Symposium*. Beacon, N.Y.: Beacon House, 1951, pp. 188-203.

Moreno, J.L., "The Prediction and Planning of Success in Marriage," *Sociometry, Experimental Method and the Science of Society*. Beacon, N.Y.: Beacon House, 1951, pp. 111-114.

————. *Psychodramatic Shock Therapy* (Psychodrama Monographs, no. 5), Beacon, N.Y.: Beacon House, 1939.

————. "Psychodramatic Treatment of Marriage Problems," *Psychodrama*, Vol. 1, Beacon, N.Y.: Beacon House, 1972, pp. 328-349.

————. "Role Theory and Role Practice," *Psychodrama*, Vol. I, 4 ed., Beacon, N.Y.: Beacon House, 1972, pp. 153-176.

————. "Table of Role Classifications," *Psychodrama*, Vol. I, 4 ed. Beacon, N.Y.: Beacon House, 1972, p. 77.

————. *Who Shall Survive? Foundations of Sociometry, Group Psychotherapy and Sociodrama*. Beacon, N.Y.: Beacon House, 1953.

Moreno, Zerka T., ed. "Building Diagrams of the Group and the Individual," in *Psychodrama in American Education*, edited by Robert B. Haas. Beacon, N.Y.: Beacon House, 1949, pp. 407-419.

Yablonsky, Lewis, "Future Projection Technique," in *Psychodrama Theory and Practice*, edited by Ira A. Greenberg. New York: Behavioral Publications, 1974, pp. 341-344.

INSTRUCTIONS TO PARTICIPANTS IN A ROLE DIAGRAM EXPLORATION

In this exploration you will be focusing on a complex network of role interactions which exist between you and the person(s) with whom you are involved in these interactions. To begin you will need to make a list of roles you determine to be the most relevant to the aspect of the relationship you wish to explore. The following comments will help you compile the list and construct the role diagram.

Role Names

1. Role names tend to be nouns which imply a group of related activities, such as teacher, listener, parent, etc. Break down large clusters of roles into identifiable acts. For example, the teacher role might focus on "preparer of lessons", "clear communicator", "discipliner", etc.

2. To check out your list, imagine the course of your day. Write down what you do and then translate these activities into role names. Also, imagine the other person, mentally role reverse with that person, and make guesses about what roles that person would consider significant.

3. The following role designations can be included in a role diagram:
   a. **Psychosomatic roles**—ongoing roles which apply to the physical functioning of the body, such as sleeper, eater.
   b. **Socio/cultural roles**—roles having a collective definition, often involving stereotyped perceptions of the role, such as Jewish mother, a real man, refugee, black militant, etc.
   c. **Psychodramatic roles**—roles referring to a specific person's perception of the role; these roles emerge from the person in response to life and are tied to a personal definition of the role, such as **a** son, **a** teacher, **a** stranger.
   d. **Active roles**—role currently active in your life.
   e. **Once active roles**—the role has died out, due to a change in situation, abilities or interests.
   f. **Future projected roles**—roles likely to be additions to the role repertoire in the future. This can include roles once active.
   g. **Ideal roles**—refers to the ideal functioning of the role, such as ideal sister, ideal ballplayer, etc.
   h. **Fantasy roles**—roles about which we dream, such as hero, movie star, landowner, etc.

4. Next, select the role diagram format which is most relevant to your situation.

5. Discuss the following with your partner:
   a. Aspect of the relationship to be diagrammed: parenting, sexual, etc.
   b. Point in time: past, present, future. Identify the year or date.
   c. Agree on the list of roles.

6. Constructing your role diagram. Use a prepared diagram format, or:
   a. On a piece of paper large enough to accommodate the list of roles, designate a space for each person as shown on the format, and use circles for females and triangles for males.
   b. Make one oval (ellipse shape) for each role name and write role name within each oval.
   c. Determine how you feel about yourself in the role and draw a list from yourself to the role, using the notational system provided. Draw the line which most closely describes the feelings you have. Next, determine how you feel about the other person in the role in relation to you and draw the line which describes that feeling. When making perceptual guesses about how another person may be feeling about themselves or you in relation to them, place yourself in their role and make guesses as if you were that person.

7. Interpreting your role diagram.
   a. Share with your partner the feelings you had while doing this. Each person experiences some degree of internal struggle in order to express feelings and responses that have validity. One line cannot speak all that is involved in any single interaction. Share with one another the difficulties which you have had.
   b. Locate those areas of strength in the relationship.
   c. Locate those areas which need further exploration and improvement.
   d. If possible, determine the effect the intrapersonal dynamic (how you feel about yourself) has on the interpersonal dynamic (your feelings about one another) and vice versa.
   e. Note the interactions where the feelings are ambivalent. What would help you to be clearer and less ambivalent?
   f. Discuss with the therapist/sociometrist the impact this exploration has had on you and what you believe would be helpful to you.

ROLE DIAGRAM DATA SHEET

NAME: _____ DATE: _____

1. The relationship I would like to explore is _____

2. The particular aspect of our relating to focus on is _____

3. I wish to include the following kinds of roles in this exploration:

    _____ a. Roles active now (A)   _____ e. Ideal roles (I)

    _____ b. Roles no longer active (OA)   _____ f. Psychosomatic roles (PS)

    _____ c. Future projected role (FP)   _____ g. Socio/cultural roles (SC)

    _____ d. Fantasy roles (F)   _____ h. Psychodramatic roles (PD)

4. The time I have chosen for this exploration is _____

    This time is important for the following reasons: _____

    _____

5. Listed here are those roles in which I interact with this person. Include the designation in parenthesis (optional).

    ROLES ACTIVE NOW (A)   ONCE ACTIVE ROLES (OA)   FUTURE PROJECTED ROLES (FP)

6. Listed here are significant roles I have outside of the relationship:

    ROLES ACTIVE NOW (A)   ONCE ACTIVE ROLES (OA)   FUTURE PROJECTED ROLES (FP)

7. Listed here are significant roles the other person has outside of the relationship:

    ROLES ACTIVE NOW (A)   ONCE ACTIVE ROLES (OA)   FUTURE PROJECTED ROLES (FP)

DIAGRAMMING NOTATION:

———+———	feels more positive now
———————	feels positive now
———–———	feels less positive now
– – –‑– – –	feels less negative now
– – – – – –	feels negative now
– – –+– – –	feels more negative now
★ ★ ★ ★ ★	indifferent
· · · · · · · · · ·	neutral
׀׀׀׀׀׀׀׀׀׀׀׀׀׀׀׀׀׀	unexamined

BLACK INK

ROLE DESIGNATIONS ARE THE SAME
AS APPEARING IN APPENDIX III.a

ROLE DIAGRAM NOTATION

This notation is provided here as a suggestion for indicating the kinds of feelings concerning role interactions. It is designed for use when reporting data in printed sources which appear only in black and white print.

ROLE DIAGRAM OF THE PSYCHODRAMA DIRECTOR: PRODUCER FUNCTION
By Linda C. Frick

How I feel about
myself in these
roles:

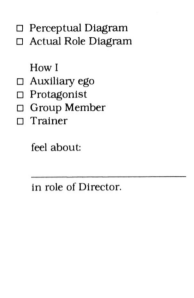

☐ Perceptual Diagram
☐ Actual Role Diagram

How I
☐ Auxiliary ego
☐ Protagonist
☐ Group Member
☐ Trainer

feel about:

_____

in role of Director.

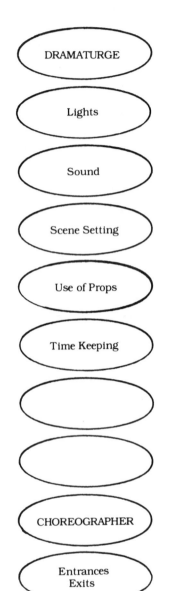

CHAPTER V   **EXAMPLE 1**   **APPENDIX IV**

ROLE DIAGRAM OF THE PSYCHODRAMA DIRECTOR: PRODUCER FUNCTION
By Linda C. Frick

How I feel about
myself in these
roles:

How I feel about
the Director in
these roles:

PLAYWRIGHT

Finding and
Following Cues

Build
Protagonist's
Story in Common
Grp. Experience

Moving from
Periphery to
Center

Flow of Drama

Aesthetic
Quality

Use of
Comic Relief

Involvement
of Group in
Production

Closure of
Scenes

Tying scenes
Together into a
Whole

Director

CHAPTER V   EXAMPLE 1   APPENDIX IV

ROLE DIAGRAM OF THE PSYCHODRAMA DIRECTOR: PRODUCER FUNCTION

How I feel about
myself in these
roles:

How I feel about
the Director in
these roles:

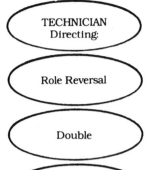

TECHNICIAN
Directing:

Role Reversal

Double

Mirror

Soliloquy

Surplus
Reality

Role
Diagram

Action
Sociogram

Empty Chair

In Situ
Encounter

Warm-up
Exercises

Self
Presentation

Directing
Co-Protagonists

Following
Rules of
Psychodrama

Utilizing
Protagonists'
Symbols

Director

ROLE DIAGRAM OF THE PSYCHODRAMA DIRECTOR: PRODUCER FUNCTION

How I feel
about myself in
these roles:

How I feel about
the Director in
these roles:

TECHNICIAN:
Adjunctive
Methods

Sociodrama

Hypnodrama

Dream Drama

Axiodrama

Bibliodrama

Playback
Theater

Living
Newspaper

Magic Shop

Role Plays

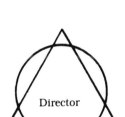

Director

EXAMPLE 1

ROLE DIAGRAM OF THE PSYCHODRAMA DIRECTOR:
ANALYST/GUIDE FUNCTION

How I feel about
myself in these
roles:

How I feel about
the Director in
these roles:

ANALYST/
GUIDE

Permission
Giver

Confidant/
Companion

Comforter

Voice of
Justice & Ethics

Facilitates
Catharsis

Link Between
Protagonist and
Group

Trains
Spontaneity

Offers Creative
Alternatives

Maximizes/
Concretizes

Tests
Hypothesis in
Action

Integrates
Other Modalities
with Psychodrama

Provides
Recovery Time

Facilitates
Sharing

Director

CHAPTER V   EXAMPLE 1   APPENDIX IV

ROLE DIAGRAM OF THE PSYCHODRAMA DIRECTOR:
SOCIAL INVESTIGATOR FUNCTION

How I feel about
myself in these
roles:

How I feel about
the Director in
these roles:

(SOCIAL INVESTIGATOR)

(Interviewer: Who, What, When, Where)

(Identifies Roles and Role Relationships)

(Establishes Protagonists' Cultural Norms)

(SOCIOMETRIST)

(Aware of Sociometric Structure)

(Provides Access to Roles)

(Investigates Role Conflicts)

(Facilitates Re-entry into Group)

(SOCIAL ATOM REPAIR)

(Explores Social Network)

(Re-establishes Sociostasis)

(Role Trains for Expansion of Role Repertoire)

EXAMPLE 1

ROLE DIAGRAM OF THE PSYCHODRAMA DIRECTOR: ELEMENTS OF PERSONAL STYLE

How I feel about
myself in these
roles:

How I feel about
the Director in
these roles:

PERSONAL
STYLE

Trust in
the Method

Spontaneity
and Ability to
Infuse Group
With It

Giving
Clear
Instructions

Aware of
Moment of
Difficulty

Willingness
to Ask for Help

Bracketing

Authentic
Body Language

Voice Control

Volume of Words

Proximity to
Protagonist

Director

GROUP MEMBER ROLE DIAGRAM

HOW I FEEL ABOUT
MYSELF AS A PERSON
WHO:

HOW _____
MAY FEEL ABOUT ME AS
A PERSON WHO:

Takes
Initiative

Expresses
Feelings
Openly

Responds
to Others

Refrains
from
Interrupting
Others

Remains
Present

Provides
Encouragement

Avoids the
Superficial

Facilitates
Others

Asks
Clearly

Establishes
Mutuality

Commands
Respect

Remains
Nonjudgemental

Contributes
Ideas

Is Supportive
During Conflicts

CHAPTER V   SAMPLE FORM #1   APPENDIX V

INTERPERSONAL ROLE DIAGRAM

How I feel about
myself in these
roles

How I feel about
my partner in these
roles in relation
to me

How I feel about
myself in these
roles

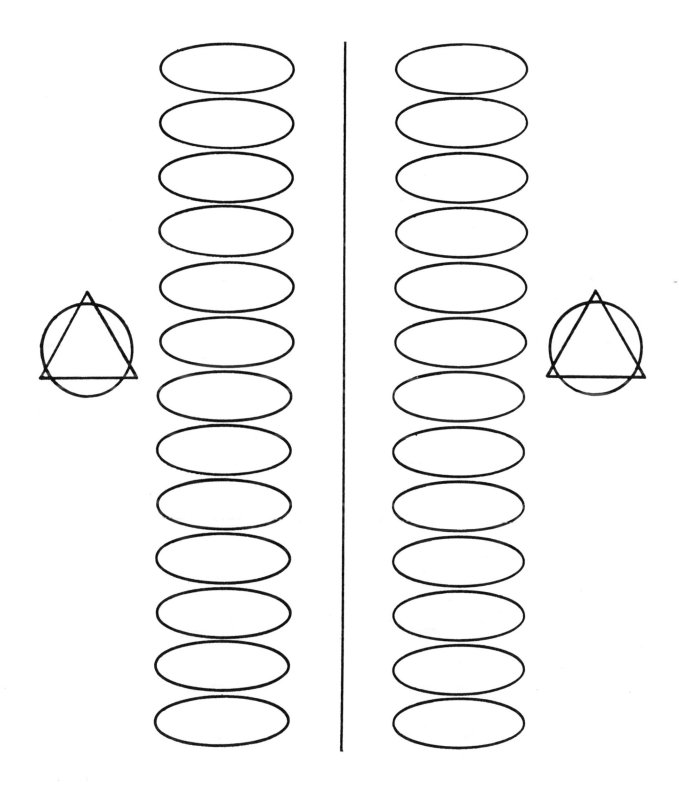

INTERPERSONAL ROLE DIAGRAM (PERCEPTUAL ASPECT)

How I feel about
myself in these
roles

How I feel about
my partner in these
roles in relation
to me

How I perceive my partner
feels about me in
these roles in relation
to him/her

How I perceive my
partner feels about
him/herself in
these roles

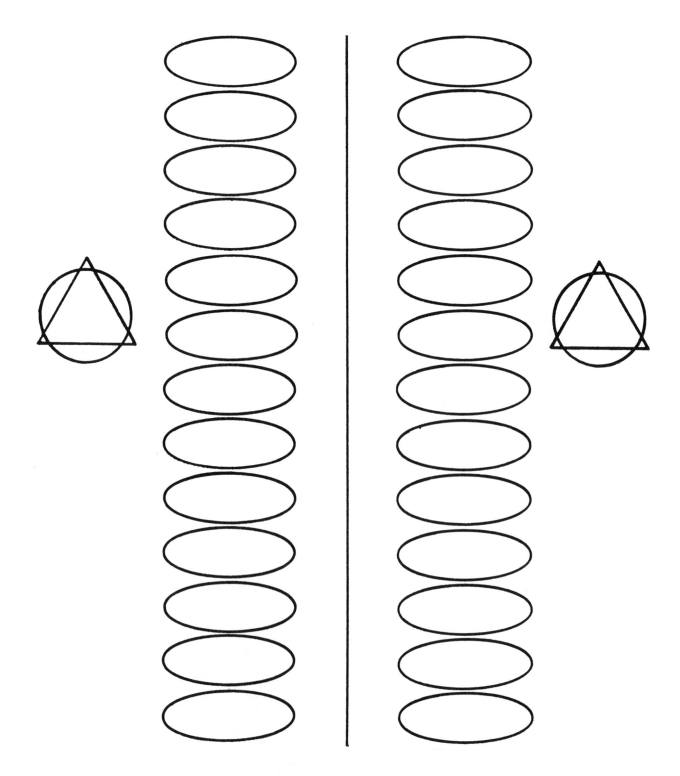

CHAPTER V   SAMPLE FORM #3   APPENDIX V

MULTILATERAL ROLE DIAGRAM:
THREE INTERACTORS, SAME ROLE CONSTRUCTION

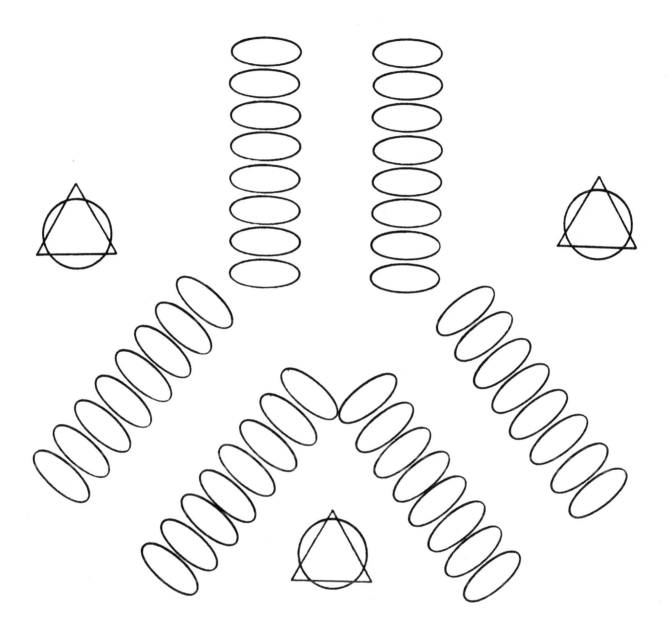

CHAPTER V   **SAMPLE FORM #4**   **APPENDIX V**

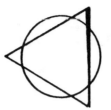

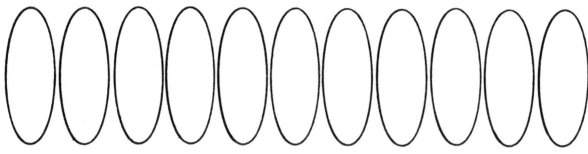

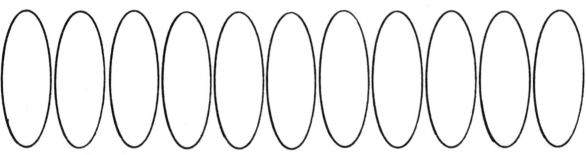

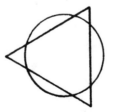

BILATERAL ROLE DIAGRAM:
ONE PERSON, TWO INTERACTORS, SAME ROLE CONSTRUCTION

CHAPTER VI
ACTION SOCIOMETRY:
A Guide for Group Leaders

"This should not be an experiment of nature without the conscious participation of the actors, but one consciously and systematically created and projected by the total group. There are many steps and more barriers which a sensitive crew of coexperimenters might encounter on the way to a scientific utopia. However little or far they advance they never fool themselves and never fool others; they prefer the 'slow' dialectic process of the sociometric experiment *in situ* to social revolutions of mass action which do not know when to start and when to end."

J.L. Moreno, *Who Shall Survive?*, p. 62-63

ACTION SOCIOMETRY: A GUIDE FOR GROUP LEADERS

Every time group members are asked to pick a partner for an activity, action sociometry is taking place. Every structured exercise, or warm-up activity, involving a group interaction, is an action sociometric event. Principles of sociometry fully apply. Every psychodrama, sociodrama, role play, encounter is a sociometric event. The choice-making is occuring in the here and now on **identifiable** criteria for selection, moment to moment, role by role—sometimes based on an actual feeling response, sometimes based on proximity or chance. The skill for group leaders and participants lies in the ability to recognize the criterion of choice, moment to moment, and to evaluate the outcome of those choices on the spontaneity level of the individuals in the group. This is sociometric consciousness in action.

A reason to engage in the "pen and paper" sociometric explorations (the sociometric test, the perceptual social atom sociogram, for example) is to train and refine one's sociometric consciousness. One makes perceptual guesses and analyzes them for their overall accuracy, an accuracy within specific choice categories. This procedure provides for the group leader and the group member, the information and confidence they need to begin conducting action sociometric events, for they now know when their observations and interventions are likely to be accurate.

Recognizing the Criterion of Choice in Action

The process of recognizing the criterion of choice in action is enhanced when one is very familiar with ways criteria are worded and he/she practices writing sociometric criteria which exactly reflect the activity, setting and intended outcome of the question. An example:

> A guy in a group has built a reputation as a belligerent person. He is never chosen to be another group member's double. What is the criterion on which he is rejected? What would be the criterion on which he could be chosen? He is rejected on the criterion: "Of the persons in the group, whom I trust to be able to monitor the intensity of their angry feelings and to stay in role as double, whom do I choose to play the role of confrontive double." The criterion on which he might be chosen is: "Of the persons in this who have had difficulty with the intensity of his/her angry feelings, whom do I choose to have as my double for a practice session in confrontive doubling."

In this example the criterion identifies the role need, and the choices, made in action, clarify whom will be chosen. On the basis of this the group studies what has to happen in order to facilitate persons having little access to roles into roles they need. In the example, the group discovers that continuing to make choices on the old criterion would prevent the person who most needs practice from having access to it. Choosing another criterion worded to facilitate access for the underchosen results in different choices and a less fixed group structure.

Some suggestions for examining choice-making in a psychodrama group:

1. Analyze a group process session in terms of criterion selection. Examples: What are the criteria on which we base our choices for whom will be the protagonist? What unconscious factors contribute to our choices? What influences with whom we spend time on breaks? How can this be translated into a criterion statement?

2. Interview a protagonist for the reasons they have made specific choices for persons to take auxiliary ego roles in his/her psychodrama. Have the group practice translating the answers into criteria. (OR, a therapist may ask a client to identify the reasons he/she has chosen a particular person for a partner in an activity. Assist the client in translating the reasons into a generalized criterion statement.

3. Draw sociograms of the choice-making activity in a psychodrama. Have the protagonist, or group, identify the overall basis for choice, and translate this into a generalized criterion.

4. Have group members engage in the "Group Exploration of Act Hunger" (page 143-145) and practice writing criteria which affect being highly chosen on the criterion of one's choice.

NAME	ROLE I HAD IN DRAMA	MY PERCEPTION OF CRITERION ON WHICH I WAS CHOSEN	ROLE I WANTED IN DRAMA	REASON I WANTED ROLE	WHAT WOULD ENABLE ME TO BE CHOSEN FOR ROLES LIKE THIS?

Figure 1.   Auxiliary Ego Role Choice: Criterion Review (may be used to assist a group in collecting information they may need in the criterion review.)

Using Action Sociometry for Dealing With Issues of Inclusion

In the beginning stages of a group it may not be clear to everyone in the group what the existing interpersonal connections are: who knows whom, what roles do certain members have in common, etc. Action methods can be used to "collect information" about the connections which exist. Some examples of how this can be accomplished are:

1. Have each person place their hand on the person in the room with whom they have had the longest relationship. The resulting configuration is likely to be several mutuals with a chain leading into a mutual. Identify the oldest relationship in the room, and the newest relationship in the room.

2. Have all those persons who are new to the situation (first-time participants) form a sub-group. Have all those familiar to the situation form another sub-group. In the newcomers' group have the group members identify, by placing their hand on the person, the people they knew before coming to the group. Next have the "old-timers" group choose any of the newcomers whom they have known before that person joined the group. This clarifies who is a potential linkage person for the newcomers into the group.

3. Have group members place a hand on the person with whom they have had the most significant contact since arrival. A variation of this would be to have the group members place a hand on the person in the group, whom they have not known before, with whom they have had a significant initial contact.

4. Place your hand on the person you would find it easy to reveal yourself to. Choose someone you do not know. Tell the person why you believe this to be true. Next, place your hand on a person in the group you would find it difficult to reveal yourself to. Choose someone whom you do not know. Tell the person why you believe this to be true. If several people choose the same person for these (which is quite likely) have the group identify and discuss what accounts for the polarities in disclosure dynamics.

5. Place your hand on the person whom you perceive to be similar to you in a significant way, more similar than with any other person in the group. Have the group members sit in the same configuration as the resulting action sociogram. Ask each person to tell the group what it is about the person they have chosen that is significantly similar. Next, reverse the process. Have the group members identify the person who is most unlike him or her in some significant way.

6. Chain action warm-up: Have one person start off this exercise. Go up to a person in the group and place your hand on him or her and tell the person what you see them having that you don't have; the person just takes in the information with little or no response; that person then moves to another group member and does the same, with the first person still connected; this continues until all persons in the group have been included in the chain. Have the group react to the statements and the effect that it had on their perceptions of people in the group.

7. Have group members line up according to their experience (most or least) in some field or with some activity. (Example: The most experienced mother to the least experienced mother.)

One of the ways to use action sociometry is to check out the degree of change that has taken place since a previous sociometric exploration. You can have group members place their hands on the first choice that they made on a previous sociometric test. Then have them consider whom they would choose here and now for their first choice using that same criterion. It also helps if group members are given the opportunity to state what the reasons are for the choices they are making here and now. This is one way that action sociometry makes it possible to have an indication of the changes in choices that are being made.

Counteracting the Sociodynamic Effect

This term, **sociodynamic effect**, is used for "the concentration of many choices upon few individuals and weak concentration of few choices on many individuals."[1] The highly overchosen person is considered to be sociometrically wealthy, or a "star". In terms of actual, or potential connection to others, he/she has a surplus of possible interactors, and consequently, a surplus of opportunities to access roles of his/her choice. When a group leader asks participants to choose a partner for an exercise, the choice pattern may resemble Figure 2.a below, **if** the sociodynamic effect is in evidence.

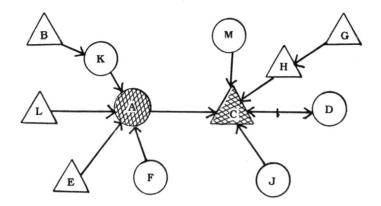

Figure 2.a   First choice for partner

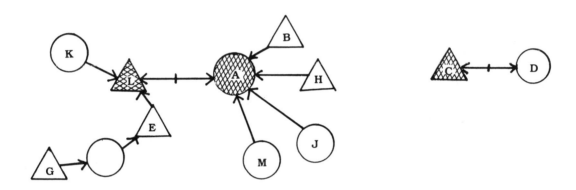

Figure 2.b   Second choice for partner

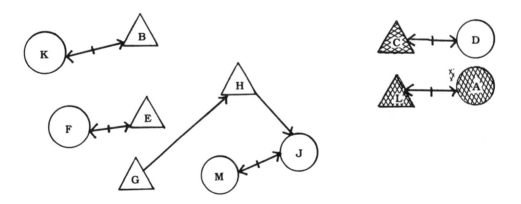

Figure 2.c   Third choice for partner

As you can imagine the choice-making represented in these illustrations takes place quickly. Moreno also defined the sociodynamic effect as "persistently leaving out a number of persons in a group."[2] The "stars" get their first or second choices and the rest accept a third choice or less. This process has impact, yet far too often group leaders avoid the impact and go right on to task. Since the interpersonal process of choosing hasn't been explored openly, any unfinished business which may have resulted from it impedes the group's progress. Incomplete warm-up will affect the meaningfulness of future actions.

This sort of choosing happens so often that it becomes "unconscious". Group leaders may believe that by asking people to make "spontaneous" choices (meaning they are free from choosing on the basis of the leader's instructions) that something spontaneous is happening. When the sociodynamic effect is in evidence this is **not** the case; rather, the choice-making is conserved. By making the choice-making **more** conscious, asking people to be aware of the impact of their choices, spontaneity can come more easily into being. A rule of thumb for counteracting sociodynamic effect is: go to the level of choice (1st, 2nd, 3rd, etc.) which produces the highest level of mutuality, particularly of the less highly chosen. If first choices produce one mutual, but ten unreciprocated choices, as in Figure 2.a, go on to second choice and so on, until those underchosen and less easy to satisfy with a partner of high value, have a reciprocated choice, or at least a partner who is neutral, rather than negative to them.

"Moreno experimented with random choice to see if chance-related selection resulted in another spread of distribution."[3] It was found that random selection produced a higher middle group and reduced the extremes of highly overchosen and significantly underchosen.[4] Moreno also developed "assignment therapy" for the groups he studied. Spontaneous choice was only one of the contributing factors in the access to roles in a group.[5] Increased consciousness-raising on the part of members can result in pressure within a group to distribute roles of high value more evenly, with some group members taking "assignment" to roles.

A Suggestion for Forming Pairs and Small Groups in Action

1. Have group assemble in a circle, facing inward.
2. "Look around the group and notice those persons you usually choose."
3. "Ask yourself: Is this the time when it is important to choose them again, or might a choice for someone new be important. Think it over a moment."
4. "Be aware if you want to choose, or would rather wait to be chosen. Put out your right foot if you want to choose. Look around the circle and notice what other people prefer."
5. "Hold your arm out level with your eyes, and look with your arm extended toward a person you choose. Waggle your fingers."[6]
6. "Now move toward your choice and place your hand on him/her."
7. "Before we go on, stand with your partner and look at the choices others have made. Is anyone dissatisfied with the result of this process?" Explore any dissatisfaction with the group before proceeding.

Act Hunger

The sociodynamic effect and the power imbalances which result is a major factor in the creation of act hunger. The group leader may recognize act hunger in the following behaviors:

1. participant's excess energy
2. impulsivity
3. participants not listening to each other
4. inability to listen, or retain, leader's instructions
5. a resistance to problem-solving, or other serious concerns
6. inability to accurately role reverse

The chaotic nature of the group when act hunger is present can discourage the novice group leader from employing action methods; however, these groups really need action to provide a vehicle for exploring the power imbalances which are contributing to act hunger. After all, these behaviors are primarily symptoms and serve an extremely positive function in alerting the group to the role demands of their members.

Moreno described act hunger as a syndrome comprised of the elements of total involvement in the striving for an act, total absorption in the role enactment, absence of the observing ego and total involvement in the moment.[7] The act, in this instance, is the rawest, most elemental form of choice, a choice subject to the urgency of the moment, the urgency of drive for completion. If interrupted, the person will seek another point of completion. The warm-up will begin again.

It becomes important to trace what circumstances provoked the act hunger and called into play this pathological form of spontaneity. The following conditions can increase act hunger.

1) **Lack of access to roles of high value**
   Exactly which roles are of high value can be determined by discussing this with the group, or may be subject to individual definition.

2) **Lack of an interactor of one's choice**
   The person of choice may be absent, never existed, or, if present, may choose not to reciprocate.

3) **Lack of the audience or setting of one's choice**
   The present audience may be inappropriate or contra-indicated for the action and will deny access to the role.

4) **Lack of spontaneity starters**
   Inadequate warm-up creates anxiety, or sparks pathological spontaneity, which infuses the setting with disjointed interactions and inadequate true spontaneity for the role.

5) **Role is in conflict with existing role repertoire**
   The group, or a member of the group, may be fixed in their choices for specific roles; or, the person cannot act when one role appears to be in conflict with another. Example: the existing role repertoire permits crying as a way of expressing disappointment. Angry feelings have no outlet and therefore become contained, until some urgency to express the feelings becomes sparked. The expression of anger is now in conflict with the existing role repertoire.

6) **Presence of inhibitors**
   (a) Parental injunctions; (b) group norms; (c) scripts; (d) fears, such as rejection, intimacy, guilt, failure, success, loss of control, humiliation, the unknown, etc.

7) **Lack of skill for the role**
   The person may lack the necessary skill for the role, or may not be perceived as a person having necessary skill due to the lack of exposure in the role.

It is important in identifying act hunger to also identify the frame of reference of the person generating the behavior. Moreno stresses this in *Who Shall Survive?*:

> "Spontaneity state is not only an expression of a process within a person, but also a relation to the outside through the spontaneity of another person. It is a meeting of two different states."[8]

An example of act hunger:

> The group has elected to enact *Cinderella* as a way to explore the dynamics of searching for a partner in life. Group members choose roles they wish on the basis that the roles they choose may benefit them. The action moves along well until it is time for the ugly stepsisters to order Cinderella around, ironing ball gowns, etc. Five people chose to play stepsisters and they are being very nasty in the role, having a wonderful time bossing poor Cinderella. The leader, sensing that the action is more than called for, stops the action, calls for a soliloquy from the stepsisters and role-reversals with Cinderella. The role reversal provided a moment to be aware of the consequences of their action on the person in the role of Cinderella, and the soliloquy gave each person a chance to recognize the high energy they have for the role of powerful, arrogant and rather mean sibling. The "stepsisters" acknowledged they were enjoying the role relief from always being "nice." Two "stepsisters" mentioned that they may have been a little hard on Cinderella because they were somewhat resentful of not being chosen for the role. (This was explored further during the sharing discussion following the role play.) The action resumed with the focus of the role play expanded to include the role relief dimension. Role reversal was increased.

The group leader is encouraged to allow for act hunger, to incorporate the high energy into moments of action, and check-in using the "stop action" approach. Whenever a person takes liberties in role, call for an immediate role reversal, repeat the action in order for both parties to experience the action from the other's role. As well, the group leader seeks those opportunities to facilitate the sharing of sociometric wealth: for the underchosen, facilitation into roles of high value, and for the overchosen, the role relief of peripherality.

A Note About the Therapeutic Impact for Group Leaders in Non-clinical Settings:

There are many group leaders who utilize action methods and sociometry for education and training purposes who wish to make a distinction between a training event and a therapeutic one. No matter what emphasis a group has, or its objectives, the group has a potential for being therapeutic. There are roles to be taken, interactors chosen, and norms for relating to be set. Whatever the group's purpose, a skilled group leader can maximize the usefulness of the group by tending to these socio-therapeutic issues. The group's functioning may be enhanced, as well as having the added benefit of the learning being immediately applicable to a person's own life experience.

(Additional action sociometric methods may be found in Chapter 2, page 25 and in Chapter 3, p. 57-58.)

CHAPTER VI

FOOTNOTES

1. J.L. Moreno and Helen Hall Jennings, "Statistics of Social Configurations" in *The Sociometry Reader* (Glencoe, Ill., The Free Press, 1960), p. 30.

2. J.L. Moreno, *Who Shall Survive?* Beacon, N.Y.: Beacon House, 1978, p. 226.

3. Ann E. Hale, "Sharing the Sociometric Wealth: the sociometric dimension of group process in the psychodrama network." Keynote presentation, Joint Conference of the Western Regional, American Society of Group Psychotherapy and Psychodrama and 6th Annual Meeting of the Federation of Trainers and Training Programs in Psychodrama, Tucson, AZ, January 28, 1983, in *Federation News* (1983) vol. IV, no. 1, p. 5.

4. J.L. Moreno and Helen Hall Jennings, "Statistics of Social Configurations," p. 36.

5. *Ibid.,* p. 21.

6. Joe W. Hart, University of Arkansas, refers to this process as "twinkling."

7. J.L. Moreno, *Psychodrama,* Volume 1, Beacon, N.Y., Beacon Press, 1946, p. 47-48.

8. J.L. Moreno, *Who Shall Survive?,* p. 335.

BIBLIOGRAPHY

Hale, Ann E., "Isolation and Its Effects on the Psychodrama Network," *Federation News,* 1982, Vol. III, no. 1.

_____, "Sharing the Sociometric Wealth: the Sociodramatic Dimension of Group Process in the Psychodrama Network," *Federation News,* 1983, Vol. IV, no. 5.

Hale, Ann E. and Carolyn Gerhards Gagnon, "Advanced Sociometry Training Group: A Sociometric Analysis and Comprehensive Report of a Week-long Residential Workshop." Unpublished paper. Roanoke, Va., 1980.

Hart, Joe W., "Socioeconomic Sociometry and Socioeconometry: Moreno's Sociodynamic Effect Revisited." *Handbook of International Sociometry,* Vol. VI (1971).

Moreno, J.L., *Psychodrama,* Vol. 1, Beacon, N.Y., Beacon Press, 1946.

_____, *Who Shall Survive?* Beacon, N.Y.: Beacon Press, 1978.

_____ and Helen Hall Jennings, "Statistics of Social Configurations," in *The Sociometry Reader.* Glencoe, Ill., The Free Press, 1960.

CHAPTER VI

GROUP EXPLORATION OF ACT HUNGER
FOR ROLES OF HIGH VALUE

This exercise is designed to increase awareness in group members of the criteria on which you and others wish to be most highly chosen. You are asked to make perceptual guesses about choices others are making for you in the here and now. The information will be shared with the group in action sociograms using the process described on the second page.

I. In the columns below identify three criteria on which you would like to be most highly chosen in this group. (That is, if this group did a sociometric exploration on the basis of this criterion, you would emerge as highly chosen, or "star.") Indicate your perceptual skills by guessing who else in this group would be chosen on this criterion.

CRITERION	REASON	WHO ELSE WOULD BE CHOSEN FOR THIS ROLE
1.		
2.		
3.		

II. Re-write the criteria you have listed in such a way as to limit the group's choices for others and effect you being the "most highly chosen." Avoid constructions such as: "Of the women in the group wearing a pink sweater, whom would you choose to confide in about a problem?" Prefer something along this line: "Of the persons in this group who have not been visible in the director role, whom do you choose to direct you in a scene setting exercise?"

1.

2.

3.

III. Action portion of the exploration of act hunger for roles of high value:

Group members will be able to check out their perceptions and share with the group those roles which have high value for them, and the reasons for their importance.

1. A person reads one criterion from his/her list.

2. Group members consider for a moment and then place a hand on the shoulder of the person in the group who would be their first choice.

3. The person shares with the group his/her perception about whom would be highly chosen on this criterion.

4. If the person reading their criterion is not significantly highly chosen, have him/her read the re-written version of the criterion, and have group members declare their choices once again.

5. If the rewritten criterion does not limit choices in such a way as to have the person be star on the criterion of his/her choice:
   a. Have the person discuss the reasons the role is of high value
   b. Have the group brainstorm criteria which meet this need
   c. Discuss ways the person could inform the group (give clues) about his/her readiness for the role.
   d. Check out any new criteria in action.

6. Allow time for persons to share with each other about the impact of this exploration on him/herself.

7. Repeat the process with another group member.

CHAPTER VI   **APPENDIX II**

EXPLORING YOUR ACT HUNGER

This exercise is designed to increase your awareness of the factors which influence the accessibility of roles in this group. The information may be kept private, or the group may wish that group members share what they have written. Discuss this in the group and come to a decision.

  I. Identify roles which have been missing thus far in your stay here:

  ROLE

  II. Identify some persons in this group with whom you have wished to be involved in the following roles, and which has not yet occurred.

  PERSON   ROLE   REASON FOR INACTION

 III. Review the above and then identify the following:

  A. What parental injunctions ("shoulds") have affected your involvement in this group?

  B. Identify group norms which have affected accessibility to roles and your involvement in this group.

  C. Identify leadership styles which have affected accessibility to roles and your involvement in in this group.

  D. What skills do you need to develop in order to facilitate yourself into roles of your choice?

© Ann E. Hale, Roanoke, Va.

GLOSSARY OF TERMS

The terms below are defined in numerous places in the literature of sociometry, psychodrama and interpersonal dynamics. While every attempt has been made to honor standard usage, the definitions offered here have been phrased with reference to their usage in sociometry. Citations for the source of the definition have been provided using the following abbreviations: WSS - *Who Shall Survive?*; SR - *Sociometry Reader*; PD1 - *Psychodrama,* Volume I; SOC(15) - *Sociometry* journal with the volume number in parentheses. An (*) after the definition indicates a definition attributed to the author.

Acquaintance diagram—a sociogram showing persons acquainted, without any further emotional or social connotations, merely "knowing each other." WSS, p. 145.

Acquaintance volume—a certain number of individuals with whom one is acquainted, which may change from birth to death in terms of number, range and geographical distribution. WSS, p. 618.

Ambiequal—a mutual; someone who reciprocates.

Aristo-tele—is the form of tele in relationships where one person, relatively unknown, exerts through the medium of other individuals a far-reaching effect upon masses of people; the form can be said to be Aristocratic. WSS, p. 318.

Axiodrama—application of the psychodramatic method for concerns which deal with the activation of religious, ethical and cultural values. WSS, p. xxvi.

Bilateral role diagram—a role diagram depicting the relationship two persons have with the same person; affecting reciprocally both sides or parties. The role construction is the same.(*)

Centrifugal aspect of choice—the choices the group, or a person makes are consistently for persons outside of the group. WSS, p. 647.

Centripetal aspect of choice—the choices the group, or a person makes are constantly for persons within the group, with little, or no connection to outside groups. WSS, p. 647.

Chain—an open series of mutual choices on any criterion; A chooses B, B chooses A, B chooses C, C chooses B, C chooses D, etc. WSS, p. 720.

Chance—the degree of likelihood of being chosen on a random basis. SR, p. 28.

Choice—the expression of preference for one thing or person over another.

Classoid—sociometric structure of the social classes. WSS, p. 81.

Cleavage—discrepancy between official and secret value systems, causing a break or a split in the group structure. WSS, p. 62.

Clinical Sociometry—aspect of sociometry focused upon the psychological and socioemotional interventions, relationship therapy and change.

Clustering effect—term used for the effect of transfer of spontaneity from role to role within the same role cluster, made possible by familiarity with a role which has similar elements. PDI, p. 175.

Cohesion—in groups, the force holding the individuals together within the groupings. SR, p. 46.

Collective social atom—refers to the minimum number of meaningful groups to which a person belongs.

Counter-transference—term used to describe what occurs when two persons each have a transference reaction to the other. Neither person is able to see the other person as he/she sees himself or herself. WSS, p. 296.

Creative neutrality—a neutral response that is elected as a creative alternative despite positive or negative feelings which may actually be present; bracketing feeling state in order to explore other ranges of feeling.

Creativity—the capacity to be, to act and to create; a phenomenon which results when spontaneity comes into contact with the cultural conserve and changes it in some novel way. WSS, p. 74.

Creatocracy—a collection of actors creating their existence. WSS, p. 74.

Criterion—an established basis for choice activity; the question one asks when making a choice. SR, p. 255.

Cultural atom—the focal pattern of role relationships around an individual. SR, p. 53.

Cultural conserve—the finished product of a creative process which has a capacity for usefulness which lies dormant until it comes into contact with spontaneity. WSS, p. 20.

Deconserving—the gradual removal of cliche from a person's behavior and relating. WSS, p. 543.

Diagnostic sociometry—application of sociometric methods for the purpose of social classification. WSS, p. 52.

Emotional expansiveness—the number of persons an individual chooses to relate to and sustains in their social atom. WSS, p. 317.

Empathy—one-way tele; the expression of positive feelings without reciprocation. WSS, p. 644.

Encounter—a meeting of two, eye to eye, face to face; able to become each other in role reversal. WSS, p. 65.

Expanded role diagram—a role diagram that is expanded to include roles the persons have outside of their relationship with each other. (*)

External reality—official institutional structures which are structured in their relationships based on public, visible elements. WSS, p. 57.

Extramural roles—roles existing outside the boundaries of a particular relationship. (*)

In situ—in the situation; designated for study in the here and now. WSS, p. 60.

In statu nascendi—in the state of birth, meaning, the beginning or source of an act, or role. WSS, p. 58. PD1, p. 37-38.

Incongruity—incompatibility or lack of reciprocity.

Indifference—an undifferentiated interest or lack of interest; absence of tele.

Infra-tele—a form of attraction which is positive and unreciprocated. WSS, p. 64.

Interpersonal—involving relations between persons.

Intrapersonal—involving the dynamics which exist within a person affecting his/her self-perception.

Isolate—a person who does not choose or reject, and who is not chosen or rejected. WSS, p. 257.

Linkage—a connection between two persons, or two sub-groups.

Locogram—a space and movement diagram. WSS, p. 142.

Matrix of all identity—the infant's social world, in which all identity is incorporated into his/her own world. PD1, p. 74.

Matrix of all reality—the identity of a person allows for differentiation of self and other. PD1, p. 75.

Mutuality—reciprocity.

Negative—reaction or feelings which imply absence of satisfaction resulting in feelings of irritation, anger, dislike, repulsion and/or unwillingness to relate.

Neutral—neither a positive or negative response; a category which may be elected deliberately (as in "openness") in order to allow for further exploration.

Omnitele—consensus of the group; a catharsis of integration resulting in a group decision. SOC (15), p. 366.

Perception—comprehending through awareness; conscious of the feelings and responses of others.

Perception test—a test given following an objective sociometric test which measures person's ability to perceive choices of others for self and other by comparing it with data from the objective test.

Pivotal person—a person whose sociometric position is located between two key persons or groups. (*)

Positive—a response with feelings of satisfaction; pleasurable, effective and desirable.

Psychetelic—response to a person for a role which is based on personal (private) and/or leisure-related motivation. SR, p. 100.

Psychodrama—a dramatic means for exploring interpersonal relations and private worlds. WSS, p. 81-87.

Psychodramatic roles—roles which have an evolving definition which comes directly from the evolving person; roles which evolve from the imagination and surplus reality. WSS, p. 76.

Psychological social atom—the smallest number of persons required by an individual to achieve sociostasis, and support creativity. WSS, p. 618.

Quasi-sociometric—methods which have been adapted in such a way as to produce data which has specific limitations; studies with less than maximal participation. WSS, p. 102.

Rejectee—a person not chosen (or significantly overchosen negatively). WSS, p. 257.

Role—a unit of conserved behavior implying specific acts or behaviors. WSS, p. 689.

Role cluster—a group of related actions encompassed under a role name, for example, "parent". PD1, p. 175.

Role creating—infusing the role with a high degree of spontaneity by developing new starters, new actions and new responses to the role. WSS, p. 689-690.

Role diagram—a visual representation of the role construction of one or more relationships. (*)

Role enactment—physically portraying or acting the function of a role. PD1, p. 163.

Role expectation—the anticipation of a specific enactment of a role.

Role model—a person or fictional character who portrays a role which is then imitated by others.

Role perception—awareness of the functions and action which comprise a role. PD1, p. 164.

Role playing—dramatic enactment of a scene which has a purpose of providing familiarity to a role, or revitalizing conserved roles by permitting a degree of freedom to the individual playing the roles. WSS, p. 75.

Role repertoire—the supply of roles available to a person.

Role resuscitation—the revival of inactive roles.

Role reversal—taking the role of another person and experiencing that person as fully as one may experience oneself. WSS, p. 87.

Role taking—taking a role as proscribed by society and enacting the role as conserved (stereotyped). WSS, p. 689.

Role test—a measure of role behavior in a structured situation, designed to measure the degree of differentiation a specific culture has had on an individual. PD1, p. 161-175.

Role training—exploring alternative role interpretations and role interactions. Practicing variations of relating within a role. WSS, p. 503.

Roles in ascendence—roles becoming more central and significant.

Roles in descendence—roles becoming more peripheral, less significant.

Self-rating—guessing what others' feelings may be and determining a possible reason for their response to oneself. WSS, p. 221.

Social atom—nucleus of relations comprising a social structure belonging to a person. It is the smallest functional unit within society. WSS, p. 52, 70.

Social expansiveness—the number of relationships a person can sustain. WSS, p. 317.

Social network—collective formations of social groupings which are interconnected, and which may, or may not, be fully realized by the persons who comprise the network. WSS, p. 67-79.

Social reality—merging of external reality (visible and public) and the sociomatrix of interpenetrating responses between persons in the group (less visible and personal). WSS, p. 57.

Social threshold—the definite line of demarcation between acquaintance volume and the nucleus of intimates. SR, p. 55.

Sociatry—treating and healing the pathological syndromes of normal society, of interrelated individuals and of interrelated groups. WSS, p. 119.

Sociodynamic law—science of the structure of social aggregates. WSS, p. 5.

Sociodynamic effect—distribution of choice in favor of the more highly chosen, as against less highly chosen. When the number of choices allowable increases, an even greater distance between highly chosen and the unchosen becomes evident. WSS, p. 36.

Sociogram—a visual representation of the placement of individuals in a group, and the interrelations of individuals. WSS, p. 95-96.

Sociogroup—a group whose sociometric structure is based on work-related criteria which is collective in nature. SOC (10), p. 71.

Socioid—cluster of atoms linked together to form a network. WSS, p. 80.

Sociomatrix—a chart on which all the choices of group members for each other are entered, thereby displaying choices of persons and choices for persons. WSS, p. 142.

Sociometric test—an investigation of the choice activity among group members. WSS, p. 92-95.

Sociometry—generic term to describe all measurements of societal and interpersonal relations. WSS, p. 16.

Socionomy—science of social laws; explains and treats the laws of social development and social relations. It is within the system of socionomy that the metaphorical We, the mass, the community, has its place. SR, p. 127.

Sociostasis—that configuration of relations having sufficient numbers and quality to effect balance and equilibrium. WSS, p. 285.

Sociotelic—response to connection with another person is based on reasons having to do with visible, work-related reasons. SOC (10), p. 71.

Spontaneity—operates in the present and is an unconservable energy which propels the individual toward an adequate response in a new situation and a novel response in an old situation. WSS, p. 42.

Spontaneous interaction diagram—the recording via graphic means of all fundamental variables in a life situation, i.e., time, space, number and type of persons present, acts, pauses, initiative, simultaneity, leadership, change and ending. WSS, p. 140.

Star—most highly chosen in a choice category (positive, negative and neutral).

Surplus reality—an experience which is novel and which extends the subject's experience of reality; a reorganization of the self in situations other than one's current reality provides, resulting in an integration of new roles and perceptions of roles. WSS, p. 85.

Tele—the current of feeling which exists and flows between two or more persons. It is "insight into" "appreciation of" and "feeling for" the actual makeup of the other person(s). It is the cement that holds individuals and groups together. PD1, p. 247, 277.

Theometry—metric universe of God's creation. WSS, p. xx.

Transference—the psychopathological branch of tele, transference is the factor responsible for the dissociation and disintegration of social groups; a projection of feelings onto a person or a group which has been experienced incompletely; often an unreciprocated process. WSS, p. 311-321.

Universalia—the sociometric universalia are the most elementary social relations independently existing regardless of social context; found in all societies although they vary widely in organizational development. They may also be called social "axioms". WSS, p. 617.

Unexamined responses—undetermined response due to a lack of information or peripherality. (*)

Warming-up process—the operational expression of spontaneity; the process of generating readiness for a specific act. WSS, p. 42.

NAME AND PLACE INDEX

Allport, Gordon W., p. 13
American Psychiatric Association, p. 3
Anderson, Walt, p. 13
Armstrong, Renate G., p. 126
Attneave, Carolyn, p. 10, 18, 28
Ausubel, David P., p. 54, 63

Bales, Robert F., p. 63
Barbour, Alton, preface, p. 18, 25, 28, 63, 109
Barnlund, Dean C., p. 96
Beavin, Janet Helmick, p. 109
Beebe, John, p. 109
Benne, Kenneth D., p. 61, 63, 109
Beum, Corli O., p. 63
Bischof, Ledford J., p. 126
Blake, Robert R., p. 60, 62
Bradford, Leland F., p. 61, 63, 109
Branham, Eya, p. 98
Bratescu, Gheorghe, p. 13
Brind, Anna B., p. 109
Brind, Nah, p. 109
Brunner, Jerome S., p. 64
Boguslaw, Robert, p. 13
Bonney, Merl E., p. 63
Borgatta, Edgar F., p. 61, 63, 77
Bronfenbrenner, Urie, p. 61, 63

Campbell, Donald T., p. 42, 61, 63
Carlson-Sabelli, Linnea, preface
Columbia University, p. 4
Cook, S.W., p. 63
Criswell, Joan H., p. 54, 63

Danielsson, Clare, p. 63, 126
Deutsch, Morton, p. 100, 109

Fessenden, Seth A., p. 63
Fox, Jonathan, preface
Frick, Linda C., p. 120-126
Frost, Joyce Hocker, p. 101, 109
Fructer, Benjamin, p. 60, 62

Gagnon, Carolyn Gerhards, p. 61, 63
Gendlin, Eugene T., p. 109
Gibb, Jack R., p. 61, 63, 109
Ginn, Robert, p. 99
Ginn, Ildri Bie, p. 99
Goldberg, Alvin A., p. 109
Greenberg, Ira A., p. 13, 126

Haas, Robert B., p. 126
Hale, Ann E., p. 10, 18, 21-22, 28, 61, 63, 105
Hare, A. Paul, p. 63
Hart, Joseph W., p. 13, 63
Haskell, Martin, p. 126
Hollander, Carl, p. 10, 17-18, 21-22, 28, 61, 63, 96, 109

Impromptu Group Theater, p. 3

Jackson, Don D., p. 109
Johoda, Marie, p. 63
Jennings, Helen Hall, p. 3, 17, 28, 55, 62, 63, 78
Johnson, David W., p. 107, 109

Katz, L., p. 63
Kerstetter, Leona, p. 126
Kogan, Nathan, p. 64

Lawlor, Gerald W., p. 126
Leavitt, Harold J., p. 38, 61, 63
Leman, Sharon, p. 17, 28, 63
Levy, Ronald B., p. 63
Lindzey, Gardner, p. 61, 63
Loomis, Charles, p. 17, 28, 63, 64

MacElveen-Hoehn, Penny, p. 28

Martin, Colin, preface
Mendelsson, Peter Dean, preface, p. 13, 62
Meyer, Henry J., p. 13
Moreno Institute, p. 4
Moreno, Florence Bridge, p. 4, 126
Moreno, Jacob Levy, p. 1-12, 18, 28, 35, 45, 51, 52, 61, 63, 64, 109, 126
    Biographical, p. 3-4
Moreno, Jonathan David, p. 4
Moreno, Nissom, p. 3
Moreno, Pauline Wolf, p. 3
Moreno, Regina, p. 4
Moreno, Zerka Toeman, p. 4, 13, 36, 50, 61, 126
Mouton, Jane Srygley, p. 60, 62
Mueller, Barbara, p. 28
Mueller, Ronald A.H., p. 38, 61, 63

Nath, Raghu, p. 63
Naugher, Jimmy B., p. 61, 64
New School of Social Research, p. 4
New York State Training School for Girls, at Hudson, NY, p. 3
New York University, p. 4
Nolte, John, preface
Northway, Mary, p. 10, 45, 48-49, 62, 64

Pepinsky, Harold, p. 17, 63
Powell, J.H., p. 63
Proctor, p. 64

Rubin, Vick, p. 23, 28

Sabelli, Hector, preface
Schiff, Herbert, p. 62-64
Schloss, Gilbert A., p. 109
Schurr, David, p. 126
Simmel, Georg, p. 64
Siroka, Ellen K., p. 109
Siroka, Robert W., p. 109
Smucker, Ogden, p. 62, 64
Sociometric Institute, p. 3
Speck, Ross, p. 18, 28

Tagiuri, Renato, p. 54, 64

Vander May, James, p. 18, 21-22, 28

Warner, G. Douglas, p. 98, 99, 109
Watzlawick, Paul, p. 109
White, William Alanson, p. 3
Whiteley, Marko, p. 18, 26, 28
Wigdor, Blossom T., p. 62, 64
Wilmot, William W., p. 101, 109
Wolff, Kurt H., p. 64
Wysong, William J., p. 13

Yablonsky, Lewis, p. 126

Zeleny, Leslie D., p. 61

SUBJECT INDEX

Acquaintance diagram, p. 157
Acquaintance volume, p. 18, 157
Act hunger, p. 5, 6, 58, 70, 145, 149-150, 153-155
Acting out technique, p. 3, 132
Action sociometry, p. 31, 143-151
Ambiequal, p. 157
Ambivalent response, p. 35-36, 122
Aristo-tele, p. 55, 157
"As if", p. 5
Assignment therapy, p. 56-60, 149
Attraction, p. 11, 17, 22
Audio-video equipment, p. 125
Auxiliary ego, p. 12, 89, 107, 123, 124, 145
    role choice, p. 146
Auxiliary world, p. 12
Axiodrama, p. 3, 5, 133, 157

Behavior training, p. 106

Canon of Creativity, p. 2, 4, 5, 6, 7, 12
Catharsis, p. 3, 5, 107, 134
    action, p. 3
    group, p. 3
    social, p. 3
Central concern, p. 70
Chain configuration, p. 50-51, 57, 147, 157
Chance, p. 48, 145, 157
Change, p. 11, 56, 72, 87, 124
Children, p. 3
Choice-making, p. 11, 17, 32, 35, 52-55, 71-72, 78, 145, 149
    centrifugal, p. 157
    centripetal, p. 157
    overchoosers, p. 157
    perception, p. 36-38
    reasons for, p. 22, 32, 35-37, 71
    record-keeping, p. 78
    revealing, p. 38, 78
    underchoosers, p. 52
    unconscious, p. 149
Classoid, p. 157
Cleavage, p. 55, 157
Clinical sociometry, p. 157
Clique, p. 50
Clustering effect, p. 157
Cohesion, p. 11, 54, 55, 99
Communication, p. 95-97, 103, 105, 127
Communication facilitation, p. 103
Community building, p. 5, 17, 126
Concretization, p. 7, 134
Conflict de-escalation, p. 104
Conflict resolution, p. 33, 51, 100-108
    facilitator role diagram, p. 101-104
        analyzer function, p. 101-102
        communicator function, p. 101, 103
        conflict manager function, p. 101, 104
    facilitator training model, p. 93, 101, 105-108
        role of trainer, p. 107
Conflict warm-up, p. 100
    facilitator training model, p. 93, 101, 105-108
Connectedness, p. 17, 18, 71, 93, 106, 147
Contracting, p. 106
Cooperation, p. 106
Creative neutrality, p. 5, 12, 36, 157
Creative revolution, p. 4
Creativity, p. 1, 3, 4, 6, 7, 157
Criterion, p. 17, 33, 56, 70, 157
    actual, p. 34
    diagnostic, p. 34
    examples of, p. 73-74

hypothetical, p. 34, 59
one-way, p. 34
personal, p. 34
recognition, p. 145-146
selection, p. 33, 58, 71, 145
social, p. 34
two-way, p. 34
wording, p. 34-35, 145-146, 153-154
Cultural atom, p. 17, 158
Cultural conserve, p. 1, 4, 6, 7, 11, 158

Daimon, p. 3
Depersonalization, p. 11
De-roling, p. 24
Double, p. 94, 105, 106, 107, 132
Dramatic methods, p. 12
    approximation, p. 94
    soliloquy, p. 150
    "stop action", p. 57, 108, 150
    ventilation, p. 105-107
Dream drama, p. 133
Drum warm-up, p. 98

Ego, p. 7, 8, 54, 126, 150
Emotional expansiveness, p. 52, 78, 158
Empathy, p. 5, 11-12, 70, 96, 103, 158
Encounter, p. 5, 91-109, 124, 132, 145, 158
    facilitation, p. 101-108, 132
        role diagram, analyzer function, p. 102
        role diagram, communicator function, p. 103
        role diagram, manager function, p. 104
    warm-up to, p. 95-96
    warm-ups, p. 97-100
Energy, p. 6
External reality, p. 8-9, 158

Facilitator role, p. 101-108
Fairy tale, p. 3
Family social atom, p. 18, 24
Fantasy methods, p. 18, 24, 59
Fear of failure, p. 122
Fear of rejection, p. 122
Feedback, p. 28, 54, 59, 72, 101
"feeders to leaders", p. 55
Future projection, p. 69, 124

God, p. 4
Group cohesion, p. 99
Group dynamics, p. 9, 10, 45, 70
    sociometric configuration, p. 51
Group member role diagram, p. 137
Group Metaphor, p. 56-57
Group norms, p. 54, 155
Group psychotherapy, p. 3, 5, 12
Group role repertoire, p. 89
Group sculpture, p. 56
Group structure, p. 34, 39, 70, 71
    sub-group, p. 45, 70
Group therapy, p. 3
Groups, p. 55
    psychegroups, p. 55
    sociogroups, p. 55
    stages, p. 70

Here and now, p. 3, 5, 6, 21, 22, 23, 38, 72, 124, 125
Hypnodrama, p. 133

Improvise, p. 7, 56
Incongruity, p. 5, 38, 41-44, 53-54, 158
    perceived, p. 44
Indifferent response, p. 5, 17, 22, 35-36, 158
Infra-tele, p. 158
Inhibitors, p. 150
Intergroup conflict, p. 51
Interpersonal conflict, p. 51
Interpersonal Relations, Theory of, p. 4, 5, 11-12, 97
Isolate, p. 11, 33, 50, 58

Leadership, p. 55, 143-151, 155
Learning, p. 7, 151
Leisure role cluster, p. 85-86
"Life boat" exercise, p. 59
Linkages, p. 17, 50, 147, 158
Listening, p. 94-95, 96, 103
Living Newspaper, p. 133
Locogram, p. 158

Magic Shop, p. 133
Matrix of all identity, p. 158
Matrix of all reality, p. 158
Metacommunication, p. 96
Mutuality, p. 5, 11, 38, 41-44, 53-54, 71, 149, 158
    perceived, p. 44
Mirror, p. 94, 95, 123, 124, 132

Near sociometry, p. 34, 59
Nearness to distance factor, p. 17-18, 23, 35-36
Negative expansiveness, p. 41, 52
Negative response, p. 5, 35-36, 38, 53, 72, 158
Neutrality, p. 17, 32, 35-36, 38, 52-53, 104, 106, 108, 158
    creative, p. 5, 12, 36
Notational systems, p. 19, 26, 47, 122
    role diagram, p. 129
    sociogram, p. 47
    streetlight, p. 19, 26

Omnitele, p. 158

Pairing, p. 56-58, 148-149
Parental injunction, p. 105, 155
Perception, p. 22, 52-54, 122, 145, 158
    accuracy of, p. 22
    test, p. 158
Perceptual social atom sociogram, p. 21-22
Perceptual sociometry, p. 37-38
Personality, p. 113, 124, 126
Pivotal position, p. 45, 50, 158
Play, p. 6, 12
Playback theater, p. 133
Positive expansiveness, p. 41, 52
Positive response, p. 5, 35-36, 41, 72, 158
Projection, p. 11, 12, 37, 70, 107
Propinquity, p. 55
Proximity, p. 93, 145
Psychegroup, p. 15, 55
Psychetelic choice, p. 36, 158
    leisure exploration, p. 85
Pyschiatric revolution, p. 4
Psychodrama, p. 5, 95, 101, 105, 107, 123, 132, 145, 158
Psychodramatist, p. 4
    Role diagram, p. 130-136
Psychotherapy, individual, p. 5

Quasi-sociometry, p. 34, 59

Reciprocity, p. 11, 53-54, 96
Reflective listening, p. 95-96, 98
Rejection, p. 22, 70, 122
Religion, p. 3, 4, 7
    eastern, p. 7
Repulsion, p. 11, 17, 22
Research, p. 56, 60
Resistance, p. 5, 7, 33, 56, 105
Risk taking, p. 52, 70, 95
Robot, p. 3
Role, p. 5, 7, 113, 159
    access to, p. 8, 11, 54, 59, 135, 147-149, 154, 155
    active, p. 127-128
    ascendence, p. 5, 8, 113, 159
    complementarity, p. 119
    conserve, p. 7, 123, 124
    construction, p. 113, 114
    descendence, p. 5, 8, 113, 159
    emergence, p. 7
    enactment, p. 5, 8, 87, 113, 159
    expectation, p. 5, 8, 87, 113, 115, 123, 159
    high value, p. 7, 58, 149, 153-154
    low value, p. 8
    masked, p. 123
    once active, p. 127-128
    overdeveloped, p. 8
    perception, p. 5, 8, 87, 113, 115-121, 123
    psychetelic, p. 34, 158
    psychodramatic, p. 5, 8, 127-128
    psychosomatic, p. 127-128
    repertoire, p. 7, 34, 51, 87, 118, 159
    relationship, p. 113
    socio/cultural, p. 5, 8, 127-128
    sociotelic, p. 34
    somatic, p. 5, 8
    taking, p. 8, 93
Role cluster, p. 159
Role creating, p. 8, 114, 159
Role death, p. 113, 114
Role diagram, p. 9-10, 111-132, 159
    ancestral, p. 123
    bilateral, p. 101, 119, 142, 157
    construction, p. 127
    data sheet, p. 113, 128
    emergence, p. 126
    example (psychodrama director), p. 130-136
    expanded, p. 113, 118, 121, 158
        example, p. 121
    extramural roles, p. 118, 121, 158
    fantasy, p. 113, 127-128
    format selection, p. 114
    future projected, p. 113, 127-128
    group member diagram, p. 137
    ideal, p. 113, 127-128
    interpersonal, p. 10, 113, 115-118, 139-140
    intrapersonal, p. 115, 117
    interpretation, p. 127
    multilateral, p. 120, 141
    notation, p. 129
Role model, p. 124, 159
Role name, p. 113, 122, 127
Role playing, p. 3, 5, 8, 133, 159
Role rehearsal, p. 106, 125
Role relief, p. 149-150
Role Reversal, p. 5, 11-12, 93-95, 98, 106, 122, 123, 132, 150
    Double-bonding, p. 94-95, 105-106
Role taking, p. 8
Role testing, p. 5, 124, 125
Role Theory, p. 4, 5, 7-8, 12
    of personality, p. 113, 124
Role training, p. 5, 59, 124, 125, 159

Science of Action, theory of, p. 4, 5, 7, 12, 113

Scientific method, p. 4
See me warm-up, p. 98
Self-disclosure, p. 123
Self-evaluation, p. 101
Self-rating, p. 159
Sharing, p. 67, 123, 134
Similarities and Differences warm-up, p. 99
Social atom, p. 5, 9-10, 16-28, 159
    collective, p. 10, 17
    in action, p. 25
    individual, p. 10, 17
    Morenean, p. 20
    psychological, p. 10, 17, 158
    repair, p. 135
    target, p. 27
Social expansiveness, p. 52
Social investigator, p. 135
Social network, p. 7, 9, 17, 135, 159
    map, p. 9-10, 16
Social reality, p. 8-9
Social revolution, p. 143
Social threshold, p. 159
Sociatry, p. 159
Socio-atomic theory, p. 8, 35
Sociodrama, p. 3, 5, 126, 133
Sociodynamic effect, p. 11, 147-149, 159
Sociogenetic law, p. 11, 50, 159
Sociograms, p. 3, 19, 21-22, 23, 39, 71, 145, 153, 159
    action, p. 5, 56, 89
    construction, p. 45-47
    notational system, p. 47
    perceptual, p. 46, 71
    target, p. 9-10, 25, 48-49, 120
Sociogroup, p. 17, 55, 160
Socioid, p. 160
Sociomatrix, p. 8-9, 39-45, 78, 160
    perceptual, p. 44
    examples of, p. 78
Sociomatrix reader, p. 42-43
Sociometric assignment, p. 56-60
Sociometric configurations, p. 51
Sociometric consciousness, p. 35, 44, 123, 145
Sociometric data
    reliability, p. 56, 60
    revealing, p. 35
Sociometric measurement, p. 71
Sociometric set, p. 78-84
Sociometric star, p. 45, 50, 52-53, 153
    psychetelic, p. 50
    sociotelic, p. 50
    star of acceptance, p. 50
    star of incongruity, p. 50
    star of rejection, p. 50
Sociometric status, p. 54
Sociometric test, p. 5, 9, 17, 30-89, 147, 160
    warm-up phase, p. 31-33, 65
    action phase, p. 31, 33-38, 66
    sharing phase, p. 31, 38, 67
    analysis phase, p. 31, 39-56, 68
    future projection/intervention phase, p. 31, 56-60, 69
    data sheets, p. 75-76
Sociometric theory, p. 4-12
Sociometric wealth, p. 11, 51, 57, 147-149, 150
Sociometrist, p. 31, 96, 113, 123, 135
    warm-up, p. 31-32
Sociometry, p. 3, 10-12
    action, p. 31, 143-151
    action orientation, p. 51
    co-researcher, p. 11, 32, 44, 56, 143
    impact on group, p. 38
    perceptual, p. 54
    revealing data, p. 35
Sociometry and the Science of Society, theory of, p. 4, 5, 8-12
Socionomy, p. 160
Sociostasis, p. 11, 17, 18, 21, 23, 54, 122, 135, 160
Sociotelic choice, p. 36, 160

Spontaneity, p. 1, 3, 4, 6, 8, 93, 108, 123, 124, 134, 136, 149-150, 160
    pathological, p. 6
    stereotyped, p. 6
    test, p. 4
    training, p. 5
    true, p. 6
Spontaneity starters, p. 150
Spontaneity Theory of Child Development, p. 8
Staff role exploration, p. 87
das Stegreiftheater, p. 18, 26
Sub-groups, p. 39, 45, 50, 52, 147
Surplus reality, p. 5, 132, 160

Target sociogram, p. 48-49, 120
Tele, p. 5, 11-12, 32, 36, 55, 70, 160
    aristo-tele, p. 55
Tell me something warm-up, p. 99
Termination, p. 70
Theometry, p. 160
Therapeutic assistants, p. 107
Tough-Tight-Tender warm-up, p. 99
Training, p. 3, 93, 95, 105-108
Transference, p. 5, 11, 36, 70, 105, 160

Universalia, p. 160
Unexamined response, p. 35, 160

Valentine warm-up, p. 98
Ventilation methods, p. 105-107
Videotape, p. 106

Warming-up process, p. 1, 3, 5, 132, 160
    for group inclusion, p. 147
    to encounter, p. 95-100
    to role diagram, p. 122
    to sociometric test, p. 31-33
Withholds warm-up, p. 98
Weighting, p. 41-42, 57-58
Words of the Father, p. 3, 111

Zen, p. 7

Sociometric Forms and Written Exercises

These pages are perforated along inside margin to allow for ease in detaching them. The following pages are duplicates of forms and exercises contained in the body of the text. Permission is given to duplicate these exercises for educational purposes.

ANN E. HALE

Moreno's Social Atom	167
Psychological Social Atom	168
Social Atom Collective	169
Perceptual Social Atom Sociogram	170
Target for Social Atom	171
Target for Social Atom	172
Ranking Criteria of Choice	173
Ranking Criteria of Choice (continued)	174
Objective Data Sheet for Sociometric Test	175
Perceptual Data Sheet for Sociometric Test	176
Objective Data Sheet for Sociometric Test	177
Perceptual Data Sheet for Sociometric Test	178
Objective Data Sheet for Sociometric Test	179
Perceptual Data Sheet for Sociometric Test	180
Sociomatrix	181
Sociomatrix	182
Sociomatrix	183
Sociometric Choice for Central Roles	184
Conflict Warm-up	185
Role Diagram Data Sheet	186
Interpersonal Role Diagram	187
Interpersonal Role Diagram (Perceptual Aspect)	188
Multilateral Role Diagram	189
Bilateral Role Diagram	190
Group Member Role Diagram	191
Exploring Your Act Hunger	192
Group Exploration of Act Hunger	193
Group Exploration of Act Hunger (continued)	194
Auxiliary Ego Role Choice	195
Auxiliary Ego Role Choice	196

MORENO'S SOCIAL ATOM*
Nucleus of Persons Emotionally Related to You

*For additional information see J.L. Moreno, *Sociometry, Experimental Method and the Science of Society*. Beacon, N.Y.: Beacon House, 1951, pp. 57-69.

This exercise is designed to help you identify (1) those people to whom you feel emotionally related, (2) those with whom you wish to have a relationship, and (3) those persons who are acquaintances.

INSTRUCTIONS:

First   Make a list of the persons you know and indicate in the margin the number 1, 2, or 3 depending on whether they fit the category as described above.

Second   Using the symbols of circles for females ◯ and triangles for males △ place yourself in the inner nucleus and position those persons to whom you feel emotionally related within the inner circle, using nearness or distance to indicate their significance to you. Continue with category (2) placing persons in the middle circle, and (3) the outer circle.

Third   Be aware of what you experience as you proceed. Discuss the meaning this exploration has had for you with another person, or share it with the group.

PSYCHOLOGICAL SOCIAL ATOM

The smallest number of people required by you in order to feel a social equilibrium (sociostasis) is called psychological social atom.* When someone who has become central to your life is missing (temporarily or permanently) the energy that would normally be given to creative, productive endeavors becomes channeled into coping with the loss, managing the feelings evoked and searching for another person who can fit a similar place in your life. Becoming familiar with your psychological social atom and studying the dynamics of maintaining these connections can help you understand the moods and changes that occur in your life and suggest ways to handle them.

The following questions, taken from an article on intimacy by Vick Rubin,** are offered here as a means for focusing you on those persons who are central to you. In the space following each question, note the names of persons who come to mind.

1. I feel that I can confide in _____ about virtually everything.

2. I would do almost anything for _____ .

3. If I could never be with _____ , I would feel miserable.

4. If I were lonely, my first thought would be to seek _____ out.

5. One of my primary concerns is _____ 's welfare.

6. I would forgive _____ for practically anything.

7. I feel responsible for _____ 's well being.

8. I would greatly enjoy being confided in by _____ .

9. It would be hard for me to get along without _____ .

Review the names of persons listed above. Are there other people in your life who feel central to you? **Make a list** of those persons whom you perceive to comprise the smallest number of people who you need in your life to feel a social equilibrium.

Next take a sheet of paper and place your name in a circle on the page. Using circles for females ◯ and triangles for males △ place each person on the page in proximity to you according to how close or distant you feel you are **here and now.** If you feel that you are becoming closer to each other draw an arrow towards you; and, if you are feeling an increasing distance between you and the other person, draw an arrow indicating moving further away.

As you diagram your psychological social atom, note the feelings that arise. Discuss what you are experiencing with another person or share your feelings with the group.

If it seems important to diagram the feelings which exist **here and now** between you and the persons who comprise your psychological social atom, follow the directions for the Perceptual Social Atom Sociogram.

---

*Hollander, Carl E., and Sharon Hollander, *Action Relationships in Learning* Denver, Colorado, Snow Lion Press, 1978.

**Rubin, Vick, "Lovers and Other Strangers: The Development of Intimacy in Encounter and Relationships," *American Scientist*, Vol. 62, pp. 182-190.

SOCIAL ATOM COLLECTIVES EXPLORATION*

This exploration will bring into focus the collectives which are significant to you and the interconnectedness of those collectives. Because each collective implies a role repertoire, shifts and changes in your choices for these groups affect your interactions with others and how you identify yourself.

1. Make a list of the groups that are significant to you. Be sure to include significant groups even if you are no longer active in them, or groups to which you have wanted to belong.

2. Take a sheet of paper and place yourself in a circle on the page. Giving each group, or collective a name, draw circles on the page for each group, using the size of the circle to indicate its importance to you relative to the other groups. Draw lines from you to each group using the notational system given below.

3. If possible to do so in the space allowed, list the individuals in each group who are significant to you. Number them in the order of their importance to you **here and now.** Remember, importance and significance to you does not always mean that you feel positive or attracted to that person. Your feeling for the person(s) can be explored using the Perceptual Social Atom Sociogram.

4. Identify for yourself those persons who appear in more than one collective or group.

5. Identify the reason for each group's significance to you. Evaluate which groups you could do without. Of these groups, which have to be existent in order for you to feel social equilibrium or sociostasis.

6. Examine missing groups, the wished for group or the group that is inactive. How do you manage without these groups, and what plans have you for the future?

7. Discuss this exploration with another person or share what you have experienced with the group.

NOTATIONAL SYSTEM

a. Attraction _____

b. Rejection _ _ _ _

c. Indifference . . . .

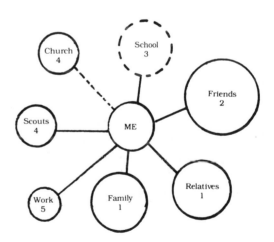

---

*This exercise is an edited version of an exercise by James Vander May: "A Perceptual Social Atom Sociogram", **Group Psychotherapy and Psychodrama,** Vol. 28 (1975), p. 129-132. Edited by Ann E. Hale, M.A.

PERCEPTUAL SOCIAL ATOM SOCIOGRAM*

The following exercise is designed to focus the feelings of attraction, repulsion, or indifference which exist between you and others by first identifying your feelings for others and, secondly, making perceptual guesses about the feelings others may have for you.

1. Identify a collective (or group) you wish to explore.

2. Make a list of names of the members of this group. If it is a large group, list the names of persons with whom you have a significant relationship, including strained relationships or persons who are deceased or who have left the group.

3. Rank each person in the collective according to their significance to you. Place a number next to each person's name. Several persons may have the same degree of significance.

4. Take a sheet of paper and place yourself in a circle at the center of the sheet. Using circles for females ◯ and triangles for males △ place each person on the sheet according to where you perceive them to be in relation to you. (This does not mean where you want them to be, or where they may want to be, but your best guess of where they stand in relation to you.) Place the ranking number to the right of their name.

5. Using the following notational system to indicate the feeling you have for each person *here and now,* draw a line using the code half-way between your circle and the symbol for the other person. Do this for each person in the collective.

6. Now make a perceptual guess about how each person in the collective may feel toward you *here and now.* In order to maximize the perceptual accuracy of the sociogram, it is necessary for you to role reverse with each person. Using the code, draw a line from each person to meet the line drawn half-way from your place on the sociogram.

7. Review the relationship you have with each person and identify what the reasons are for your feelings for each person and for their feelings for you.

8. If you are unsure or disturbed about the information which appears, find a way to check your perceptions with the persons involved. Discuss your feelings and reaction with another person or with the group.

NOTATIONAL SYSTEM:

a. Mutual attraction ————————————
b. Mutual rejection — — — — — — — — —
c. Mutual indifference ·
e. Attraction - Indifference ——————— · · · · · ·
f. Rejection - Indifference — — — — — · · · · ·

Female ◯   Male △   Missing Person ◌ △

SOCIOGRAM EXAMPLE:

---

*This exercise is an edited version of an exercise by James Vander May: "A Perceptual Social Atom Sociogram," **Group Psychotherapy and Psychodrama,** Vol. 28 (1975), p. 128-134. Edited by Ann E. Hale, M.A.

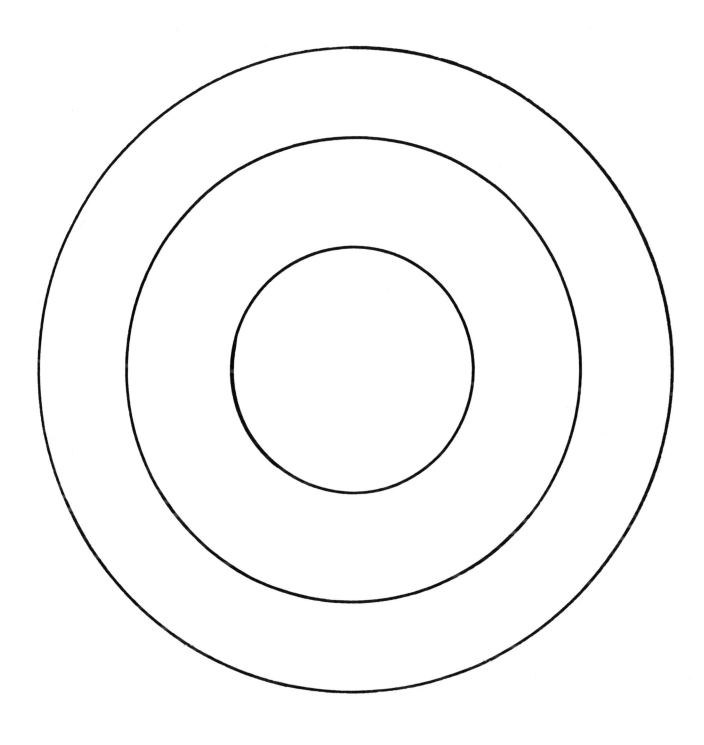

Name _____ Date _____

Criterion: _____

TARGET FOR USE IN SOCIAL ATOM EXPLORATIONS

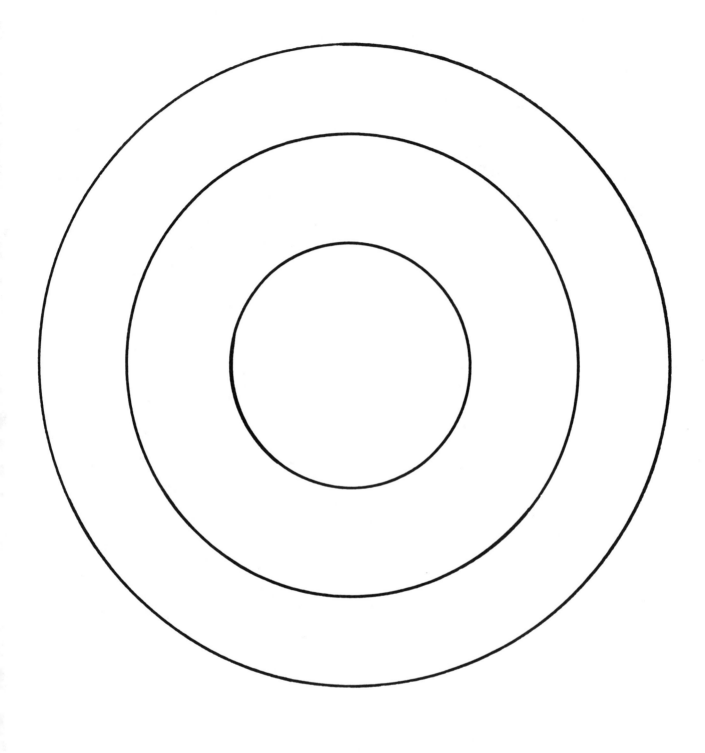

Name _____ Date _____

Criterion: _____

TARGET FOR USE IN SOCIAL ATOM EXPLORATIONS

RANKING CRITERIA OF CHOICE BY RELEVANCE, THREAT & TYPE

In the columns indicated below rank the following criteria using the scale as itemized.

THREAT

1 = No threat
2 = Mildly threatening
3 = Threatening
4 = Very threatening
5 = Overwhelmingly
    threatening

RELEVANCE

1 = No relevance
2 = Some relevance
3 = Very relevant

TYPE

P = Psychetelic
S = Sociotelic

DECISION

1 = I would urge others
    to use it as well.
2 = I would use it.
3 = I'm neutral about
    using it.
4 = I could be persuaded
    to use it.
5 = I won't use it.

THREAT	RELEVANCE	TYPE	DECISION	CRITERIA
				Whom do I choose to hold me when I need to cry?
				Whom do I choose to be a confrontive double in my psychodrama?
				Whom would I allow to practice psychodrama directing on me?
				Whom would I choose to tell about a distressing sexual incident?
				Whom do I choose to advise me about a current decision?
				With whom do I choose to take a nap?
				With whom do I choose to share a room?
				Whom do I choose to wrestle?
				Whom do I choose to spend leisure time with?
				From who do I choose to borrow notes?
				Whom do I choose to have over to my house after class (after session)?
				Of the people who are a risk for me to encounter about my angry feelings toward them, whom do I choose to encounter?
				Of the people who are a risk for me to let them know I am sexually attracted to them, whom do I choose to spend a hour with being open and direct?
				Whom do I choose to have as my partner for analyzing the data from this sociometric test?
				With whom do I choose to share the impact this sociometric test has had on me?
				Whom do I choose to tell about my first impressions of the other group members?
				With whom do I choose to draw sociograms?
				Whom do I choose to advise me about my physical appearance?
				Whom do I choose to have on my volleyball team?
				Whom do I choose to lead the group in a guided fantasy?
				Whom do I choose to lend my car to?
				Whom in the group do I choose to ask for a loan of money (over $20, less than $50)?
				Whom do I choose to dance with, to slow music, when the lights are down?
				With whom do I choose to share a weakness?
				Of the people in the group whom it would be a risk for me to have them hold me, whom do I choose to hold me for five minutes in order for me to check my perceptions?
				With whom do I choose to design a sociometric exploration for use in my work setting?
				With whom do I choose to share a massage?

THREAT	RELEVANCE	TYPE	DECISION	CRITERIA
				To whom would I go for comfort if I find myself distressed in the middle of the night?
				Whom do I choose to support me if I should be encountered in this group?
				Whom do I choose to sit across from in group sessions?
				Whom do I choose to spend an hour with exchanging feedback?
				Of the people in the group whom I know least well, whom do I choose to spend time with on the break?
				Whom do I choose to have as members of my support group?
				OTHER:

OBJECTIVE DATA SHEET
FOR
THE SOCIOMETRIC TEST

Name _____ Date _____

1. Whom in the group do I choose to _____
   List in the order of preference.
   NAME   REASON FOR THIS CHOICE

2. Whom in the group do I choose not to _____
   List in the order of least preference.

   NAME   REASON FOR THIS CHOICE

3. Whom in the group do I choose to remain neutral toward on the basis of this criterion. It is not necessary to list in any particular order.

PERCEPTUAL DATA SHEET
FOR
THE SOCIOMETRIC TEST

Name: _____   Date: _____

Criterion: _____

A. 1. Whom in the group do I perceive will choose me?

    NAME   REASON FOR THIS PERCEPTION

  2. Whom in the group do I perceive will place me in the "choose not to" category?

    NAME   REASON FOR THIS PERCEPTION

  3. Whom in the group do I perceive will choose to remain neutral toward me on the basis of this criterion?

    NAME   REASON FOR THIS PERCEPTION

B. I have chosen to make perceptual guesses about the choices of _____ .

    HE/SHE CHOSE: HE/SHE DID NOT CHOOSE: HE/SHE WAS NEUTRAL TOWARD:

OBJECTIVE DATA SHEET
FOR
THE SOCIOMETRIC TEST

Name _____   Date _____

1. Whom in the group do I choose to _____
   List in the order of preference.
   NAME   REASON FOR THIS CHOICE

2. Whom in the group do I choose not to _____
   List in the order of least preference.

   NAME   REASON FOR THIS CHOICE

3. Whom in the group do I choose to remain neutral toward on the basis of this criterion. It is not necessary to list
   in any particular order.

PERCEPTUAL DATA SHEET
FOR
THE SOCIOMETRIC TEST

Name: _____   Date: _____

Criterion: _____

A. 1. Whom in the group do I perceive will choose me?

     NAME   REASON FOR THIS PERCEPTION

   2. Whom in the group do I perceive will place me in the "choose not to" category?

     NAME   REASON FOR THIS PERCEPTION

   3. Whom in the group do I perceive will choose to remain neutral toward me on the basis of this criterion?

     NAME   REASON FOR THIS PERCEPTION

B. I have chosen to make perceptual guesses about the choices of _____ .

     HE/SHE CHOSE: HE/SHE DID NOT CHOOSE: HE/SHE WAS NEUTRAL TOWARD:

OBJECTIVE DATA SHEET
FOR
THE SOCIOMETRIC TEST

Name _____   Date _____

1. Whom in the group do I choose to _____
   List in the order of preference.
   NAME   REASON FOR THIS CHOICE

2. Whom in the group do I choose not to _____
   List in the order of least preference.

   NAME   REASON FOR THIS CHOICE

3. Whom in the group do I choose to remain neutral toward on the basis of this criterion. It is not necessary to list
   in any particular order.

PERCEPTUAL DATA SHEET
FOR
THE SOCIOMETRIC TEST

Name: _____   Date: _____

Criterion: _____

A. 1. Whom in the group do I perceive will choose me?

NAME   REASON FOR THIS PERCEPTION

2. Whom in the group do I perceive will place me in the "choose not to" category?

NAME   REASON FOR THIS PERCEPTION

3. Whom in the group do I perceive will choose to remain neutral toward me on the basis of this criterion?

NAME   REASON FOR THIS PERCEPTION

B. I have chosen to make perceptual guesses about the choices of _____ .

HE/SHE CHOSE: HE/SHE DID NOT CHOOSE: HE/SHE WAS NEUTRAL TOWARD:

SOCIOMATRIX

CRITERION   DATE:

NAMES	1	2	3	4	5	6	7	8	9	10	11	12	13	14	15	16	17	18	19	20	Positive Choices Made	Negative Choices Made	Neutral Choices Made
1																							
2																							
3																							
4																							
5																							
6																							
7																							
8																							
9																							
10																							
11																							
12																							
13																							
14																							
15																							
16																							
17																							
18																							
19																							
20																							
Positive Choices Rec'd.																							
Negative Choices Rec'd.																							
Neutral Choices Rec'd.																							
Positive Mutuals																							
Negative Mutuals																							
Neutral Mutuals																							
Pos./Neg. Incongruity																							
Pos./Neut. Incongruity																							
Neg./Neut. Incongruity																							
WEIGHTING																							

SOCIOMATRIX

CRITERION   DATE:

NAMES	1	2	3	4	5	6	7	8	9	10	11	12	13	14	15	16	17	18	19	20	Positive Choices Made	Negative Choices Made	Neutral Choices Made
1																							
2																							
3																							
4																							
5																							
6																							
7																							
8																							
9																							
10																							
11																							
12																							
13																							
14																							
15																							
16																							
17																							
18																							
19																							
20																							
Positive Choices Rec'd.																							
Negative Choices Rec'd.																							
Neutral Choices Rec'd.																							
Positive Mutuals																							
Negative Mutuals																							
Neutral Mutuals																							
Pos./Neg. Incongruity																							
Pos./Neut. Incongruity																							
Neg./Neut. Incongruity																							
WEIGHTING																							

SOCIOMATRIX

CRITERION   DATE:

NAMES	1	2	3	4	5	6	7	8	9	10	11	12	13	14	15	16	17	18	19	20	Positive Choices Made	Negative Choices Made	Neutral Choices Made
1																							
2																							
3																							
4																							
5																							
6																							
7																							
8																							
9																							
10																							
11																							
12																							
13																							
14																							
15																							
16																							
17																							
18																							
19																							
20																							
Positive Choices Rec'd.																							
Negative Choices Rec'd.																							
Neutral Choices Rec'd.																							
Positive Mutuals																							
Negative Mutuals																							
Neutral Mutuals																							
Pos./Neg. Incongruity																							
Pos./Neut. Incongruity																							
Neg./Neut. Incongruity																							
WEIGHTING																							

SOCIOMETRIC CHOICE FOR CENTRAL ROLES

Name: _____   Date: _____

This exploration focuses the group on whom is likely to be highly chosen for specific key auxiliary ego roles, and on the basis of this, who may be carrying the heaviest load of projection for a particular role. It is suggested that the group form action sociograms as a way to share the information with the group. Allow time for group members to tell the persons they have chosen the reason for the choice. Allow at least one and a half hours.

1. Whom in the group would I choose to play the role of my Mother as she used to be? List in the order of preference.

   NAME   REASON FOR THIS CHOICE

2. Whom in the group would I choose to play the role of my Father as he used to be? List in the order of preference.

   NAME   REASON FOR THIS CHOICE

3. Whom in the group is most like me? What role would I choose them to play in relation to me?
   NAME   ROLE   REASON FOR THIS CHOICE

4. Whom in the group is least like me? What role would I choose them to play in relation to me?
   NAME   ROLE   REASON FOR THIS CHOICE

5. Excluding my Mother and Father, the person with whom I have the most unfinished business, who is not a member of this group, is: _____
   Whom in the group would I choose to play the role in a psychodrama session?
   NAME   REASON FOR THIS CHOICE

6. Identify other central roles and continue making choices in action.

CONFLICT WARMUP, a paper and pencil exercise

1. Conflicts can be with people whom:
   a. we like a lot:

   (Whom?) _____ (About) _____

   b. we dislike a lot:

   (Whom?) _____ (About) _____

   c. we are neutral toward:

   (Whom?) _____ (About) _____

   Think of a conflict you have with someone who fits each category.

2. Conflicts can be over:

   small issues   to   big issues

   Think of a conflict going on in this group which is over a:

   a. small issue: _____

   b. big issue: _____

3. If you were in conflict in this group would it be with persons having:

   a. _____ Less power,   _____ Same power   _____ More power
              Influence

   b. _____ Less skill   _____ Same skill   _____ More skill

   c. _____ Less self esteem _____ Same self esteem   _____ More self esteem

4. Some conflicts seem unresolved and leave a person feeling as if the solution to it has been postponed. Can you identify a time when that has happened in this group?

5. Some conflicts seem best avoided as there appears to be little likelihood of resolution. Identify a conflict which feels this way to you.

6. In your opinion what does this group need to do in order to handle the conflicts that arise?

7. List the names of the members of this group and identify the resources you believe they have for dealing with conflict.

   NAME   **THEIR RESOURCES**

This warmup is based upon the theories of Morton Deutsch as conveyed in "A Theory of Cooperation and Competition," **Human Relations,** 2 (1949), pp. 120-151.

ROLE DIAGRAM DATA SHEET

NAME: _____ DATE: _____

1. The relationship I would like to explore is _____

2. The particular aspect of our relating to focus on is _____

3. I wish to include the following kinds of roles in this exploration:

    _____ a. Roles active now (A)   _____ e. Ideal roles (I)

    _____ b. Roles no longer active (OA)   _____ f. Psychosomatic roles (PS)

    _____ c. Future projected role (FP)   _____ g. Socio/cultural roles (SC)

    _____ d. Fantasy roles (F)   _____ h. Psychodramatic roles (PD)

4. The time I have chosen for this exploration is _____

   This time is important for the following reasons: _____

   _____

5. Listed here are those roles in which I interact with this person. Include the designation in parenthesis (optional).

   ROLES ACTIVE NOW (A)   ONCE ACTIVE ROLES (OA)   FUTURE PROJECTED ROLES (FP)

6. Listed here are significant roles I have outside of the relationship:

   ROLES ACTIVE NOW (A)   ONCE ACTIVE ROLES (OA)   FUTURE PROJECTED ROLES (FP)

7. Listed here are significant roles the other person has outside of the relationship:

   ROLES ACTIVE NOW (A)   ONCE ACTIVE ROLES (OA)   FUTURE PROJECTED ROLES (FP)

INTERPERSONAL ROLE DIAGRAM

How I feel about
myself in these
roles

How I feel about
my partner in these
roles in relation
to me

How I feel about
myself in these
roles

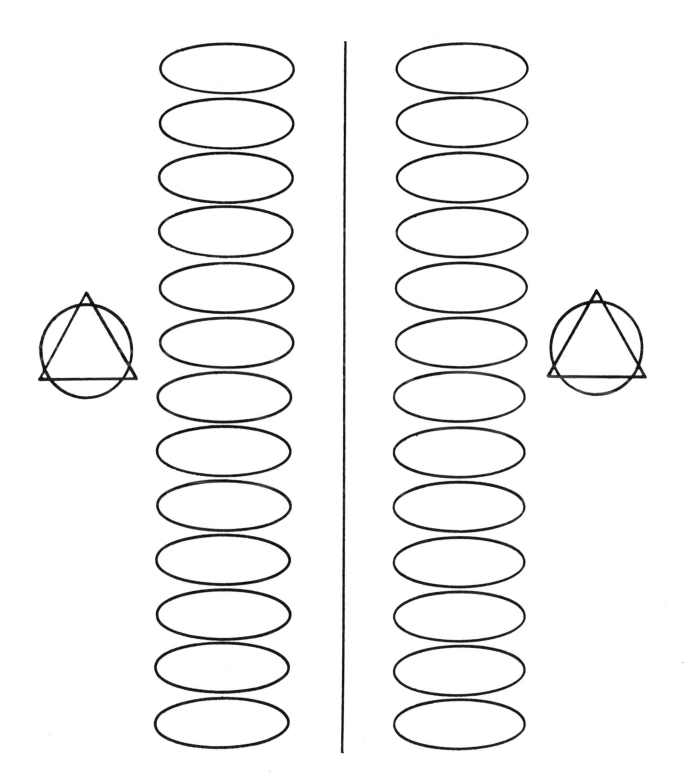

INTERPERSONAL ROLE DIAGRAM (PERCEPTUAL ASPECT)

How I feel about myself in these roles

How I feel about my partner in these roles in relation to me

How I perceive my partner feels about me in these roles in relation to him/her

How I perceive my partner feels about him/herself in these roles

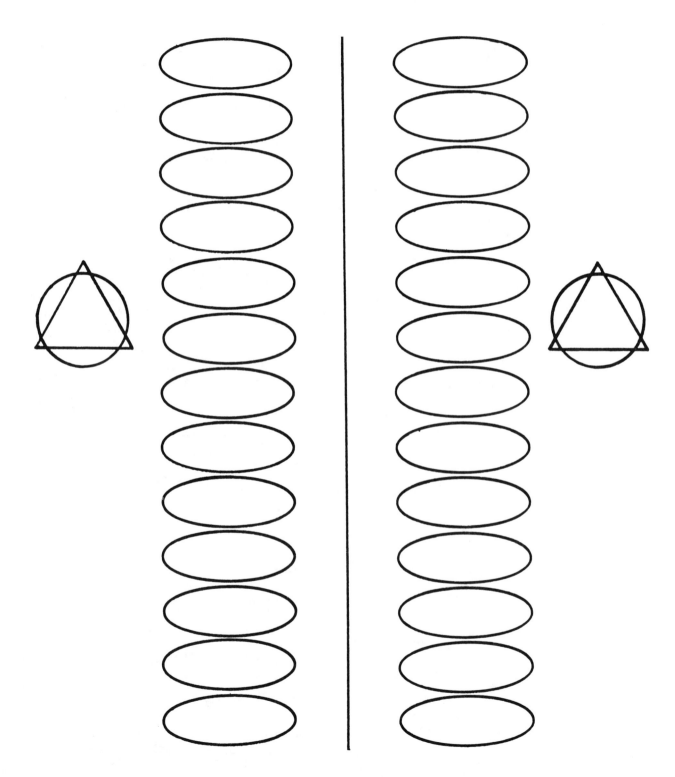

MULTILATERAL ROLE DIAGRAM:
THREE INTERACTORS, SAME ROLE CONSTRUCTION

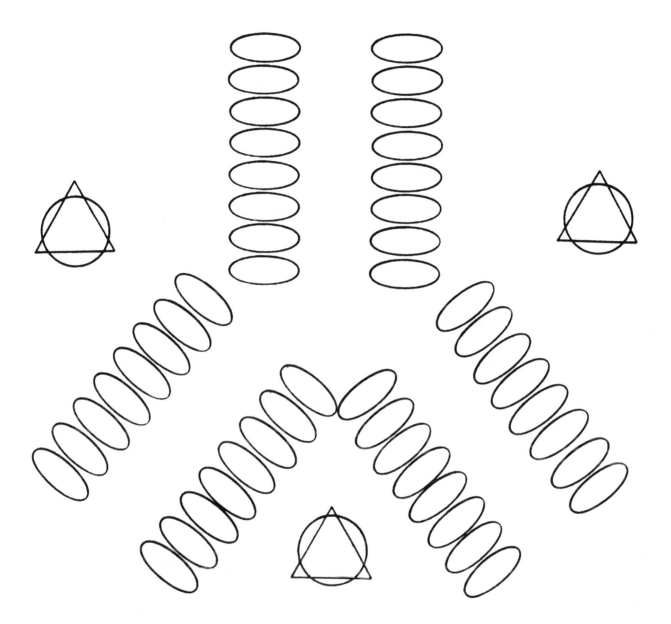

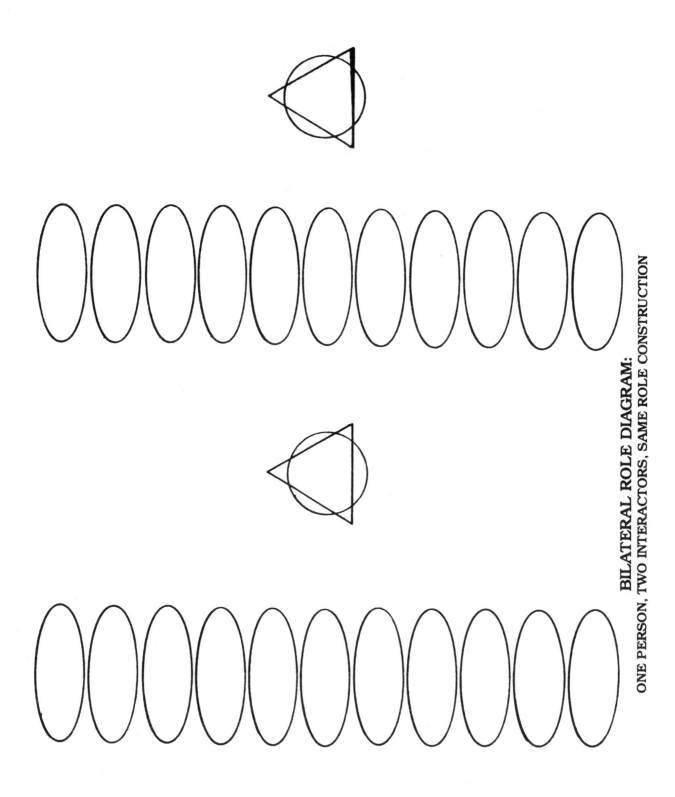

BILATERAL ROLE DIAGRAM:
ONE PERSON, TWO INTERACTORS, SAME ROLE CONSTRUCTION

GROUP MEMBER ROLE DIAGRAM

HOW I FEEL ABOUT
MYSELF AS A PERSON
WHO:

HOW _____
MAY FEEL ABOUT ME AS
A PERSON WHO:

Takes
Initiative

Expresses
Feelings
Openly

Responds
to Others

Refrains
from
Interrupting
Others

Remains
Present

Provides
Encouragement

Avoids the
Superficial

Facilitates
Others

Asks
Clearly

Establishes
Mutuality

Commands
Respect

Remains
Nonjudgemental

Contributes
Ideas

Is Supportive
During Conflicts

EXPLORING YOUR ACT HUNGER

This exercise is designed to increase your awareness of the factors which influence the accessibility of roles in this group. The information may be kept private, or the group may wish that group members share what they have written. Discuss this in the group and come to a decision.

  I. Identify roles which have been missing thus far in your stay here:

   ROLE

 II. Identify some persons in this group with whom you have wished to be involved in the following roles, and which has not yet occurred.

   PERSON   ROLE   REASON FOR INACTION

III. Review the above and then identify the following:

   A. What parental injunctions ("shoulds") have affected your involvement in this group?

   B. Identify group norms which have affected accessibility to roles and your involvement in this group.

   C. Identify leadership styles which have affected accessibility to roles and your involvement in in this group.

   D. What skills do you need to develop in order to facilitate yourself into roles of your choice?

GROUP EXPLORATION OF ACT HUNGER
FOR ROLES OF HIGH VALUE

This exercise is designed to increase awareness in group members of the criteria on which you and others wish to be most highly chosen. You are asked to make perceptual guesses about choices others are making for you in the here and now. The information will be shared with the group in action sociograms using the process described on the second page.

I. In the columns below identify three criteria on which you would like to be most highly chosen in this group. (That is, if this group did a sociometric exploration on the basis of this criterion, you would emerge as highly chosen, or "star.") Indicate your perceptual skills by guessing who else in this group would be chosen on this criterion.

CRITERION	REASON	WHO ELSE WOULD BE CHOSEN FOR THIS ROLE
1.		
2.		
3.		

II. Re-write the criteria you have listed in such a way as to limit the group's choices for others and effect you being the "most highly chosen." Avoid constructions such as: "Of the women in the group wearing a pink sweater, whom would you choose to confide in about a problem?" Prefer something along this line: "Of the persons in this group who have not been visible in the director role, whom do you choose to direct you in a scene setting exercise?"

1.

2.

3.

III. Action portion of the exploration of act hunger for roles of high value:

Group members will be able to check out their perceptions and share with the group those roles which have high value for them, and the reasons for their importance.

1. A person reads one criterion from his/her list.

2. Group members consider for a moment and then place a hand on the shoulder of the person in the group who would be their first choice.

3. The person shares with the group his/her perception about whom would be highly chosen on this criterion.

4. If the person reading their criterion is not significantly highly chosen, have him/her read the re-written version of the criterion, and have group members declare their choices once again.

5. If the rewritten criterion does not limit choices in such a way as to have the person be star on the criterion of his/her choice:
   a. Have the person discuss the reasons the role is of high value
   b. Have the group brainstorm criteria which meet this need
   c. Discuss ways the person could inform the group (give clues) about his/her readiness for the role.
   d. Check out any new criteria in action.

6. Allow time for persons to share with each other about the impact of this exploration on him/herself.

7. Repeat the process with another group member.

NAME	ROLE I HAD IN DRAMA	MY PERCEPTION OF CRITERION ON WHICH I WAS CHOSEN	ROLE I WANTED IN DRAMA	REASON I WANTED ROLE	WHAT WOULD ENABLE ME TO BE CHOSEN FOR ROLES LIKE THIS?

Figure 1. Auxiliary Ego Role Choice: Criterion Review (may be used to assist a group in collecting information they may need in the criterion review.)

NAME	ROLE I HAD IN DRAMA	MY PERCEPTION OF CRITERION ON WHICH I WAS CHOSEN	ROLE I WANTED IN DRAMA	REASON I WANTED ROLE	WHAT WOULD ENABLE ME TO BE CHOSEN FOR ROLES LIKE THIS?

Figure 1.   Auxiliary Ego Role Choice: Criterion Review (may be used to assist a group in collecting information they may need in the criterion review.)

"...eye to eye, face to face"
J.L. MORENO

CONDUCTING CLINICAL SOCIOMETRIC EXPLORATIONS:

A MANUAL FOR PSYCHODRAMATISTS AND SOCIOMETRISTS

BY ANN E. HALE

FIRST WORKBOOK EDITION
COMPLETELY REVISED • TEAR OUT WORKSHEETS
ALSO INCLUDING
THE NEW SOCIAMATRIX READER

Contents

Preface
Chapter 1 Sociometric Theory
Chapter 2 Social Atom
Chapter 3 Sociometric Test
Chapter 4 Encounter
Chapter 5 Role Diagram
Chapter 6 Action Sociometry

Indices: Glossary, Name and Subject Index

30 Worksheets that tear out

Plastic Sociomatrix Reader (insert)

Laminated paper binding

208 pages

Written for students and teachers of psychodrama, sociometry, group psychotherapy; group leaders, counsellors, social psychologists and managers of human resources.
Cost: $30.00 U.S.

"This [1st edition] is a book for the serious pursuit of the sociometric method. No one interested in the field should be without it."
ZERKA T. MORENO
Journal of Group Psychotherapy, Psychodrama and Sociometry (Fall, 1982), p. 130

ORDER FORM

Name: _____

Address: _____

_____

_____

Phone: _____

Please send me _____ copies of Conducting Clinical Sociometric Explorations. I have enclosed $30.00 for each copy ordered .... TOTAL _____

$2.00 U.S./$4.00 Overseas*/$10.00 Overseas Airmail .... POSTAGE/HANDLING (Each Book) _____

TOTAL AMOUNT ENCLOSED _____

Make checks payable to Ann E. Hale and remit with order to:

Royal Publishing Company
137 W. Campbell Ave.
Roanoke, VA 24011

Foreign orders must be accompanied by a check drawn against a U.S. bank, or pay collection fee.